# Scraplifting Inspirations

Mommy and Me

*We are lucky to have each other!*

April and Brodey  May 2008

# creating Keepsakes

## Creating Keepsakes

**Editor-in-Chief:** Jennafer Martin

**Founding Editor:** Lisa Bearnson

**Managing Editor:** Lara Penrod

**Creative Editor:** Megan Hoeppner

**Senior Editor:** Kim Jackson

**Editor:** Lori Fairbanks

**Associate Editors:**
Dorathy Gilchrist, Joannie McBride

**Online Senior Editor:** Amber Ellis

**Online Editor:** Erin Weed

**Editorial Assistant:** Ahtanya Johnson

**Contributing Writers:** Brittany Beattie, Maurianne Dunn, Ali Edwards, Elsie Flannigan, Vanessa Hoy, Jana Lillie, Beth Opel, BrianTippetts

**Art Director:** Erin Bayless

**Senior Designers:** Neko Carillo, Maren Ingles

**Contributing Designer:** Gaige Redd

**Photography:**
American Color, Symoni Johnson, BPD Studios, Vertis Communications

Library of Congress Control Number: 2011926480
ISBN-13/EAN: 978-1-60900-247-3

## Creative Crafts Group, LLC.

**President and CEO**
Stephen J. Kent

**VP/Group Publisher**
Tina Battock

**Chief Financial Officer**
Mark F. Arnett

**Corporate Controller**
Jordan Bohrer

**VP/Publishing Director**
Joel P. Toner

**VP/Production & Technology**
Derek W. Corson

**VP/e-Commerce**
Dennis O'Brien

**VP/Circulation**
Nicole McGuire

**VP/e-Media**
Eric Svenson

**Associate Publisher**
Barb Tanner

**Production Manager**
Michael Rueckwald

## Leisure Arts

**Editor-in-Chief**
Susan White Sullivan

**Director of Designer Relations**
Cheryl Johnson

**Special Projects Director**
Susan Frantz Wiles

**Senior Prepress Director**
Mark Hawkins

**Imaging Technician**
Stephanie Johnson

**Prepress Technician**
Janie Marie Wright

**Publishing Systems Administrator**
Becky Riddle

**Mac Information Technology Specialist**
Robert Young

**President and Chief Executive Officer**
Rick Barton

**Vice President and Chief Operations Officer**
Tom Siebenmorgen

**Vice President of Sales**
Mike Behar

**Director of Finance and Administration**
Laticia Mull Dittrich

**National Sales Director**
Martha Adams

**Creative Services**
Chaska Lucas

**Information Technology Director**
Hermine Linz

**Controller**
Francis Caple

**Vice President, Operations**
Jim Dittrich

**Retail Customer Service Manager**
Stan Raynor

**Print Production Manager**
Fred F. Pruss

Between school, work, birthdays, holidays, vacations, and everyday happenings, we create many memories each year. And scrapbooking all of those memories in creative ways becomes a lot easier when you have inspiration to start from. Borrowing an idea from a layout you see and utilizing it on your own layouts—or "scraplifting" as scrapbookers have come to call it—is an easy way to jump start your creative scrapbooking process. Whether you see a cute color combination, a unique title treatment, an easy-to-duplicate design, or a fun photo mat on a layout, you can copy it exactly or adapt it for your page—making scrapbooking your memories easier than ever.

In this book, you'll find more than 379 inspiring layouts showcasing memories from all kinds of events and occasions, each with lots of scrapliftable ideas. Whether you copy those ideas exactly or use them as a springboard and completely switch them up to fit your needs, they're here for your use. We hope you'll find yourself turning to this book again and again for scraplifting inspiration.

Enjoy!

JENNAFER MARTIN
Editor-in-Chief
*Creating Keepsakes* magazine

## 3 Tips to Successful Scraplifting

1. Remember, anything goes! From a clever title to a layout's design to the entire layout itself, you can scraplift anything you like.

2. Copy away. One of the best things about scraplifting is there's no reason to feel badly about copying an idea exactly. If it'll work for your layout, you can copy it completely, and there's no reason for guilt. It's not "stealing"—it's scraplifting!

3. Switch it up. When you find an idea to scraplift, you don't have to stick to it exactly. Change the colors, technique, textures—whatever aspect you'd like—to suit your layout's needs.

See page 14 for more scraplifting tips.

# creating Keepsakes : Scraplifting Inspirations

## CONTENTS

# Inspiring Layouts

**6**   10 Amazing Reader Pages

**14**   Transform It! Make a scraplifted idea your own

**15**   10-photo Layouts

**20**   A Funny Thing Happened . . .

**23**   5 Fun Ideas

**27**   Tips to Save You Time

**32**   It's All in the Details—Photos and Journaling

**35**   New Beginnings

**39**   First Signs of Spring

**43**   Spring is Here

**47**   Rites of Spring

**50**   Enjoy the Outdoors

**54**   Storytelling Shortcuts

**57**   Summer Lovin'

**60**   Fun Photo Groupings

**63**   Summer Inspiration

**67**   Memories That Matter

**71**   An International Salute

**75**   Happiness is . . .

**79**   Two-page Layouts to Inspire You

**82**   10 Tips for Great Pages

**85**   Helpful Tips

**89**   Fall in Love with Your Style

**92**   Colorful and Spunky Layouts

**95**   Photos in a Series

**99**   Sharing the Big and the Small Moments

**102**   Scrapbook Your Life

# Seasonal Solutions

129   The Inside Story

133   January Jubilation

139   Winterize Your Layouts

143   Organize Your Pages

149   Easter Extravaganza

153   Springtime and Easter

159   Nature's Majesty

163   On Being a Mother

169   Mom & Me

173   Honoring Dad

177   Pet Pages

181   Summer Traditions

187   City Celebrations

191   Down the River

197   Summer Wrap-Up

203   School Journaling With a Twist

208   6 Back-to-School Jump-Starts

213   10 Fun Tricks to Treat You

218   Lifelong Learning

222   Falling for You

229   Kid Projects for Thanksgiving

234   'Twas the Month Before Christmas

239   Holiday Journaling Ideas

# Scraplifting Tips

243   CK & Me: A reader's take on a published layout

244   Scraplifting Challenges

252   CK & Me: A reader's take on a published layout

253   Let's Make It Happen: Use your supplies to achieve your goals this year

258   Finding Your Creative Muse: Let home, outdoors and the media inspire your next page

263   Get Inspired by Library Books: Check out inspiration for your next layout

269   From Blah to Ahh: 25 simple strategies to make ordinary layouts dazzle

276   Totally Wicked Teen Layouts: Cool pages and accents you've got to see

284   Studio A: Letter to a new scrapbooker, 10 lessons every scrapbooker should know

287   CK & Me: A reader's take on a published layout

288   Hot Spot: Adorn your layout with a fancy fair ribbon

Jennifer Barksdale

Jessy Christopher

Moon Ko

Gwen Lefleur

**Top Reader Pages**

Heather Lough

April Massad

Ria Mojica

Jing-Jing Nickel

Kim Watson

Deena Wuest

# 10 Amazing

# Amazing
## READER PAGES

**Be wowed by these incredible reader-created designs**

Wow! That's all I can say. When we printed an "Amazing Pages" call in our

April 2009 issue for you to submit your layouts, I was sure we would get more

than a few submissions, but I was overwhelmed with the number of amazing

pages we received. It was extremely hard to narrow them down to this selec-

tion. Here are 10 amazing reader pages that we feel will inspire you and give

you additional layout ideas when creating your own scrapbooks. Enjoy!

**by Brian Tippetts**

*Mommy and Me* by April Massad. **Supplies** *Cardstock:* Prism Paper; *Patterned paper:* BasicGrey; *Brushes:* Funky Flowers Brush Kit by Rhonna Farrer; *Software:* Adobe Photoshop Elements 7.0; *Font:* CK Signature; *Adhesive:* Scrapbook Adhesives by 3L and The Paper Studio.

## April Massad

**Tip 1: Add a single image over both your photos and your background for a dimensional design.** Set your photo flat against your layout, and then stamp or add rub-ons that overlap both the photo and the page background. Raise your photo for more interest by adhering it with dimensional adhesive. To learn how April Massad created this technique on the computer, visit CreatingKeepsakes.com/issues/-October_2009.

**Tip 2: Add dimension to photos.** Cut your photos and adhere them to your layout using dimensional adhesive to create a 3-D effect.

## Kim Watson

**Tip 1: Include memorabilia.** Kim Watson did an amazing job including memorabilia on her layout. She positioned a recipe behind her photo for quick reference. And since she couldn't include actual food samples on her layout, she photographed the dishes to showcase them.

**Tip 2: Photograph food in natural light.** Food can be difficult to photograph in an appealing way. Kim utilized natural light from a window to help her creations look their best.

*I Love to Bake* by Kim Watson. **Supplies** *Cardstock:* Bazzill Basics Paper; *Patterned paper:* My Mind's Eye (yellow dot and check) and Scenic Route (blue dot); *Letter stickers:* American Crafts (white) and Making Memories (blue felt); *Recipe card:* 7gypsies; *Chipboard, epoxy and rubber embellishments:* KI Memories; *Brads:* BasicGrey; *Chipboard heart:* Autumn Leaves; *Embroidery floss:* Karen Foster Design (white) and unknown; *Stamp:* Croxley Stationery; *Ink:* ColorBox, Clearsnap; *Tab punch:* EK Success; *Adhesive:* Mono Adhesive, Tombow; Scrapbook Adhesives by 3L; *Other:* Thread, typewriter, tiny peg, cotton lace and staple.

**Marriage Bliss** *by Jessy Christopher.* **Supplies** *Cardstock:* Bazzill Basics Paper; *Patterned paper:* BasicGrey; *"Marriage" sticker:* 7gypsies; *Flowers and rhinestones:* Prima; *Ink:* Tsukineko; *Brads:* Making Memories; *Adhesive:* All Night Media and Elmer's; *Other:* Doily and pearl trim.

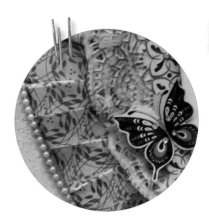

## Jessy Christopher

**Tip 1:** Create a pleated border. Pleat strips of patterned paper and connect the ends in a circle shape to create a unique look on your page.

**Tip 2:** Ink a doily for added contrast. Jessy Christopher inked a doily before putting it on her page to add an intriguing look and to soften the white in order to match the colors of the layout. Try inking a doily to match the color palette of your next layout.

**U R 2 Cute 4 Words** *by Deena Wuest.* **Supplies** *Software:* Adobe Photoshop CS2; *Patterned paper:* Purely Happy Paper Pack by Katie Pertiet; *Frame:* DoodleDo Frames No. 03 Brushes and Stamps by Katie Pertiet; *Flowers:* Lolly Rub-Ons by Michelle Martin and Anyday Brushes and Stamps by Katie Pertiet; *Brush:* Sentiments + Greetings Hand Drawn Brushes by Ali Edwards; *Fonts:* Avant Garde and Cheri.

## Deena Wuest

**Tip 1:** Use a photo for part of your title. Deena Wuest used her daughter's T-shirt as part of the title for her page. The font is one she remembered discovering a couple years ago, and she knew it would work well with the font on the shirt.

**Tip 2:** Incorporate parts of a photo in your design. Deena loves to find ways to incorporate her subject (or an item in a photo) into her layout designs. She did this with the flower border and the title.

**The Underground River** *by Gwen Lefleur.* **Supplies** *Patterned paper:* Jenni Bowlin Studio (pink bracket) and Sassafras (pink wave); *Flowers, leaves and rub-ons:* Making Memories; *Punches:* EK Success (circles) and Fiskars Americas (scallop border); *Stickers:* Jolee's, Sticko by EK Success; *Brads and photo turns:* Queen & Co.; *Photo frames:* Karen Russell for Polka Dot Potato (black digital) and My Mind's Eye (pink transparency); *Letter stickers and pen:* American Crafts; *Font:* Century Gothic; *Adhesive:* Dot 'n' Roller, Kokuyo; *Other:* Jewels.

## Gwen Lefleur

**Tip 1:** Create a visual triangle with groupings. You can create a visual triangle on your pages with three *groupings* of accents instead of three individual accents. Gwen Lefleur executed this trick with the punched circles on her layout.

**Tip 2:** Turn one accent into two. You can turn one die-cut journaling block into two accents by simply trimming one side off and adhering it in another spot on your page. Gwen included the smaller half in the collage near the left edge of her layout.

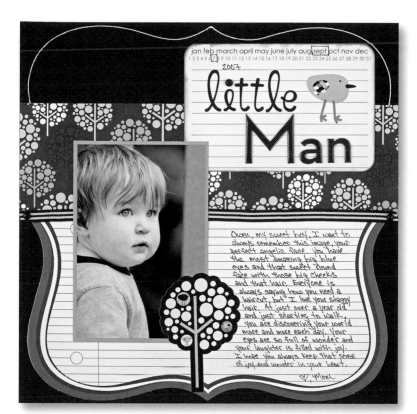

Little Man *by Heather Lough.* **Supplies** *Cardstock:* Bazzill Basics Paper; *Patterned paper:* Jenni Bowlin Studio (line) and Pebbles Inc. (tree); *Letter stickers:* Doodlebug Design (red) and Making Memories (brown); *Journaling card:* Jenni Bowlin Studio; *Ribbon:* Maya Road; *Stickers:* Pebbles Inc.; *Pen:* American Crafts (blue) and Uni-ball Signo, Newell Rubbermaid (white); *Adhesive:* Glue Dots International; Glue Glider Pro, GlueArts. *Note:* All products came from the April 2009 Scrapperie kit.

## Heather Lough

**Tip 1:** Get more from die-cut papers. If you have only half a sheet of die-cut paper, use it to create a complete look on your layout. Simply trace around it on the top of your page (see the white pen drawing Heather Lough created), and then adhere the paper itself to the bottom of the page. Cover the seam between the two with a large strip of patterned paper.

**Tip 2:** Use products for a dual purpose. Use a calendar-themed journaling card as a way to both show the date caption for your photos and to house the title.

## Jennifer Barksdale

**Tip 1:** Wrap embroidery floss or thread around letters. Wrap embroidery floss around chipboard letters for a new take—especially on a layout about teeth where the embroidery floss resembles dental floss!

**Tip 2:** Create a shaped journaling block that supports your subject. Print a clip-art image of a tooth for a fun journaling block! Jennifer Barksdale watercolored her printed clip-art to add an extra touch.

Super Star *by Jennifer Barksdale.* **Supplies** *Cardstock:* Bazzill Basics Paper; *Patterned paper:* Jillibean Soup (brown circle), Sassafras (orange stripe and die-cut border) and Scenic Route (cream); *Scallop border:* Doodlebug Design; *Chipboard:* Heidi Swapp for Advantus (letters) and Making Memories (stars); *Gems:* Westrim Crafts (clear) and unknown (orange); *Embroidery floss:* DMC; *Pen:* Sakura; *Font:* Arial Black; *Adhesive:* Scrapbook Adhesives by 3L; Zots, Therm O Web; *Other:* Staples, thread, ribbon and paint.

## Ria Mojica

**Tip 1: Ground your photo with a frame.** When your photo is surrounded by many busy elements, help ground it by adding a frame—either with rub-ons or hand-drawn with pen—in the same color as the layout's background.

**Tip 2: Use leftover letters creatively.** If you're creating a mix-and-match title, see how you can incorporate some of your rarely used letters. On this layout, Ria Mojica used an upside-down "u" for an "n."

**RDY or Not?** *by Ria Mojica.* **Supplies** *Lace cardstock:* KI Memories; *Patterned paper:* Rusty Pickle and Scenic Route; *Letter stickers:* American Crafts; *Chipboard question mark:* Heidi Swapp for Advantus; *Pens:* Newell Rubbermaid (white) and Zig, EK Success; *Adhesive:* 3M and Uhu.

## Moon Ko

**Tip 1: Tone down the colors.** Since her photos were black and white, Moon Ko filled the empty space in her photo collage with gray-tone papers instead of colored papers— it's the perfect complement.

**Tip 2: Use what you have.** The journaling strips Moon printed were supposed to be red, but the red ink in her printer was running low. Rather than run to the store to purchase a new ink cartridge, she went with the magenta color, and the result turned out spectacular!

**Holy Grail** *by Moon Ko.* **Supplies** *Cardstock, patterned paper and letter stickers:* American Crafts; *Letter dies and die-cutting machine:* Metro, Squeeze, QuicKutz; *Font:* Typewriter Condensed; *Adhesive:* Herma Dotto, EK Success.

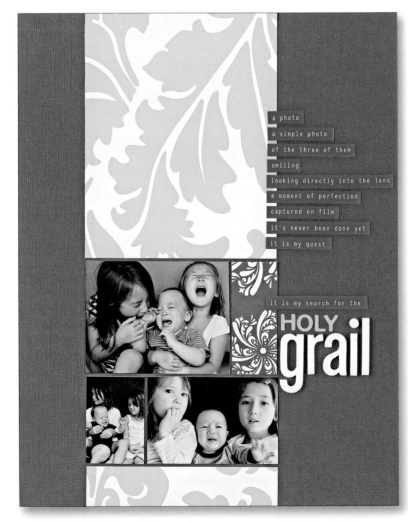

**Some Kind of Wonderful** by *Jing-Jing Nickel.* **Supplies** *Cardstock:* Stampin' Up!; *Patterned paper and chipboard circle:* BasicGrey; *Felt circles and stars:* Fancy Pants Designs; *Letter stickers:* BasicGrey (orange chipboard), Jenni Bowlin Studio (black rub-on), Making Memories (block) and Prima (black felt); *Brads and pen:* American Crafts; *Adhesive:* 3M; *Other:* Embroidery floss.

## Jing-Jing Nickel

**Tip 1:** Cut out a wavy photo frame. This page may look like it took a lot of time, but the collage of blocks is actually a piece of patterned paper from BasicGrey's Lime Rickey collection. Jing-Jing Nickel simply cut out a center portion to create a large frame for her photo.

**Tip 2:** Stitch a multicolored border. Stitch a border with multicolored thread for the perfect border to a multicolored design!

**Tip 3:** Create a layered paper look. Since Jing-Jing had extra paper squares from where she cut out a place for her photo, she trimmed some small squares to use as journaling blocks, which she adhered to the layout with dimensional adhesive for extra pop. **ck**

# TRANSFORM IT!

Designer Kimber McGray was asked to transform a layout about a child's birthday to one of a totally different subject matter. She really hit the spot with her parade-themed approach.

"CELEBRATING 2" BY SUSAN WEINROTH, AS SEEN IN THE FEBRUARY 2010 ISSUE, P. 99.

**Parade Time** *by Kimber McGray.* **Supplies:** *Cardstock:* Core'dinatinos; *Patterned paper and stickers:* Jillibean Soup; *Brads:* Bazzill Basics Paper; *Rhinestones:* Darice, Me and My Big Ideas, and Zva Creative; *Punch:* We R Memory Keepers; *Die-cutting machine and die:* Provo Craft; *Pen:* Newell Rubbermaid; *Adhesive:* Scrapbook Adhesives by 3L.

**To make this page your own, follow Kimber's lead.**

- Create your own sketch of the original as needed.
- Choose an appropriate color scheme.
- Create a hanging title design that reflects your subject.
- Change up the accents to go with your theme.

**You could also**

- Replace a photo or two with accents or journaling.
- Vary the photo sizes.

**This layout design is great for photos**

- of one event,
- taken as a series, or
- showing progression.

*Challenge:* Create your own layout about an everyday topic based on these two designs, using dark or masculine colors.

# { 10-photo layouts }

As a tribute to the year of 2010, let's take a moment to think of all things "10." At the top of my list are 10-photo layouts, which is what you'll find in this issue's "Reader Gallery." I hope these pages will inspire you and give you new ways to get more pictures onto layouts.

*fit more pictures on your pages!*

**Toddler Lives Here** *by Summer Johnson.* **Supplies** *Cardstock:* Die Cuts With a View; *Patterned paper:* Bella Blvd (blue), Doodlebug Design (brown dot) and Love, Elsie for KI Memories (line); *Chipboard:* American Crafts (blue letters), Creative Imaginations (house) and Love, Elsie for KI Memories (flowers); *Stickers:* American Crafts (journaling spot), Doodlebug Design (letters), Heidi Grace Designs (velvet trim) and SEI (flower border); *Brad:* Making Memories; *Pen:* American Crafts; *Adhesive:* EK Success and Therm O Web; *Other:* Chipboard heart and embroidery floss.

Fresh Face *Summer* Johnson owns her own PR firm but works from home because being a mom is her first priority. She loves all crafts, including sewing, cooking and baking. She credits scrapbooking for helping her slow down and appreciate the little things about the great journey of life.

**CREATIVITY TIP:**
Summer keeps a small notebook with her at all times so she can put together ideas and sketches when she has a few minutes in a line or while her husband drives.

**BY JOANNIE McBRIDE**

*Keri* Babbitt has been scrapbooking since high school, and she's found that she scraps more quickly and efficiently by keeping a row of five open embellishment containers within reach. Her accents of choice are buttons, rhinestones, trims and ribbon, letters and small stamps.

**PHOTO TIP:**

For visual interest, crop your photos in a variety of basic shapes. Keri used five squares, three rectangles and two circles.

**March at a Glance** by Keri Babbitt. **Supplies** *Cardstock:* Bazzill Basics Paper; *Patterned paper:* My Mind's Eye; *Letter stickers:* American Crafts (pink), Making Memories (white block) and October Afternoon (blue); *Pearls:* Kaisercraft; *Border punch:* Fiskars Americas; *Font:* Vrinda; *Adhesive:* Therm O Web.

**My Best Buds** by Jennifer Larson. **Supplies** *Cardstock:* Stampin' Up!; *Patterned paper:* BasicGrey, Die Cuts With a View and Making Memories; *Calendar die cuts and label sticker:* Jenni Bowlin Studio; *Chipboard letters:* BasicGrey; *Metal word:* Making Memories; *Glitter:* Doodlebug Design; *Glitter glue:* Stickles, Ranger Industries; *Embroidery floss:* DMC; *Adhesive:* Fiskars Americas, Tombow and Xyron; *Other:* Photo corners.

*Jennifer* Larson teaches high-school English. She is a cross-stitcher, a gardener, a reader and a huge fan of the TV series *Buffy the Vampire Slayer*. She also makes terrific cookies!

**TIME-SAVING TIP:**

Rather than spending hours figuring out how to position numerous photos on a layout, use a grid positioned on a large photo mat to organize multiphoto layouts in no time at all.

**The Long and Short of It** *by Ria Mojica.* **Supplies** *Cardstock:* Bazzill Basics Paper and Die Cuts With a View; *Patterned paper:* Collage Press; *Journaling paper:* Fancy Pants Designs; *Chipboard letters:* KI Memories; *Word stickers:* 7gypsies; *Border punch:* Fiskars Americas; *Glitter letters, circle accent and pen:* American Crafts; *Adhesive:* 3M; *Other:* Ribbon and rickrack.

*Ria* Mojica enjoys cake decorating and makes all her kids' birthday cakes. She loves waking up before anyone else in her house when her mind is fresh and the house is quiet so she can finish scrapbook pages faster.

**DESIGN TIP:**

When using multiple photos on a layout, choose one or two pictures as your focal photo(s) and accent the layout with smaller, cropped photos.

**How Does Our Summer Grow?** *by Jing-Jing Nickel.* **Supplies** *Cardstock:* Prism Papers; *Patterned paper:* Adornit - Carolee's Creations and Collage Press; *Circle die cuts:* Collage Press; *Letter stickers:* Collage Press (black) and Sassafras (blue); *Border punch:* Fiskars Americas; *Font:* CK Journaling; *Brads:* Bazzill Basics Paper; *Adhesive:* 3M.

*Jing-Jing* Nickel is an IT engineer and loves to travel. Her collection of trip photos inspired her to start scrapbooking, and her favorite aspect of this craft is telling the story behind the photos.

**PHOTO TIP:**

The photos Jing-Jing used on her layout are all 3″ x 4″. They are collaged together using free software (Picasa 3) and were printed out as 4″ x 6″ prints in groups of two photos per print.

*Heidi* Sonboul is a vegetarian and a singer who loves being a mom to her two overly active boys. Her favorite time-saving technique is to start a layout with the photos. From there, she decides on colors and textures to fit the idea of her layout.

**TECHNIQUE TIP:**

To re-create this elegant border, pleat your ribbon while stitching it to the page, and then adhere pearls over the stitching to hide it.

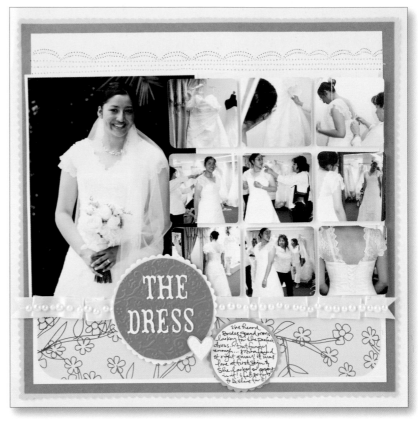

**The Dress** *by Heidi Sonboul.* **Supplies** *Cardstock:* Bazzill Basics Paper; *Patterned paper:* GCD Studios; *Pearls:* BasicGrey; *Ribbon:* Anna Griffin; *Embossing die and machine:* Cuttlebug, Provo Craft; *Adhesive:* 3M; *Other:* Thread.

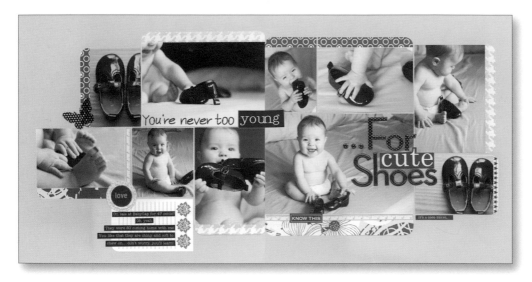

**You're Never Too Young for Cute Shoes** *by Lisa Kisch.* **Supplies** *Cardstock and punches:* Creative Memories; *Patterned paper:* Collage Press, KitoftheMonth.com, Making Memories and October Afternoon; *Stickers:* Jenni Bowlin Studio and Making Memories; *Acrylic butterfly:* Heidi Swapp for Advantus; *Chipboard:* Scenic Route; *Rub-ons:* FontWerks; *Journaling spot:* Jenni Bowlin Studio; *Adhesive:* Creative Memories and Scrapbook Adhesives by 3L.

*Lisa* Kisch is a stage actress who is currently appearing in *The Sound of Music* in downtown Toronto. Scrapbooking since 2003, Lisa finds that creating memories for her two daughters provides a similar creative thrill to appearing on stage.

**DESIGN TIP:**

For more visual interest, pull out a bold accent color from your focal-point photo to use as the background color in your journaling strips and title.

Stay-at-home mom *Brigid* Gonzalez loves to travel and take pictures. She also enjoys getting her hands dirty with home-improvement and decorating projects. Her favorite time-saving tip is to keep her layouts simple and clean. This mother of three uses embellishments sparingly and often uses text as her only accent.

**TECHNIQUE TIP:**

Give numbers stamped on photos a translucent look. You can replicate this technique with number stamps and white paint by adding gel medium to your paint to soften the color. Or stamp once onto scratch paper before stamping your numbers onto your photos.

**How to Have Fun on a Rainy Day** by Brigid Gonzalez. **Supplies** *Software:* Adobe Photoshop CS3; *Fonts:* Kalinga and Times New Roman.

**Dreams Come True** by Annette Pixley. **Supplies** *Patterned paper:* Scenic Route; *Letter stickers:* American Crafts, BasicGrey and Webster's Pages; *Chipboard:* Colorbök; *Mickey Mouse button:* Creative Imaginations; *Rhinestones:* Heidi Swapp for Advantus; *Adhesive:* 3M.

Journaling is *Annette* Pixley's favorite aspect of scrapbooking. She loves to capture what she calls "the perfect words," and she will often use journaling as the platform for her pages. She volunteers for the Boy Scouts of America helping to organize and maintain records.

**TECHNIQUE TIP:**

Use a variety of styles, sizes and colors of letters to create a unique title for your layout, but don't use more than three styles if you want to maintain unity on your pages.

# a *funny* thing happened...

Looking back on the year 2008, so many fond memories made me laugh. For instance, I'm always entertained by the funny things my four-year-old son says. One afternoon, after I had picked Ben up from his sitter, he asked me, "Mom, why did you name me *Benjamin*?" I told him that his dad and I both really liked that name. He replied, "I really like peanut butter and jelly. You should have named me that."

I keep a journal of conversations like this because I never want to forget them. Following are five memorable layouts our readers shared that highlight a funny event in their lives. I hope you enjoy them as much as I do—and that you scrapbook one of *your* funny stories this month!

laughter is *contagious* and should be shared

**You Make Me Laugh** *by DeAnna Heidmann.* **Supplies** *Software:* Adobe Photoshop Elements 4.0; *Patterned paper and letters:* Fletcher PageSet by Anna Aspnes; *Textured paper:* Mail Room No. 02 Paper Pack by Katie Pertiet; *Tape:* Expressions Tapes by Katie Pertiet; *Brushes:* Love All Around Stickers and BrushSet by Anna Aspnes and DoodleDo Circles Brushes-n-Stamps by Katie Pertiet; *Overlay, flower and orange tag:* Orange Crush Kit by Lynn Grieveson; *Brad:* Brad Bonanza by Pattie Knox; *Font:* CK Ali's Writing.

I love how *DeAnna* Heidmann tells her story with journaling and only a few highlight photos. Says DeAnna, "It's important to scrap a story, even if you don't have pictures of the entire event. In the end, if you scrap what you have and write the story down with it, the memories will flood back just the same."

### YOU CAN DO THIS!

1. Choose a solid and a patterned paper and cut the second into a rectangle.
2. Arrange and crop three pictures and your title to form a smaller rectangle on top of the patterned paper. Place an oval embellishment over the photos and trim them to match the curves.
3. Add journaling and a few embellishments as desired. >>

**BY JOANNIE McBRIDE**

**Gravity** *by Jill Deckard.* **Supplies** *Patterned paper, flowers, presents, cupcake, candles, ribbon, string and frame:* So Delightful, Weeds & Wildflowers Design; *Peeled and revealed action:* Marcie Reckinger; *Font:* CK Classical.

At a birthday party for *Jill* Deckard, someone close to her accidentally dropped the cake. The silence in the room could only mean one thing . . . everyone was shocked. Soon nothing but laughter filled the room. End of story, right? Not quite. A couple months later Jill surprised her friend with a birthday cake. This time it was Jill who dropped the cake right on top of her sister's head! Maybe ice cream or cookies would be a better fit for future birthdays. Then again, with photos like these . . . let's bring on the cake!

**YOU CAN DO THIS!**

❶ Create a block of stacked patterned papers near the left side of the layout.

❷ Position three photos over the papers, then add ribbon around their edges for frames.

❸ Assemble the title elements (letters, candles and ribbon) in the lower-right corner.

❸ Add journaling and embellishments to complete the layout.

---

*Julie* Fairman could have become upset when her daughter rubbed nontoxic paint all over her body. Instead, she decided to make the best of it and took photos to create a memory that will last forever. Julie cleverly titled her page "I Put on Scunscreen," which documents her daughter's pronunciation of the word at the time. Love it!

**YOU CAN DO THIS!**

❶ Place three vertical photos across your background (just trim a bit of the vertical edge on two of the 4" x 6" photos).

❷ Place your title across the top of the page and use strips of patterned paper to border above and below the photo strip.

❸ Draw vertical lines for your journaling block, then add journaling and an accent.

**I Put on Scunscreen** *by Julie Fairman.* **Supplies** *Cardstock:* Scenic Route; *Foam letters:* Miss Elizabeth's; *Letter stickers:* Provo Craft; *Pen:* Zig Millennium, EK Success.

Jonny Calvin *by Shannon Brouwer.* **Supplies** *Cardstock:* Bazzill Basics Paper; *Stickers:* Heidi Swapp for Advantus; *Chipboard letters:* Heidi Swapp for Advantus and Scenic Route; *Brads:* BasicGrey, Bazzill Basics Paper and Making Memories; *Ink:* ColorBox, Clearsnap; *Comic strip: The Indispensable Calvin and Hobbes* by Bill Watterson; *Font:* 2Peas Quirky.

*Shannon* Brouwer loves pages that tell a story, and this layout is about her youngest son. He has many nicknames, but the one used most often is "Jonny Calvin." She stated that he looks—and at times acts—just like Calvin from the "Calvin and Hobbes" comic strip. Her husband pointed out this particular strip after Shannon showed him the results from an attempted photo shoot. What a funny boy!

**YOU CAN DO THIS!**

❶ Trim the edges of red cardstock to make a frame for your page and add it to blue cardstock.

❷ Add three 4" x 6" pictures across the lower middle section of the layout. Add a comic strip (you can use more photos in place of this to tell your story or replace it with patterned paper).

❸ Add your title, journaling strip and embellishments.

**Blush Much** *by Pam Callaghan.* **Supplies** *Cardstock:* Bazzill Basics Paper; *Patterned paper and die cuts:* My Mind's Eye and Tinkering Ink; *Letter stickers:* American Crafts and Scenic Route; *Jewels:* Heidi Swapp for Advantus; *Ribbon:* American Crafts; *Button:* Autumn Leaves; *Font:* Georgia.

Blushing is nothing new for *Pam* Callaghan. She confesses that not only is she easily embarrassed but she is also accident prone. In the layout here she shares some of her most embarrassing times.

**YOU CAN DO THIS!**

❶ Print out one 5" x 8" photo and two 4" x 4" photos. Mat them together on an 8½" x 11" piece of white cardstock. Add a title to the left side of the photos.

❷ Type out journaling on an 8" x 11" piece of white cardstock.

❸ Add striped paper strips above and below the blocks of white cardstock. Embellish your layout with flowers, buttons and ribbon.

# 5 *fun* ideas

I love the fresh start that January brings. For me, January is all about optimism. It's the one time of year that I can believe anything is possible. Those Italian language CDs I didn't dust off last year? I'll study those this year, for sure! All those photos I still have to print out and scrap? I've got 364 days to catch up this year. Five of them will be easy—I can work from one of these amazing layouts. Until next month . . . ciao!

Joy submitted this page as a general submission, and her action shots captured our attention. Notice the fun effect of showing the first photo series with one background and the second series with her daughter in front of another backdrop.

**JOY'S PHOTO TIP**

■ Use the sports mode on your camera to take continuous shots. Who knows what you'll end up with?

*see our*

*faves*

*from readers like you*

BY VANESSA HOY

**Practice Makes Perfect** *by Joy Bollinger.* **Supplies** *Cardstock:* Bazzill Basics Paper; *Patterned paper:* me & my BIG ideas (polka dot) and Pebbles Inc. (pink); *Letter stickers:* BasicGrey ("makes") and me & my BIG ideas ("practice"); *Chipboard letters:* Heidi Swapp for Advantus; *Circle and corner-rounder punches:* EK Success; *Font:* Arial Narrow, Microsoft Word.

You have no idea what having a baby is like until you actually have one • don't say "I will never do that" regarding how you will raise your kids • despite what babywise says, you can never hold your children too much • sometimes one hard knock is worth a million words of warning • a child is definately more demanding than the world's toughest boss, but more fun • you have a new understanding of the sacrifice God made giving His only son for you once you have a child of your own • sweet potatoes stain really badly • discipline really does hurt you more than it hurts them •

when your child is hurt, you would give anything in the world to take away the pain • get the expensive car seat & stroller • sippy cups leak • little arms hugging around your neck is the best feeling in the world • the scariest place in the world is the church nursery during flu season • sometimes, you just have to give it all over to God...

**LESSONS learned**

*Katie,* a 2007 Honorable Mention in our Hall of Fame contest, originally submitted this layout as the technique assignment for her entry. We loved the way Katie used her handwritten journaling as a design element. Notice how the two blocks of journaling naturally flow around her photograph.

*Kelly* originally submitted her layout to our November call for Becky's Sketch pages. After making a few adjustments, she resubmitted it to our call for January layouts. I love how she captures all her significant memories using a list format and combines 16 photos of the previous year!

**Lessons Learned** *by Katie Burnett.* **Supplies** *Software:* Adobe Photoshop CS2, Adobe Systems; *Cardstock:* Crate Paper; *Rub-ons:* Heidi Swapp for Advantus; *Fabric:* SEI; *Buttons:* Autumn Leaves; *Other:* Medical tape and beads.

'06

one GREAT year

**One Great Year** *by Kelly Purkey.* **Supplies** *Cardstock:* Bazzill Basics Paper; *Patterned paper:* American Crafts and Creative Imaginations; *Stickers:* American Crafts and Doodlebug Design; *Ribbon and brads:* American Crafts; *Labels:* Martha Stewart Crafts for EK Success and Heidi Swapp for Advantus; *Button:* KI Memories; *Pin:* Heidi Grace Designs; *Punch:* Fiskars; *Font:* Claredon, downloaded from the Internet.

Congratulations to

*Colleen!*

She submitted this layout to our Fresh Face call. Notice how she documented all the fun her sons had while waiting for the midnight release of the final Harry Potter book. This layout is definitely one they'll enjoy for years to come.

### COLLEEN'S MULTI-PHOTO SOLUTION

■ Too many pictures and not enough space for journaling? Colleen likes to crop photos to focus on her subjects, then handwrite a few details on label stickers as captions.

**Waiting for Harry** *by Colleen Stearns.* **Supplies** *Patterned paper:* Jenni Bowlin Studio and Scenic Route; *Overlay:* Hambly Studios; *Flowers and chipboard letters:* Heidi Swapp for Advantus; *Label stickers:* Jenni Bowlin Studio; *Gems:* Junkitz; *Labels:* Dymo; *Pen:* American Crafts.

# 2 reader trends

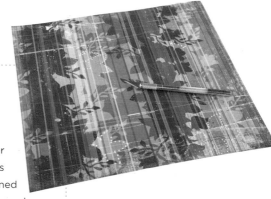

I spotted the following trends on pages from readers this month:

**TEENY, TINY ACCENTS.** Little accents, such as paper flowers, buttons and jewels, are big this month. Whether grouped together to accent a focal-point photo or arranged around a title for emphasis, these tiny accents are a huge hit! Look for pretty jewels, buttons and flowers from companies like Doodlebug Design (*www.doodlebug.ws*), Making Memories (*www.making-memories.com*), Prima (*www.primamarketinginc.com*) and Queen & Co. (*www.queenandcompany.com*).

**PAPER CUTOUTS.** Readers are creating custom page accents by either cutting hand-drawn images from cardstock and patterned paper (think hearts and stars) or cutting out designs and borders from the patterns on their patterned paper.

**Imagine** by Shanah Gordon. **Supplies** *Patterned paper and flower: Jackie Eckles, www.designerdigitals.com; Pink paper: Feminine by Denise Docherty, www.designerdigitals.com.*

## Shanah's

wishful thinking struck a chord with me. Shanah originally submitted this playful layout for (what else?) our winter pages call. Says Shanah, "Scrapping is therapy for me, and during the brutally cold and drab New York winters I find myself dreaming of a new and improved sort of winter...one with colors and flowers. Much better, don't you agree?" I sure do!

# tips to *save* you time

What better month than February—the shortest month of the year—to talk about quick solutions to get more done? You'll find simple tips and techniques here to help you scrapbook the everyday moments with less hassle. You'll enjoy scrapbooking, and these tips will save you time, so you can do even more activities you love to do!

be *inspired* by reader layouts you'll love!

You can find *Jennifer* Davis hiking in the Northwoods with family or reading a book when she's not paper crafting. She also enjoys baking, sewing and taking photos.

**TIME-SAVING TIP:**

Jennifer keeps her in-process projects out on her desk so she can work on bits of her project here and there, as time permits.

**BORDER TIP:**

Create your own border by stamping a phrase stamp repeatedly across the layout.

**BY JOANNIE McBRIDE**

**Thursday Morning Waffles** *by Jennifer Davis.* **Supplies** *Cardstock:* Bazzill Basics Paper; *Patterned paper:* KI Memories; *Letter stickers:* American Crafts (orange and green) and Doodlebug Design (white); *Acrylic hearts:* Heidi Swapp for Advantus; *Buttons:* Creative Café; *Circle sticker:* Heidi Grace Designs, Fiskars Americas; *Die-cutting machine:* Cuttlebug, Provo Craft; *Punches:* Fiskars Americas (scallop border) and Marvy Uchida (scallop circle); *Stamps:* Hero Arts; *Ink:* VersaMark, Tsukineko; *Adhesive:* Therm O Web and Tombow; *Other:* Pen, embroidery floss and thread.

*Andrea* Friebus is a stay-at-home mom who enjoys reading and longs to have a pink Mini Cooper. She loves to purchase scrapbook supplies and has found ways to stretch her money and her imagination. She handcrafted the heart accent on her page using scraps of ribbon.

**TIME-SAVING TIP:**

To save time, Andrea used a Mad-Lib style journaling block to help her record her story on the layout.

**RIBBON TECHNIQUE:**

Weave several pieces of ribbon together and tape them onto cardstock. Place another piece of cardstock with a heart shape cut out of it on top of the ribbon, and stitch the pieces together. Cut around the stitching, leaving a small border, and adhere the accent to your page.

**Embrace** by Andrea Friebus. **Supplies** Cardstock: American Crafts; Patterned paper: American Crafts and KI Memories; Transparency frame: Fancy Pants Designs; Die-cutting machine: Slice, Making Memories; Journaling block: Ella Publishing Co.; Ribbon: Home Shopping Network and Oriental Trading Company; Brads: Making Memories and Oriental Trading Company; Ink: Clearsnap; Embroidery floss: DMC; Adhesive: Therm O Web; Other: Felt, pen, flowers and buttons.

On the Train by Pam Young. **Supplies** *Patterned paper, transparency overlays, stickers and die cuts:* My Little Shoebox; *Letter stickers:* Making Memories; *Pearls:* Hero Arts; *Embroidery floss:* DMC; *Adhesive:* Tombow.

*Pam* Young is fond of reading, writing, painting, quilting and paper crafting. She finds joy in the everyday moments of life!

**TIME-SAVING TIP:**
Pam sets aside pages she knows she wants to add a bit of stitching to, and she pulls one out while watching a favorite TV show. It's an easy way to add her personal hand-stitched touches.

**PAPER TECHNIQUE:**
Cut the center from a piece of scalloped-circle paper. Use the outside as a border on your page, and save the middle piece to use on another layout.

*Lisa* Dorsey keeps herself busy by volunteering at her daughters' school, attending weekly Bible studies and running her two active girls to sporting events. A scrapbooker for 14 years, Lisa has learned many techniques that give her pages a personal touch and make use of extra pieces of scraps.

**TIME-SAVING TIP:**
If you don't have time to sew, use a white pen to add more detail to your accents. Lisa selected a dot border for several accents on her layout.

**BUDGET-SAVING TIP:**
To create the scallop border on her page, Lisa cut circles from a piece of patterned paper, cut them in half, placed them in a line and added a paper strip over the top.

You're a Star, Baby by Lisa Dorsey. **Supplies** *Cardstock:* Bazzill Basics Paper; *Patterned paper:* Bo-Bunny Press, Melissa Frances, Scenic Route and We R Memory Keepers; *Flower button:* Making Memories; *Chipboard:* Magistical Memories (stars and bracket) and Scenic Route (circle); *Letter stickers:* American Crafts (white) and Making Memories (black); *Ink:* Clearsnap; *Rhinestones:* Prima; *Paint pen:* Newell Rubbermaid.

**Snow Day** *by Kathleen Summers.* **Supplies** *Software:* Adobe Photoshop Elements; *Patterned paper:* A Bit of Grunge Paper Pack and Soft Breeze Paper Pack by Katie Pertiet; *Snowflake, flourishes, ribbon and felt:* Frosted by Michelle Coleman; *Sparkles:* Magic Sparkle Overlays by Anna Aspnes; *Clips and ribbon:* Tied Fasteners No. 03 by Katie Pertiet; *Stitching:* Milly Molly Kit by Lynn Grieveson (glittered) and Stitched by Anna Crème No. 03 by Anna Aspnes (white); *Letters:* Vibe Alphabet Brushes and Stamps by Art Warehouse; *Font:* Pea Olson.

*Kathleen* Summers has been fortunate enough to work in the scrapbooking industry and hopes to do so again someday. She started scrapbooking traditionally eight years ago but has been digitally scrapping for a year.

**TIME-SAVING TIP:**
Don't be afraid to crop photos into shapes. Cropping a 4" x 6" print into a 4" square or circle is much faster than spending hours shuffling your pictures to create an arrangement that fits.

**TECHNIQUE TIP:**
Stitch around a photo for a fun design element.

*Amy* LeJeune is a physician, happily married and the mother of four young-adult sons. She likes photography and gardening. Amy was a Fresh Face in the May 2009 issue of *Creating Keepsakes*. She loves scrapbooking and uses it as a creative outlet that allows her to express her love for her family.

**TIME-SAVING TIP:**
As a digital scrapbooker, Amy saves time by using a page template. If you're a traditional scrapper, use the digital template like you would a sketch.

**Proof** *by Amy LeJeune.* **Supplies** *Software:* Adobe Photoshop CS3; *Page template:* Filmed layered Template No. 02 by Katie Pertiet; *Patterned paper:* Baby Pink Patterns + Solids Papers by Ali Edwards (pink swirl); Naturally Krafty No. 03 Paper Pack by Katie Pertiet (green, recolored); Smoothie Shop Paper Pack (floral) and Bright Days Paper Pack (stripe and check) by Jesse Edwards; *Ribbon:* Cherry Festival Kit by Lynn Grieveson; *Title block:* Edges Brushes and Stamps by Katie Pertiet; *Overlay:* O.M.G. PageSet by Anna Aspnes; *Letter stamps ("Proof"):* Wood Type Alphabet by Ali Edwards; *Postmark stamp ("Captured Moment"):* Postmarked New Years 2009 Brushes and Stamps by Katie Pertiet.

**2009 Summer Vacation** *by Lisa Pate.* **Supplies** *Software:* Adobe Photoshop Elements and Adobe Lightroom; *Patterned paper:* Ocean Solids Paper Pack by Andrea Victoria; *Month tabs:* Tabbed Dates by Katie Pertiet; *Clock:* Clock Parts Elements by Katie Pertiet; *Photo arrangements:* Photo Clusters No. 17 by Katie Pertiet; *Text overlay:* All You Need Overlays No. 05 by Katie Pertiet; *Letter stamps ("Road Trip"):* Messy Stamped Alphabet No. 02 Brushes and Stamps by Katie Pertiet; *Stitching:* Stitched by Anna White No. 01 by Anna Aspnes; *Word art ("Summer Vacation"):* Hello Summer Hand Drawn Brushes by Ali Edwards; *Brad:* Brad Bonanza by Pattie Knox; *Circle text:* Memories Circles No. 01 Brushes and Stamps by Art Warehouse; *Distressing:* Worn Page Edges No. 02 by Lynn Grieveson; *Font:* Arial.

*Lisa* Pate teaches junior-high math and enjoys baking, taking photographs and spending time with her family. Lisa's layout is a Readers' Pick page selected for publication by readers on *CreatingKeepsakes.com*. Cast your vote today—you'll find more details at *CreatingKeepsakesBlog.com*.

**TIME-SAVING TIP:**

Lisa created two folders on her computer to house her digital elements. One folder is for kits and embellishments, and the other is for papers. Each item is saved as a thumbnail so Lisa can look through them and find the perfect accent or paper to complete her project.

**TITLE TECHNIQUE:**

If you're creating a travel layout, search the Internet for fonts with a similar look or feel of the signs as your destination.

# it's all in the *details!*

When you schedule an appointment or plan a trip, you likely first write down a list of the details. What? When? Where? Who? These are the things you don't want to forget. Scrapbooking is much the same. Through it, we record a piece of history and capture an important time in our lives. Whether you prefer to journal a lot or a little on your pages, don't forget to add in the things that matter—the what, when, where and who. Future generations will appreciate your attention to detail!

**do your photos and journaling *tell* the story?**

**Jen** Jockisch began scrapbooking four years ago. Looking for a way to store her wedding photos, she stumbled onto a scrapbooking website and hasn't looked back. In addition to memory keeping, Jen loves to cook and is an avid reader. When she created this layout, she had just picked up knitting. Although the hobby is no longer something Jen spends time doing, she created a page about it and has recorded a piece of her life for herself and her family.

### JEN'S PROCESS

1. I placed my photos in the vertical center of the page.

2. I chose assorted patterned-paper strips and layered them around the photos. (I left a lot of room for my title because it was large.)

3. I added my title and accents.

**Like I Need Another Hobby** by Jen Jockisch. **Supplies** Cardstock: Bazzill Basics Paper; *Patterned paper:* 7gypsies, BasicGrey, October Afternoon, Scenic Route and Sitrah Paper; *Chipboard letters, acrylic stars and chipboard asterisks:* Heidi Swapp for Advantus; *Rhinestones:* Swarovski; *Index tab:* Autumn Leaves; *Date stamp:* FontWerks; *Ink:* Fluid Chalk, Clearsnap; *Epoxy stickers:* Love, Elsie for KI Memories; *Brads:* SEI; *Felt flower and pen:* American Crafts; *Font:* 2Peas Tubby; *Other:* Ribbon and staples.

**BY JOANNIE McBRIDE**

**Tracie** Radtke wanted to capture everything about her visit to Molly's—right down to the bright, yellow countertop with extra toppings, the heart-shaped sprinkles on top of the red-velvet cupcake, the pretty pink plate her cupcake came on and the wooden swings that replaced barstools. This layout just screams happy! Anyone else feel like making cupcakes?

*Cupcakes by Tracie Radtke.* **Supplies** *Borders and swirls:* Wild Thing Mini-Kit by Emily Powers; *Cupcake:* Let Them Eat Cupcakes by Kate Hadfield and Angela Powers; *Letters:* Candied Apple by Emily Merritt and Kate Hadfield; *Font:* Century Gothic.

**Gina** Hanson submitted her page for the Fresh Face call last July, and I was instantly drawn to how she captured her daughter's true beauty and personality in these photos. Gina enjoys setting up photo shoots of her children in their backyard. Like most of us, she'll usually come away with a few great shots from the hundreds she takes, and that's okay. If a picture is worth a thousand words, then snap away!

### CREATE BEAUTIFUL BUTTERFLIES

1. Punch, trace or die cut a butterfly shape onto cardstock.

2. Wrap embroidery floss around the middle of the body, then knot the ends at the top to create the antennae.

3. For added dimension, use a scissor edge to distress the butterfly edges.

**Life Ain't Always Beautiful** *by Gina Hanson.* **Supplies** *Cardstock and brads:* Bazzill Basics Paper; *Patterned paper, die-cut cardstock and letter stickers:* Pink Paislee; *Flowers:* Heidi Swapp for Advantus and Prima; *Mini eyelets:* Making Memories; *Butterfly die cuts:* AccuCut; *Fiber:* DMC; *Font:* Pea Girly Girls Print.

*Lynne* Ashcraft created this page for an online challenge at Twelve-of-Twelve. Blog-spot.com. Strictly an event-based scrapper back in March 2008, Lynne has since been inspired to scrapbook photos about everyday life as well. This helps her include interests like her love for taking photographs, baking, reading and doing anything crafty!

### ACCENT IDEA

To fill white space in a subtle way, stamp a flourish (or another accent) in opposite corners of the layout. Lynne added a flourish to the top-right and bottom-left corners.

**The Details** by Lynne Ashcraft. **Supplies** *Digital journaling frame:* Ali Edwards; *Transparency:* Fancy Pants Designs; *Fonts:* Bookshelf Symbol 7 and CK Ali's Handwriting.

**Bike Wash** by Laina Lamb. **Supplies** *Cardstock:* Archiver's; *Patterned paper and journaling block:* Glitz Design; *Dimensional letters:* American Crafts; *Stickers and coaster board:* Imagination Project; *Arrow punch:* EK Success for Stampin' Up!.

### YOU CAN DO THIS!

❶ Mat photos onto white cardstock in a horizontal line across the pages.

❷ Add patterned-paper strips with rounded corners above and below the photos to accent them.

❸ Apply title, journaling circle and two accent circles.

*Laina* Lamb's layout--selected as a reader favorite at the website CreatingKeepsakes.com—shows her son happily washing his bike just like he does every Saturday morning. Note how she includes her own handwriting as well—Laina feels like her pages are incomplete without it.

# *new* { beginnings }

Well, it's almost the end of winter here in Utah. As new leaves and flowers begin to sprout, I find myself bursting with energy and ready to start my spring cleaning. And what better time to introduce five talented contributors? Four are Fresh Faces (that means it's their first time being published in *Creating Keepsakes* magazine!). Once you take a peek at their pages, you'll see why I had to include them in Reader Gallery this month.

4 fresh faces *inspire* with their talent

**1234 Years** *by Davinie Fiero.* **Supplies** *Cardstock:* WorldWin; *Patterned paper and rub-ons:* Pink Paislee; *Sticker:* American Crafts; *Ribbon* C.M. Offray & Son; *Button:* Making Memories; *Embroidery floss:* DMC; *Font:* Souvenir.

*Davinie* Fiero wanted to show on this layout just how much her daughter Morgan has changed over the years. While the photos reflect the changes, they also show how much Morgan looks the same.

I love the idea of using a series of photos to capture different stages of a child's life. You can use this concept for anything stage-related, including pregnancy or home improvement.

**note:** Notice how Davinie used three circle elements to create a visual triangle on her page.

BY JOANNIE McBRIDE

A few of *Mary* MacAskill's favorite things are being a stay-at-home mom, baking cupcakes, reading and watching romantic comedies. Being the photographer in her family, Mary wanted to capture her daughter's tiny fist. She enlisted the help of her husband, who was able to snap these photos of baby Sadie's tiny hands at just two weeks old. A fun fact: this page includes over 100 flowers.

### YOU CAN DO THIS!

❶ Trim patterned papers and attach to layout. *Optional:* Stitch into place with a sewing machine.

❷ Create the title block with stamps and attach letter stickers. Attach title block to layout and add a decorative paper strip. Embellish with ribbon and a tag.

❸ Add photos. Print journaling and trim into strips. Add buttons and eyelet.

*Little Fingers by Mary MacAskill.* **Supplies** *Cardstock:* Bazzill Basics Paper (brown) and SEI (yellow and pink); *Patterned paper:* Bo-Bunny Press (dot) and SEI (flower); *Tag, ribbon and iron-ons:* SEI; *Decorative paper strip:* Doodlebug Design; *Stickers:* American Crafts; *Stamp and gem:* Hero Arts; *Ink:* ColorBox, Clearsnap; *Eyelet:* We R Memory Keepers; *Font:* AL Uncle Charles; *Other:* Thread.

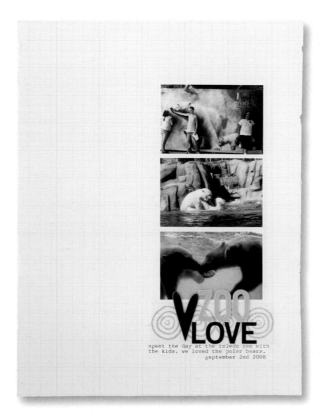

*Staci* Compher is another Fresh Face this month! She originally submitted her page in September 2008 and was contacted a month later to have her work published. I love that she used an old typewriter for the journaling on this page. Besides scrapbooking, Staci enjoys taking photographs. She also spends a lot of time caring for her two daughters, three cats and four chickens.

When Staci first started working on her page, she ripped the side of the paper. Instead of throwing out the paper, she distressed the edges to make it look like she meant to rip it. Great tip for making what you have work for your page!

### YOU CAN DO THIS!

❶ Print three small photos in 3" x 2" format.

❷ Line up the pictures, then add the title and journaling below them.

❸ Distress the edges of the layout.

*Zoo Love by Staci Compher.* **Supplies** *Patterned paper:* Dream Street Papers; *Letter stickers:* American Crafts; *Chipboard heart:* Heidi Swapp for Advantus; *Rub-on word:* Scenic Route; *Sticker:* Colorbök.

Blomster by Marianne Hope. **Supplies** *Cardstock:* Bazzill Basics Paper; *Other:* Paint, felt, buttons, notebook paper, thread, paper flower and seam rub-on.

## YOU CAN DO THIS!

❶ Pick the photo or photos you want to use and find a background that goes with them. The white background on this layout is neutral and really makes the photos and elements stand out.

❷ Find a color in the photos that you want to highlight and paint behind or around the photos using this color. Pick letters for your title that go with the photos. Don't be afraid to cut the letters out by hand to make them fit your layout.

❸ Use embellishments that tie the colors and the design together. Marianne used buttons and a paper strip, and she repeated them to connect the different elements of the layout.

*Marianne* Hope, another Fresh Face, is Norwegian and lives with her husband and three children in the Netherlands.

Marianne's page is about her love of "blomsters" (flowers). Here is the translation for her journaling: "No summer is without flowers. I have always dreamt of having my own garden with lots of flowers like lavender, roses, hydrangea and colorful climbers. In our garden here in the Netherlands, we have all those flowers and more!"

## make your own felt letters

❶ Write your title letters on a scrap of felt.

❷ Cut your title out.

❸ Adhere your letters to your page. If your title has an "O," you can replace it with a flower accent.

**Owls** *by Jaime Ward.* **Supplies** *Software:* Adobe Photoshop Elements 5.0; *Patterned paper and flowers:* LivE Designs; *Scallop circle mask and stitching brush:* Jessica Sprague; *Paper swirl:* Amanda Rockwell; *Notebook journaling paper:* Erica Zane; *Title letter:* GG Digital Designs; *Journaling tab:* Katie Pertiet; *Fonts:* CK Ali's Writing and LB Typewriter Thin.

Fresh Face *Jamie* Ward created this "Readers' Pick" page in less than an hour, and it received the most votes when we asked our online audience to choose a favorite. Congratulations!

Jaime loves to spend time with her family, and she enjoys reading anything she can get her hands on. Her husband's family lives in a rural farming community, and the photos here were captured in their backyard. One thing Jaime loves about this page is that even though it's digital, the design makes it easy to re-create as a traditional paper layout as well.

**YOU CAN DO THIS!**

❶ Place a circle (cut out by hand, digitally created or premade) on your background.

❷ Layer your photos on top of the circle. Consider placing your photos in a grid. The circle provides a good contrast to the linear feel of the photos.

❸ Add elements and journaling. Jaime clustered elements around the bottom corners of the photos to draw the eye to them.

# first signs of *spring*

At the first signs of spring, it's not just leaving the coat behind that puts a smile on my face . . . it's seeing all the fun, bright pages our readers submit. And it's no surprise that most of these pages feature outdoor photos, whether celebrating special family traditions or just the loveliness of spring! So, what caught CK's eye this month? Read on!

see our
*faves*
from readers like you

**Recipe for Always Active and Adorable Girl** *by Stephanie Ruda.* **Supplies** *Cardstock:* Making Memories; *Patterned paper:* KI Memories; *Circle cutter:* Creative Memories; *Colored pencils:* Prismacolor, Newell Rubbermaid; *Bird and flowers:* Stephanie's own designs; *Ink:* Cat's Eye, Clearsnap; *Decorative scissors:* Fiskars; *Pens:* Slick Writers, American Crafts; *Fonts:* Lemon Chicken and CatholicSchoolGirls BB, Internet.

**CONGRATULATIONS** to Stephanie—it's her first time being published in CK! She submitted this layout to our Fresh Face call, and we loved how the doodling complements the happy photos of her daughter. Stephanie revealed that she is new to doodling and loves making her own embellishments, including the little bird and recipe card on this page. Way to go!

**STEPHANIE'S FRAMING TIP**
Use circles to frame your photo, then add title words around it for emphasis.

BY VANESSA HOY

*Mary Jo* caught our attention in an instant with her gallery submission—a clever page with birthday pictures assembled in the shape of a cake (with a candle on top). What a great solution for this typical multiphoto event!

**MARY JO'S CLEVER BORDER IDEA:**
To add definition to a "cake" page design, use border rub-ons to outline the layers of the cake.

**1st Birthday Cake** *by Mary Jo Johnston.* **Supplies** *Cardstock:* Bazzill Basics Paper; *Patterned paper:* Creative Imaginations; *Cardstock stickers:* Heidi Grace Designs; *Rub-ons:* Creative Imaginations and Heidi Grace Designs; *Rhinestones:* Gartner Studios; *Paper frills:* Doodlebug Design; *Ink:* ColorBox, Clearsnap.

Design a tiered "photo cake" on your page!

*Shaunte* submitted this layout to our "Spring Pages" call. (She confessed that she scrapped everything spring that weekend!) I love the story behind her title. Says Shaunte, "I originally cut 'Spring,' and as the Silhouette started to cut the 'P' I thought it was a 'T' and that I had typed 'String' by accident. Then I realized it fit anyway! I love a good title."

**Spring Requires String** *by Shaunte Wadley.* **Supplies** *Cardstock:* Prism Papers; *Patterned paper:* Cactus Pink; *Lettering template, nameplate and photo corner dies:* Silhouette, QuicKutz; *Brads:* Karen Foster Design; *Fonts:* Elise (used with QuicKutz) and American Typewriter, Internet; *Other:* Thread.

**God's Garden** *by Lisa Wear.* **Supplies** *Cardstock:* Bazzill Basics Paper (lavender) and Wish in the Wind (black); *Lettering dies:* George, Cricut, Provo Craft; *Butterfly stickers:* Creative Memories; *Other:* Vellum and brads.

*Lisa's* brilliant photo mosaic made her Fresh Face submission a true standout. Says Lisa, "I get a lot of my inspiration from nature. I love taking pictures of flowers, sunsets and other scenery. Great pictures create great pages."

**LISA'S SECRETS TO SUCCESSFUL MOSAICS:**

First, decide what part of the picture is the most important. Then, cut a series of photos into 1" squares and blend them to make everything look as if it were one scene. You can include or exclude squares depending on what fits with the picture next to it.

# 2 reader trends

What are our readers doing right now? I spotted the following trends on reader pages:

**BRIGHTS!** Nothing says *spring* like a splash of bright color. Readers are embracing bright colors this month, adding them to neutral backgrounds or letting them shine atop black backgrounds.

**CIRCLES.** Designing around circles is still very popular. And it's no surprise—this eye-catching shape lends vibrancy and energy to the photos on a layout.

**Junking** *by Layle Koncar.* **Supplies** *Cardstock:* Bazzill Basics Paper; *Acrylic letters:* Heidi Swapp for Advantus; *Rub-ons:* me & my BIG ideas (white) and Scenic Route (blue arrow); *Letter stickers and labels:* Scenic Route; *Pen:* Uni-ball Signo, Newell Rubbermaid; *Bird:* Bam Pop; *Other:* Staples.

*Layle* originally submitted this layout to our "Recent Pages" call. We loved how she balanced colorful photos of her antiquing trips against a black cardstock background.

**LAYLE'S TIPS:**

- Did you notice that I didn't use any patterned paper? Instead, I used rub-ons and my favorite white pen to create a background.

- For some of my easiest journaling ever, I wrote my comments on label stickers.

# ····{ *spring* is here! }····

Don't you just love springtime? Buds sprout and the sun peeks gently from behind the clouds, assuring us that warmer days are just around the bend. Take advantage of the extra daylight by going on family outings, preparing your garden for planting or even taking walks with family and friends. Here are five great layouts about spring and the memories captured during its delightful moments. Enjoy!

five *fresh* looks from our readers

**Take Time** *by Kim Moreno.* **Supplies** *Cardstock:* Core'dinations; *Patterned paper:* BasicGrey (orange scallop), Pink Paislee (background), Sassafras (decorative strips) and Scenic Route (green); *Stickers:* American Crafts (title), Melissa Frances (brown date) and Scenic Route (strip); *Rub-ons:* American Crafts; *Flowers:* Bazzill Basics Paper; *Ribbon and stick pin:* Maya Road; *Buttons:* Sassafras; *Die cuts:* Crate Paper; *Ink:* Stampin' Up!; *Paper clip:* Making Memories; *Other:* Vintage bird tag.

*Kim* Moreno creatively cropped the photos on her page to disguise the real meaning behind them. While it may appear that Kim's daughter is taking a leisurely walk through the trees on their property, in reality she was setting up soda cans for her family's target practice with an air pistol. So clever, Kim! These photos are beautiful.

### TIPS FOR SUCCESS

❶ When using a series of photos, back them with white for a uniform look and to help them stand out against the background.

❷ Lay your photos out on your page, then use strips of patterned paper and borders to visually "ground" them.

❸ Pulling matching embellishments ahead of time (in this case from a kit) and collage elements quickly to finish off a page.

**BY JOANNIE McBRIDE**

**First Spring Day** *by Kim Watson.*
**Supplies** *Cardstock:* Bazzill Basics
Paper; *Patterned paper:* My Mind's
Eye and Sassafras; *Paper flowers,
letter stickers and brads:* Making
Memories; *Buttons:* Autumn
Leaves and Making Memories;
*Butterfly die cuts:* Cricut, Provo
Craft; *Adhesive:* Mono Adhesive,
Tombow; *Other:* Thread, glass
beads, typewriter and lace.

*Kim* Watson created this layout to highlight a spring day that she and her son
shared. They were exploring a field down the road from their home. Hoping to find the
field full of wildflowers, they searched and searched. Finally Kim's son found a lone
daisy and presented it to his mom. Although this year spring was slow to come, Kim's
memories of springtime in the Cape include fields of white wild daises. What things
remind you of spring?

❶ Cut strips of lace for the flower
stems. Adhere lace to page.

❷ Adhere paper flowers to stems
and embellish flowers with buttons and brads.

**YOU CAN DO THIS!**

❶ Create background paper by
penciling shapes onto your
paper, then stitching around
the pencil lines.

❷ Add a border strip of patterned paper, followed by
ribbon, lace or trim.

❸ Add journaling and embellishments.

**Hunt** *by Wendy Sue Anderson.* **Supplies** *Cardstock:* Bazzill Basics Paper; *Patterned paper and chipboard accents:* Heidi Grace Designs; *Chipboard letters:* Doodlebug Design; *Letter stickers:* Scrap Pagerz; *Ribbon and string:* Making Memories; *Buttons:* Autumn Leaves; *Pen:* American Crafts; *Ink:* Tsukineko.

*Wendy* Sue Anderson loves reading when she has spare time, baking when it's cold outside and spending time with her children and husband anytime. On her layout, Wendy combined blacks and browns with her pastels to create a unique color combination that's really quite lovely. For her title, she used black ink to color white chipboard letters and heat embossed them to set the color.

### YOU CAN DO THIS!

❶ Cut two strips of patterned paper and two pieces of cardstock to place on green cardstock for the layout's background.

❷ Next, add three 4" x 6" photographs, ribbon, buttons and journaling.

❸ Use black ink to change white chipboard letters to black, then set the color with a heat gun.

*Jennifer* Jorgensen is a stay-at-home mom to three children and has a fourth on the way. Although she's had three other pregnancies, this is actually the first layout Jennifer's completed about being pregnant. The photos were taken by her five-year-old daughter—amazing! Jennifer states that she has a hard time scrapping about herself. She made it a goal to document the journey of this last pregnancy, and this layout is the result.

**Last Time** *by Jennifer Jorgensen* **Supplies** *Software:* Adobe Photoshop Elements 4.0; *Page elements:* Moments in Time kit by Kristen Cronin-Barrow; *Template:* Created by Cindy Schneider and designed by Sara Gleason; *Fonts:* Porcelain and Typist.

**Backyard Boyz** by MaryRose Lovgren. **Supplies** Software: Adobe InDesign CS3; Button and overlay: Shabby Princess; Fonts: Amelie (journaling), Base 02 (title) and FG Jeana (title).

In *MaryRose* Lovgren's layout, she describes a typical spring day when Dad is in charge of her boys. This photo session yielded over a hundred photos, so it was easy for MaryRose to choose her favorite baker's dozen! I love that she included so many photos of this single event on her layout and captured her sons' unique personalities. Notice how the grid pattern gives her layout a clean look, while the larger photo on the left-hand page serves as her focal point.

## YOU CAN DO THIS!

❶ Select one focal-point photo and position it on the bottom-left side of the layout.

❷ Choose a dozen other photos that support the main photo and the layout's general story. Place them in an evenly spaced grid. Position three of the twelve photos on the left-hand page and the other nine on the right-hand page.

❸ Use fonts that reflect the layout's theme for both the title and the journaling. Add an element on the right-hand side to make a focal triangle (title to element to focal-photo).

# {rites of spring}

With so many layout ideas and lovely pages coming in (and being forwarded to me from other CK editors), it's impossible not to be inspired to scrapbook this month! I've seen so many "can't resist" ideas for multiphoto pages and clever journaling. Check out these layouts by readers just like you!

**See our faves from readers like you**

KIM submitted this layout to our call for recent pages in October. The bright, happy colors of the flowers surrounding her photograph instantly caught my eye.

Did you notice that she also tucked a shaped booklet under the big flower in the top-right corner? The little booklet is ideal for adding extra journaling and photos!

**KIM'S PICTURE-PERFECT JOURNALING TIP**

"Don't be afraid to try something that could potentially 'ruin' a photograph," says Kim. "For a long time I was reluctant to stamp, write or paint directly onto a photograph, especially if it was an enlargement. But nowadays with digital pictures, if for some reason we make a mistake that cannot be rescued, we can simply reprint the photograph."

**BY VANESSA HOY**

**Bloom** by Kim Watson. **Supplies** Cardstock: Bazzill Basics Paper; Patterned paper: K&Company; Photo turns: Queen & Co.; Buttons and vinyl letters: Autumn Leaves; Paint: Heidi Swapp for Advantus; Brads: Making Memories; Pens: Zig Photo Signature and Zig Millennium, EK Success; Adhesive: Mono Adhesive, Tombow; Other: Ribbon and embroidery floss.

The third time's a *charm* for Vinnie Pearce, who reveals that she has three versions of this layout. Says Vinnie, "I always play with different compositions before deciding a layout is complete!" Her layout caught our attention with this engaging photograph and the clever title treatment framing it.

**VINNIE'S LAYOUT REMINDER:**
"It's important to scrap family members that you hardly see," notes Vinnie. "My son loves his Uncle VJ, but this year VJ is studying, so unfortunately we don't see him as much as we would like to."

**Uncle** *by Vinnie Pearce.* **Supplies** *Software:* Adobe Photoshop Elements 3.0, Adobe Systems; *Digital buttons:* Katie Pertiet, www.designerdigitals.com; *Digital patterned paper:* Nostalgia No. 3—Paper, www.jenwilsondesigns.com; *Digital distressed brushes:* Distressed ToolSet, Anna Aspnes, www.designerdigitals.com; *Digital brads:* Signature No. 1 Elements, www.jenwilsondesigns.com; *Digital stamps:* Worn Foam Stamps 2, www.jenwilsondesigns.com; *Font:* CK Script, www.scrapnfonts.com.

*I always* take tons of photos whenever my husband and I do anything, including building snow dogs in the front yard. So I simply loved the way Julie combined so many photos of this snow activity on her layout, which she initially submitted to a Seasonal Solutions call.

**Snow Family** *by Julie Laakso.* **Supplies** *Cardstock:* Bazzill Basics Paper; *Patterned paper:* Daisy D's Paper Co. and Sweetwater; *Letter stickers:* American Crafts; *Stamp:* 7gypsies; *Rub-ons:* Hambly Studios; *Buttons:* Daisy D's Paper Co.

**CINDY'S PREMADE ACCENT TRICKS:**

"Premade ermbellishments are awesome and can make for quicker scrapbooking, but sometimes I like to dress them up a bit," shares Cindy. "To embellish my chipboard flower, I carefully pulled apart the chipboard circle and blossom, sandwiched a silk flower between the pieces, added gems and glitter rub-ons, then outlined the glitter."

*Who can resist* the appeal of the first warm day after a long, cold winter? When I saw Cindy's layout (submitted to our "March Pages" call), I knew I couldn't! This is definitely a moment to scrapbook. The bright strip of framed photos adds the perfect touch to this joyful layout!

**1st Warm Day** *by Cindy Tobey.* **Supplies** *Cardstock:* Bazzill Basics Paper; *Patterned paper, chipboard and rub-ons:* We R Memory Keepers; *Clear label sheet:* Avery; *Flower and gems:* Heidi Swapp for Advantus; *Accents:* Westrim Crafts; *Ink:* Tsukineko; *Paint and journaling paper:* Making Memories; *Flower strips:* Paper Frills, Doodlebug Design; *Pens:* American Crafts and Sakura; *Font:* Lucida Console, Microsoft; *Other:* Thread.

*Congratulations* to Erin! She submitted this layout to a "recent pages" call in September. We loved how she scrapbooked this memorable, unplanned event with humor and the attention of a journalist. The photos and detailed journaling help document the unfortunate circumstance of losing keys in the ocean!

**Depoe Bay and the Lost Keys** *by Erin Benaim.* **Supplies** *Cardstock:* Bazzill Basics Paper; *Patterned paper:* Collage Press, KI Memories and My Mind's Eye; *Chipboard letters:* Heidi Swapp for Advantus; *Scallop accent:* Waste Not Paper; *Word stickers:* 7gypsies; *Velvet rickrack:* Maya Road.

# enjoy the outdoors

Last spring, my husband and I finally went on a cruise. The experience was absolutely amazing, with perfect weather and stunning scenery, and we returned with fond memories of scrumptious food, new friends and incredible sights.

Whether you visit an exotic location, camp in the mountains or simply spend time in your own backyard this month, remember to relish the beauty of the great outdoors. Here's how spending time outside with the ones you love can help create memories that will last a lifetime.

check out these *multiphoto* layouts

**Off We Go** by Denine Zielinski. **Supplies** *Cardstock:* Bazzill Basics Paper; *Patterned paper:* Fancy Pants Designs (orange dot), Making Memories (yellow stripe), My Mind's Eye (green) and Sassafras (blue stripe and scallop edge); *Letter stickers:* My Mind's Eye; *Die-cut stickers:* 7gypsies and Scenic Route; *Epoxy sticker and rub-on phrases:* Creative Imaginations; *Chipboard circle:* Technique Tuesday; *Buttons:* BasicGrey; *Brads:* Making Memories and Prima; *Embroidery floss:* DMC; *Pen:* Sakura; *Font:* Garamond; *Other:* Thread.

*Denine* Zielinski submitted this page in mid-December, and I requested it shortly after. I love how she trimmed down the 12" x 12" paper so that her photo collage could hang slightly over the sides. The colors are bright and express the excitement felt by family members getting ready to embark on their family vacation. The letter stickers in the title are actually six years old—way to go making your stash work for you, Denine.

### YOU CAN DO THIS!

❶ Mount patterned paper on cardstock with only a ½" border showing. Add strips of patterned paper and die-cut stickers to the right-hand side.

❷ Add a photo-collage strip across the page.

❸ Add title, journaling and embellishments.

**BY JOANNIE McBRIDE**

# boost a border

Want to add more pizzazz to border strips? Try this idea:

❶ Cut a 1" x 12" strip of patterned paper (circle print) and adhere it vertically near the right-hand edge of the page.

❷ Choose several different buttons. Place the buttons over the strip for reference and use them as templates to poke holes in the strip.

❸ Adhere buttons to page with embroidery floss.

**Daddy's Little Helpers** by Claude Campeau. **Supplies** Cardstock: Bazzill Basics Paper; Patterned paper: My Mind's Eye and We R Memory Keepers; Letter stickers: American Crafts; Journaling stamp: Autumn Leaves; Decorative paper strips: Doodlebug Design; Felt star: Fancy Pants Designs; Star die cut: My Mind's Eye; Ink: Inkadinkado; Pen: Staedtler.

*Claude* Campeau is a Fresh Face who submitted this page as a general submission. Married to her husband Keith for seven years, she is a stay-at-home mom to two young children. Besides scrapbooking, Claude enjoys meeting up with friends at their local Starbucks. Her children thought it would be cool to help their dad fix a broken bench, so Claude snapped photos of "Daddy's little helpers," and the idea for this layout came to life.

## YOU CAN DO THIS!

❶ Add a black border around a yellow piece of cardstock.

❷ Mat pictures on a single block of red cardstock, then mat the red block on patterned paper and add border strips to the sides.

❸ Finish with the title, journaling and embellishments.

*Terri* Davenport's page at left was requested a week after she submitted it. Seeing photos of the children side by side is a powerful reminder of how quickly the years go by, and I am inspired to create a similar page of my five children.

Terri's photos were taken at an annual family-vacation spot. Do you have a favorite vacation spot or a family tradition that you revisit every year? Be sure to capture the new memories that will someday be past memories for you and your family to treasure.

**Five Years Later** by Terri Davenport. **Supplies** *Software:* Adobe Photoshop CS2; *Patterned paper:* Hear It for the Boys Supplement Paper Pack and All Natural Solids Paper Pack by Jesse Edwards; *Digital elements:* 12 x 12 Page FotoBlendz Clipping Masks No. 01 and Scanty Journal Lines by Anna Aspnes; 4 x 6 Photo Templates No. 2, Hinged Frames No. 2, Messy Stamped letters No. 5 and Vintage Photo Frames No. 1 by Katie Pertiet; Dot Templates by Kellie Mize.

**Together** by Amy LeJeune. **Supplies** *Patterned paper:* Free July 2008 Computer Tricks digital kit at CreatingKeepsakes.com by Michelle Coleman; *Squares:* Snap Frame Flourished Squares No. 02 by Katie Pertiet; *Calendar stamp:* Digital Dates Stamps by Katie Pertiet; *Frames:* Little Vintage Frames Curled and Flat by Katie Pertiet; *Font:* Pea Jay.

*Amy* LeJeune is an internal medicine physician and is married to an internist. They have four young-adult/teenage sons that keep their lives interesting and full. She also loves photography and gardening. This particular layout was inspired from an ad Amy saw in a magazine. She knew it would be the perfect template for a layout about their family vacation. I love how she was able to include so many photos—you'll find 13 pictures on this layout!

**YOU CAN DO THIS!**

1 Take lots of photos of an event. Choose one photo and enlarge it to use as the focal-point photo.

2 Use frames, mats or slide mounts to frame the accent photos on your layout.

3 Add embellishments such as the timeline across the top of the page. Use a date stamp at the bottom.

*Kayleigh* Wiles is not only a Fresh Face, but her page is also this month's online Reader's Pick. Besides enjoying time with her family, Kayleigh enjoys cooking and is a huge fan of The Food Network and *Top Chef*. She loves to create two-page layouts because she can add lots of photos and likes how the layouts look in her albums. You'll notice that the right-hand page of the layout is a mirror image of the first, making for a fast and balanced design.

### YOU CAN DO THIS!

1. Start with a sketch to make your page design simple and quick.
2. Pull colors from your photos with coordinating papers.
3. Add embellishments, stamps and journaling to complete the layout.

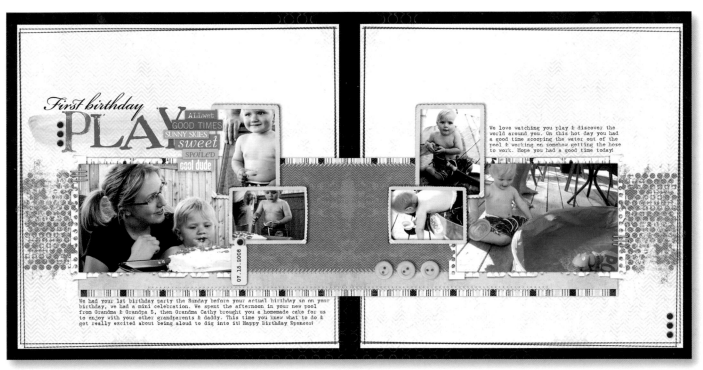

**First Birthday** *by Kayleigh Wiles.* **Supplies** *Page template:* Katie Pertiet; *Patterned paper:* Boy Star Kit by Mindy Terasawa; *Brushes:* Watery Washes Brushes-n-Stamps and Spot Dots No. 04 Brushes-n-Stamps by Katie Pertiet; *Staple, button and word strips:* Simple Classics No. 03 Kit and Cut Ups: Destination Collection by Katie Pertiet; *Brown stitching:* Stitched by Anna Brown No. 01 by Anna Aspnes; *Brads:* Anchors Its! by Pattie Knox; *Fonts:* Batik Regular and Bickman Script Pro.

# { storytelling *shortcuts* }

For me, what really brings a layout to life is the journaling—the sweet story behind the memorable photo or the crazy adventure where the fun is all in the details. So I love seeing all the creative techniques readers use to share their stories and record their memories. Here are five favorite layouts this month and five gotta-try journaling starters I plan to use, too!

*favorite* layouts and quick journaling help

**Go** *by Michelle Alynn Clement.* **Supplies** *Patterned paper, felt shapes and journaling card:* Fancy Pants Designs; *Letter stamps:* Hero Arts; *Ink:* StazOn, Tsukineko; *Date stamp:* Making Memories; *Chipboard letter stickers:* American Crafts; *Dimensional globes:* Magic Scraps; *Other:* Staples, paint, watercolor pencils, sandpaper, buttons, journal page, embroidery floss and cardboard circle.

## WAY TO GO, MICHELLE!

This Fresh Face graduated from film school and works at an animation studio in Vancouver, British Columbia. She created this whimsical layout as the title page for an album about a trip she won to France. For her photos, Michelle used the index prints so she could document all the great times and people she met through **"thought bubble" style journaling** stemming out from her main photo.

## MICHELLE'S EASY-ACCENTS SOLUTIONS

No circle stamp? Michelle didn't have one either, so she used the edge of a cardboard tube from an empty roll of Glue Dots. Just brush paint around the edge and voila . . . an impromptu circle stamp.

**BY VANESSA HOY**

On our second day at the cottage, the boys decided to take a little trip around the lake in the canoe. Now, from these pictures, you would think that they had a nice relaxing time. What you don't see is that, after a few random turns around the water, and after several warnings, Tim decided to stick his oar down into the water like a gondolier and flipped the boat over! The boys called for Sarah and I and we ran down to the beach to see them flailing around while trying (unsuccessfully!) to flip the boat back into an upright position. The boat just kept on filling up with water! Although they'd tell you differently, Sarah and I thought that it was too funny that the guys wanted us to help them as we had no way to do so! As we watched them in the lake, we devised several crazy rescue schemes like paddling out on the air mattress, and flipping the boat over with our super-human strength. Eventually, a neighbour came out with his motorboat, helped the boys into the back, flipped the canoe, tied it to the boat and towed it back to our dock. Cameron and Tim still insist that it was scary, but I still laugh when I think about this crazy adventure and wish I'd had my camera with me to capture the moment!

the CANOE adventure

*Lisa* says she regrets not grabbing the camera when her husband and son called her name during their canoeing misadventure. Fortunately, she **chronicled their tale** with this layout and the photos she'd taken earlier that day.

### LISA'S DIGITAL TRICKS

- Add glitter swirls below photos on the water to mimic waves.
- Rearrange premade frames to fit your layout. These postage-stamp frames were originally in a different configuration, then Lisa cut and rearranged them to fit her design.

**Canoe Adventure** *by Lisa Habisreutinger.* **Supplies** *Software:* Adobe Photoshop CS, Adobe Systems; *Paper and flourish:* Leora Sanford, www.littledreamerdesigns.com; *Digital stitching:* Shabby Princess, www.shabbyprincess.com; *Digital letters:* Missed the Bus Alpha by Britt-ish Designs, www.scraphead.com; *Digital frame:* Lindsay Jane Designs, www.lindsayjanedesigns.blogspot.com; *Fonts:* CK Love Life, www.scrapnfonts.com; AvantGarde, Internet.

the STELLER SEA LION

Our captain said that in the 9 years he has worked for the Kenai Fjords Tours he has never seen the Sea Lions this far up the rocks and thought it might have something to do with the high waves the day before. According to the Kenai Fjords Alaska Heritage Tours 'Wildlife Guide' the Steller Sea Lion is the largest member of the eared seal family. They live in the Kenai Fjords and along the coast of the North Pacific year round. The Sea Lion is an endangered species. They hunt nocturnally for fish like pollock, herring, cod, salmon and rest on the rocks during the day. They are exceptional climbers.

Although *Laura,* a photographer, lived in Anchorage for a few years as a teenager, she had never gone on a boat tour until this vacation to the Kenai Fjords National Park with her husband, where she captured these incredible wildlife photos. She **used information from the tour brochure** to write her journaling about the sea lions and what she learned.

**Steller Sea Lions** *by Laura Vanderbeek.* **Supplies** *Software:* Adobe Photoshop CS2, Adobe Systems; *Digital paper:* Autumn Blend Paperset by Nancie Rowe Janitz, www.scrap-artist.com; *Digital stamped block flourish:* Katie Pertiet, www.designer-digitals.com; *Fonts:* SBC Stone Inscription and Century Gothic, Internet.

*Natalie,* a scrapbooker since she was in seventh grade, kept her embellishments to a minimum so she could feature as many photos of this kite-flying experience as possible. Notice how she placed both her **title and journaling elements on the swirls** in the center of her layout.

**NATALIE'S SECRETS FOR A GREAT MULTIPHOTO LAYOUT**

- Make your own paper swirls—Natalie created these fun kite-string embellishments by freehand cutting her paper. ("I'm not much of a measure-and-sketch girl," she admits.) Notice how the paper swirls perfectly mimic the kite images in her photos.
- Trim premade embellishments (such as these crystal swirls) to fit your design. Don't be afraid to alter accents to make them fit your layout.

**Kite Strings** *by Natalie Call.* **Supplies** *Patterned paper:* Fancy Pants Designs; *Letter stickers:* Making Memories; *Rub-ons:* Scenic Route; *Crystal swirls:* Prima.

*Annette* creates a similar layout every year with **the same questions for her children.** What a wonderful way to document what changes and what remains the same from year to year!

**ANNETTE'S INTERACTIVE JOURNALING TRICK**

- Use lined paper to make it easier for children to write their answers.

**Fifth** *by Annette Pixley.* **Supplies** *Patterned paper:* Creative Imaginations; *Chipboard:* Junkitz; *Stickers:* American Crafts and EK Success; *Pen:* American Crafts.

# { summer lovin'! }

It's beginning to feel a lot like summer! If you're like most of us, you and your family are starting to spend more time outdoors soaking up the sun. Whether your idea of a great time is camping, fishing, swimming or even visiting your favorite summer places, be sure to pack your camera so you can capture these everyday moments. Don't forget to get out from behind your lens—it's important that you're in the photos as well!

enjoy summer *fun* with five readers

Fresh Face *Jana* Eubank is a stay-at-home mom to four children. Besides scrapbooking, she likes to decorate her home and hang out with family. Her son looks forward to their annual camping trips and the chance to go fishing. Although he's never caught a fish on his own, he is very serious about it and does not like to be distracted. Jana's kids don't want to catch a fish for dinner anyway— they want to bring one home as a pet!

**Casting for a Spell** by Jana Eubank. **Supplies** *Cardstock:* Bazzill Basics Paper; *Patterned paper:* 7gyp-sies (red floral), Collage Press (brown and journaling block) and Pink Paislee (scallop circle); *Letter stickers:* American Crafts ("spell"), Collage Press ("for a") and Sassafras ("casting"); *Word and border stickers:* Scenic Route; *Label sticker and paper clip:* 7gypsies; *Buttons:* Fancy Pants Designs; *Pen:* American Crafts; *Other:* Thread and embroidery floss.

**BY JOANNIE McBRIDE**

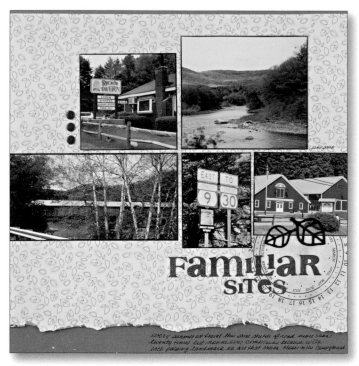

**Familiar Sites** by Jennifer Arble. **Supplies** *Cardstock:* The Paper Company; *Patterned paper:* Canson; *Journaling card:* My Mind's Eye; *Leaf die cuts:* Accent Essentials Cartridge, Cricut, Provo Craft; *Letter stickers:* BasicGrey; *Brads:* American Crafts; *Pens:* Pigma Micron, Sakura; Slick Writers, American Crafts.

*Jennifer* Arble is a Fresh Face, and her layout is this month's online Reader's Pick page. Congratulations! Jennifer drew inspiration for her title and the rolled-paper technique from friends she met online. She created the page to serve as a reminder to her and her family of the beautiful places they pass repeatedly on the way to their summer home in Vermont.

### YOU CAN DO THIS!

❶ Crop five 4" x 6" photos in various sizes (Jennifer's photos are, from top left to bottom right, 3½" x 3½", 4½" x 4½", 3" x 6", 2½" x 3¼" and 3¼" x 3"). Use a photo pen or marker to outline the edges of each picture.

❷ Lightly dampen the bottom edge of an 11" x 12" block of double-sided patterned paper. While it's damp, tear the edge and roll the paper up slightly to show the reverse side. Adhere the paper to your background ¼" from the top.

❸ Arrange pictures and adhere to page. Add title, embellishments and journaling.

*Heidi* Sonboul has been creating scrapbook pages since she was twelve. Her inspiration for this page came from a road sign. Very cool. Don't be afraid to use shapes on your page. They can add a whimsical feel to a layout and offer a unique way to showcase favorite photos.

**The Great Outdoors** by Heidi Sonboul. **Supplies** *Cardstock:* Bazzill Basics Paper; *Patterned paper:* Cosmo Cricket; *Paint:* Crayola; *Ribbon:* Anna Griffin; *Pen:* American Crafts.

If you ask *Kim* Watson about her life, she'd tell you it's pretty close to perfect. She gets to stay home with her son. She is a vocalist in her church band alongside her guitar-playing husband. She enjoys making low-fat and gluten-free baked goods and reading a good "whodunit" novel. A great tip Kim shares is to not throw away your scraps. Her philosophy? As long as the colors are complementary, you can mix manufacturers and seasons. That's right!

**Uncle Steve** by Kim Watson. **Supplies** *Cardstock:* Die Cuts With a View (lime green); PaperMates, WorldWin (red); Tinkering Ink (avocado green); *Digital papers:* Jenni Bowlin Studio (blue damask) and PrintablePaper.net (blue graph); *Patterned paper:* 7gypsies (black text), Luxe Designs (yellow and lime stripe), Making Memories (green stripe and green dot), October Afternoon (pale yellow), Pebbles Inc. (green and blue stripe) and Scenic Route (blue dot); *Letters:* American Crafts (blue), Bo-Bunny Press (red) and Making Memories (black); *Stamps and buttons:* Autumn Leaves; *Ink:* StazOn, Tsukineko; *Brads:* BasicGrey; *Punches:* EK Success (butterfly, scallop circle, tab and corner-rounder punch), Making Memories and Marvy Uchida (circle); *Edge distresser:* Making Memories; *Pen:* Pentel; *Software:* Adobe Photoshop 7.0; *Font:* Another Typewriter; *Other:* Typewriter and thread

*Kristina* Proffitt is a stay-at-home mom to one daughter. She loves photography, everyday photos, Target and Robin Egg Blue. (That is a great color!) The flowers she chose for this layout highlight her daughter's swimsuit perfectly. She wanted to capture her daughter in her swimsuit, and once Kristina purchased these flowers she knew exactly how to scrapbook this everyday moment.

**Sweet Suit** by Kristina Proffitt. **Supplies** *Cardstock:* Bazzill Basics Paper and The Paper Company; *Letter stickers:* Doodlebug Design; *Felt flowers:* Heidi Swapp for Advantus; *Buttons:* American Crafts; *Stamp:* Autumn Leaves; *Pen:* Newell Rubbermaid; *Other:* Decorative scissors.

# { *fun* photo groupings }

While I don't often scrapbook from sketches, I'm always on the lookout for interesting photo groupings and treatments that I can use for my photos. This month, readers submitted so many great layout ideas. Here are my five favorite tips!

*5 easy tricks* for stunning pages

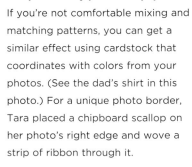

**CONGRATULATIONS, TARA!**
This Fresh Face has submitted to CK for four years, and she's thrilled to share this layout that includes a favorite photo of her husband and daughter! Tara recently submitted this layout as a general submission.

**PHOTO TREATMENT TIP #1:**
**Layer an uncropped photo over complementary patterned papers.**
If you're not comfortable mixing and matching patterns, you can get a similar effect using cardstock that coordinates with colors from your photos. (See the dad's shirt in this photo.) For a unique photo border, Tara placed a chipboard scallop on her photo's right edge and wove a strip of ribbon through it.

**BY VANESSA HOY**

**Father's Day** *by Tara Pakosta.* **Supplies** *Cardstock:* Archiver's; *Patterned paper:* K&Company; *Chipboard scallop:* Fancy Pants Designs; *Orange flower, vinyl letters and brown brad:* American Crafts; *Green flower:* Prima; *Button:* Autumn Leaves; *Stamps:* Great Impressions and Hero Arts; *Ink:* StazOn, Tsukineko; *Letter stickers:* Making Memories; *Ribbon:* May Arts; *Pen:* Sharpie, Newell Rubbermaid.

*Overexposed* by Melissa Sill. **Supplies** *Software:* Adobe Photoshop Elements 6.0, Adobe Systems; *Digital title:* Coconut Creamer kit by Laura Deacetis, www.sweet-shoppedesigns.com; *Digital paper:* Michelle Coleman and Lori Barnhurst, www.littledreamerdesigns.com; *Circle arrow and man:* Stamp Works by Laura Alpuche, www.oscraps.com; *Orange tag:* Summer Beginnings by Melany Violette, www.simplycleandigiscraps.com; *Rusty screw:* Baby Days 3.0: Busy Bee Kit by Sarah Jones, www.thedigichick.com; *Staple:* Diva Kit by Daniela Peuss, www.scrapartist.com; *Photo corner:* Katie Pertiet, www.designerdigitals.com; *Accent:* Glitter Mesh by Emily Merritt, www.thedigichick.com; *Fonts:* Arial, Microsoft (journaling); Aristamp, Internet ("over").

**MELISSA** submitted this eye-catching layout to our Fresh Faces call in January. Way to go! I loved the way she created an artistic effect with an overexposed photo. Says Melissa, "Sometimes layouts work out with overexposed or underexposed photos—you just have to look for the beauty in imperfection."

### PHOTO TREATMENT TIP #2:

**Blend an overexposed photo with your background.** Even if a cherished photo is not technically perfect, find ways to make it work for your layout. Melissa let this overexposed photo blend into the white background of her layout. It created the perfect spot for journaling around her photo in the white space.

*Faces of Hunter* by Summer Ford. **Supplies** *Cardstock:* The Paper Company; *Chipboard:* AMM and Heidi Swapp for Advantus; *Rub-ons:* Scenic Route and Making Memories; *Stamps:* Hampton Arts, Hero Arts, Kolette Hall and Stampin' Up!; *Ink:* Ranger Industries and Tsukineko; *Pen:* Martha Stewart Crafts; *Tag:* Rusty Pickle; *Safety pin:* Making Memories; *Eyelet brad:* Karen Foster Design; *Square punch:* Marvy Uchida; *Ribbon:* C.M. Offray & Son; *Font:* Adolescence, Internet; *Other:* Thread.

When she's not scrapbooking or running to and from her children's various sports and school activities, scrapbooker **SUMMER FORD** is a self-proclaimed organizing and decorating addict. She'd been studying CK recently, noticing how many layouts in this column originate from general submissions, when she decided to send a few layouts for us to consider.

### PHOTO TREATMENT TIP #3:

**Create a photo block with one large photo and several cropped photos.** Sometimes I find myself with several similar photos from a photo shoot. They're all darling, but in some ways nearly identical. What to do? I love Summer's idea of pairing one large focal-point photo with three similar images cropped into squares and lined up right next to the larger one.

AUTUMN originally submitted this to Seasonal Solutions, but when I saw this clever photo and journaling treatment I just knew it was the perfect fit for my collection of reader-inspired photo tips. Autumn admits that when she first looked at these photos she almost didn't print anything out . . . but lucky for us (and her family), she did.

PHOTO TREATMENT TIP #4:

**Design a page like a magazine article, choosing photos to illustrate your journaling.** Autumn created this layout as if it were a page in a fictional book called "The Happy Parent's Guide." She came up with a "Rule of Mess" to determine which messes she would let the kids make and which just weren't worth the cleanup time. She discusses six activities, including the one illustrated by the photos.

**Rule of Mess** by Autumn Baldwin. **Supplies** *Cardstock:* Bazzill Basics Paper; *Ribbon:* May Arts; *Fonts:* Copperplate Gothic Light and Copperplate Gothic Bold, Microsoft.

When I contacted KATHY for this pretty layout, she was thrilled to share the news with her daughter, Emma, and Emma's two friends—the subjects of her layout. Kathy submitted this layout to CK's call for recent pages and said that its inspiration was the song "All I Ever Wanted" by Brian Melo, the 2007 Canadian Idol. "It's on the radio all the time!" she jokes. "One day, I was singing along and realized how much the lyrics remind me of Emma and her friends."

**The Time of My Life** by Kathy Thompson Laffoley. **Supplies** *Cardstock:* Scrapbook Sally; *Patterned paper and epoxy stickers:* me & my BIG ideas; *Font:* Century Gothic, Microsoft.

PHOTO TREATMENT TIP #5: **Create a photo strip.** This is my favorite technique when working with several photos from one event. I simply pick my favorites, crop in on my subjects, choosing a size that works well for all the photos, and lay them out in a strip. Notice how well this design works for these photos even though they are zoomed in at different distances.

# summer
## *inspiration*

..... { } .....

With the sunshiny, enjoyable days of July in full swing, there's so much you'll want to record. That's why I've gathered five layouts, along with photo and journaling prompts, to help you document some of the daily routines your family participates in during the lazy days of summer.

**how do you** *document* **the summertime?**

JACK JONES · FIFTH TOOTH · SELF EXTRACTION
## THE GREAT GAPSBY

**The Great Gapsby** *by Cassie Jones.* **Supplies** *Software:* Adobe Photoshop CS4; *Patterned paper (altered):* Graphic Garden No. 02 Paper Pack by Katie Pertiet; *Brushes:* Title Line Brushes-n-Stamps by Jesse Edwards; *Fonts:* Andes and Avant Garde.

*Cassie* Jones is the creator of this month's Readers' Pick layout choice. Congratulations! She loves to play with her kids, experiment with her camera and spend time with her girlfriends. Her "The Great Gapsby" page showcases a milestone for her son. He lost so many teeth during this time that she wanted to make sure to capture the big moment!

## journaling ideas

Don't forget to journal these milestones that will occur this summer as well:

- Birthday
- Graduation
- Firsts

**BY JOANNIE McBRIDE**

**Authentic Art** *by Iris Babao Uy.* **Supplies** *Patterned paper, chipboard and felt:* Fancy Pants Designs; *Stickers and pen:* American Crafts; *Adhesive:* UHU.

*Iris* Babao Uy loves scrapbooking so much that not a day passes without her spending some time doing something scrapbook related. "Authentic Art" took less than thirty minutes to create. The drawing is an actual sketch her daughter drew of Wall-E, scanned and resized to fit her page. Consider documenting indoor-play photos such as enjoying board games, tea parties and dress-up playtime.

## photo ideas

Photograph your kids enjoying these activities this summer:

- Cooking or baking together
- Watching summertime movies
- Reading favorite books

*Lisa* Truesdell is a stay-at-home mom to three boys. Although Lisa was originally going to delete the right-hand photo on her "Run" layout from her camera because her son was running out of the frame, she decided to save it. It makes a perfect finishing point to her page!

## photo ideas

The great outdoors provide opportunities for numerous outdoor play shots, such as:

- Recreational league games
- Water play
- Backyard or park play

**Run** *by Lisa Truesdell.* **Supplies** *Patterned paper:* Cosmo Cricket (yellow, green and dot), Creative Imaginations (background), October Afternoon (text, red and blue) and Pink Paislee (orange); *Letter stickers:* October Afternoon; *Chipboard buttons:* Scenic Route; *Felt flower:* Creative Café, Creative Imaginations; *Stamps:* Hero Arts; *Ink:* Brilliance, Tsukineko; *Other:* String.

*Jen* Jockisch has been scrapbooking for four years, and her "Favorite Photos in 2008" page was requested just two weeks after she submitted it. A design secret she shared with me was that the yellow circles only came about because she was trying to cover up some stray ink marks that ended up on the white cardstock. Great cover-up, Jen!

**Favorite Photos in 2008** *by Jen Jockisch.* **Supplies** *Cardstock:* American Crafts; *Kit:* ScrapInStyleTV.com; *Patterned paper:* BasicGrey (yellow and white circles), October Afternoon (file folder) and ScrapInStyleTV. com (all others); *Punches:* EK Success and Martha Stewart Crafts; *Letters and chipboard heart:* Heidi Swapp for Advantus; *Index tab:* October Afternoon; *Ink:* Clearsnap; *Pens:* American Crafts and Uni-ball Signo, Newell Rubbermaid; *Adhesive:* Pop Dots, All Night Media, Plaid Enterprises; EK Success; *Other:* Vinyl ribbon and staples.

## photo and journaling ideas

Make it a point to record your favorite summertime photos. Here's a quick list to consider:

- Annual vacation spots
- Preferred summer foods
- Seasonal family photos you love

### YOU CAN DO THIS!

❶ Layer file folders, journaling cards or paper scraps in the center of a page to create a rectangle shape.

❷ Adhere six wallet-size photos on top of the collage.

❸ Adhere a title to the side of the photos, and then add rub-ons, ribbon and index tabs over the photos.

*Kristin* Hayne loves photography, reading, lampwork beading, gardening and participating in anything to do with the outdoors.

She also loves to buy new shoes! On her "New Kicks" layout, Kristin stapled a torn piece of a shoe box to create a unique background shape.

**New Kicks** *by Kristin Hayne.* **Supplies** *Cardstock:* Bazzill Basics Paper; *Patterned paper:* Creative Imaginations and Teresa Collins Designs; *Letter stickers:* American Crafts; *Journaling block:* Teresa Collins Designs; *Pens:* EK Success and Newell Rubbermaid; *Adhesive:* Therm O Web; *Other:* Rubber shelf paper, shoelaces and staples.

## photo and journaling ideas

Follow Kristin's lead and snap photos of your favorite outfits, and then scrapbook why you love them. Consider:

- Team uniforms
- New outfits photographed with an old favorite to show a difference in size or style
- An array of outfits and shoes showcasing a favorite color in your wardrobe

### YOU CAN DO THIS!

1. Layer 12" long paper strips onto black cardstock.

2. Tear part of a decorative shoe box and staple it to your layout. *Note:* Spray it with deacidification spray first.

3. Layer photos, and then add your title and journaling block on top of the paper and shoe box.

# *memories* that matter

There isn't anything I enjoy more than spending time with my family. As a family, we spend time doing many things together including cooking, four-wheeling, watching movies and traveling for our daughter's softball tournaments. Whatever you do together, be sure that you record those memories. Here are some great page ideas from five readers this month!

document *memories* with family

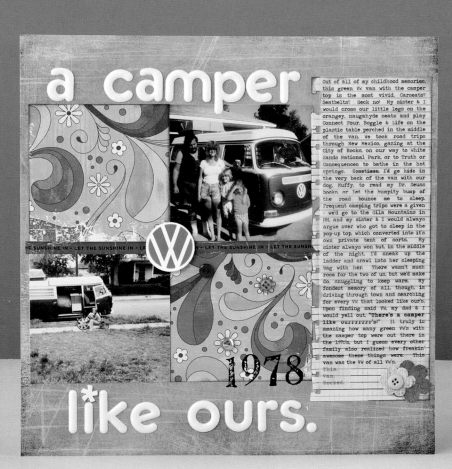

**A Camper Like Ours** *by Emilie Scoggins.* **Supplies** *Patterned paper:* BasicGrey and We R Memory Keepers; *Rub-on:* BasicGrey; *Stickers:* American Crafts and Cosmo Cricket; *Chalk:* ColorBox, Clearsnap; *VW logo:* Emilie's own design; *Font:* Traveling Typewriter; *Adhesive:* Dot 'n' Roller, Kokuyo.

*Emilie* Scoggins is a Fresh Face! She normally scrapbooks about her daughter, but on this page she captured her own childhood. Emilie chose patterned paper and letter stickers that would add to the retro feel of her page.

**YOU CAN DO THIS!**

❶ Choose a solid color of paper for your background.

❷ Cut two 4" x 4" squares from a sheet of patterned paper and print two 4" x 4" photos to create an 8" x 8" square on your layout.

❸ Place your text on the side and your title on the top and bottom of your page.

BY JOANNIE McBRIDE

**Puppy Love** *by Renee Lamb.* **Supplies** *Cardstock:* Imagine That! and The Paper Company; *Patterned paper:* Making Memories; *Letter dies:* QuickKutz; *Heart accents:* Renee's own designs; *Ribbon:* Michaels; *Tag:* K&Company; *Buttons:* The Paper Studio; *Vintage photo distressing ink:* Tim Holtz, Ranger Industries; *Font:* Pupcat; *Adhesive:* All Night Media, Plaid Enterprises, Tombow.

Congratulations to *Renee* Lamb for being the designer of this month's Readers' Pick layout and a Fresh Face! Some of Renee's interests include hiking, bike riding, enjoying the sun and watching horror movies. To create the flower border under her photos, Renee cut them out of patterned paper. She also created the scallop strip on top of her page by simply following the curves of the flowers on the patterned paper.

**YOU CAN DO THIS!**

❶ Print one 4" x 6" photo plus three smaller photos.

❷ Cut a thin strip of paper with a contrasting color to use as a border.

❸ Trim a notebook or use ledger patterned paper to use as your journaling strip.

*Kim* Watson created this page by using easy-to-do techniques. She used a golf tee to stamp the red circle around the 35 mark on the tape measure. Kim also likes to practice writing her journaling by placing a piece of tracing paper over the spot she intends to place her messaging.

**YOU CAN DO THIS!**

❶ Arrange your photos and embellishments on the page before you sketch out the arrow shape.

❷ Apply the red paint to a photo and let dry.

❸ Cut out an arrow shape to fit between your photos.

❹ Stitch with turquoise thread around the red-paint photo.

**Lil' Skater Dude** *by Kim Watson.* **Supplies** *Patterned paper:* Antalis, Bo-Bunny Press, K&Company and Making Memories; *Chipboard letters:* American Crafts, Enmarc and Making Memories; *Ink:* ColorBox, Clearsnap; *Paint:* Ranger Industries; *Circle template:* Coluzzle, Provo Craft; *Labels:* Dymo; *Pen:* Uni-ball Signo, Newell Rubbermaid; *Adhesive:* Scrapbook Adhesives by 3L; Mono Adhesive, Tombow; *Other:* Chipboard, thread, metal buttons, paper tape measure and masking tape.

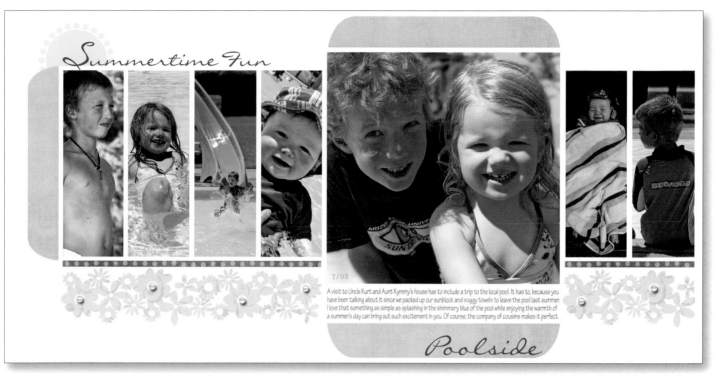

**Summertime Fun—Poolside** *by Heather Paulding.* **Supplies** *Software:* Adobe Photoshop Elements 3.0; *Patterned paper:* Wonderful by The Shabby Princess, *Yellow strip and blue flourish:* Color My World by Rhonna Farrer; *Sun:* Summertime by Jeri Ingalls for Autumn Leaves; *Rhinestone brads:* Bohemian Summer by Michelle Coleman; *Fonts:* Liorah, Pica 10 Pitch and Tekton Pro.

*Heather* Paulding is another Fresh Face this month. She originally submitted her layout to a different call. I contacted her several weeks later to be featured in this month's issue. Heather used bright colors and white space to reflect the feeling of a summer day.

## YOU CAN DO THIS!

❶ Crop six photos to 2″ x 6″ and crop one main photo to 7¼″ x 7¼″. Line the photos across the two-page layout (leaving some white space between each picture).

❷ Attach a narrow strip of patterned paper and flowers below the line of photos. Embellish with a sun, extending the sun beyond the edge of the photo. Cap off the end of the photo lineup with a blue paper strip rounded at the outer corners. Do the same for the top and bottom of the main photo.

❸ Add a title above the photos on the left page, starting the title in the center of the sun. Complete the title on the blue strip below the journaling.

❹ Create some sparkle by adding gems to the centers of the largest flowers in the flower border.

❺ Finish the layout by making a splash with a blue flourish in the bottom-left corner.

**July 2008** *by Sheri Horton.* **Supplies** *Software:* Microsoft Paint Shop Pro 9; *Patterned Papers, flowers and tags:* Bloom & Grow Mega Kit by Zoe Pearn; *Letters (re-colored):* Free Spirit Alphabet by C.D. Muckosky; *Sketch:* Dunia Stella Acaian; *Border and word art:* Life 365 by Gina Marie Huff; *Numbers:* Cozy Comfy Fall Mega Kit, "It's a Girl" graphic: Baby on Board by Kristin Cronin-Barrow; *Font:* Typenoksidi.

*Sheri* Horton is currently on maternity leave with her second child. (She gets a whole year off in Canada!) Sheri's goal this year is to take photos every day. At the end of each day, she adds her favorites to her personal blog. At the end of the year, she plans to print her blog as a book for her family to enjoy.

**YOU CAN DO THIS!**

❶ Gather photos to highlight a particular month, week or day. You want to have photos that reflect your everyday happenings along with the major highlights.

❷ Resize the photos into squares and put them onto one sheet before printing them, or use a square punch to punch out the main focus of the photo.

❸ Gather various paper scraps, along with a few embellishments, and arrange them on your page.

❹ Add journaling. You want your journaling to reflect the big highlights from that particular month, week or day, but you also want to include the everyday stuff. It's amazing how quickly you forget the little things in life.

# an *international* salute

Inspiration can come from anywhere—from a pretty wildflower on the side of the highway to a retro sign hanging in a store window. It isn't hard to find once we learn to see the possibilities around us. And no matter where we live or where we come from, we can always find inspiration in the art of others. Today we're celebrating the inspiration gathered throughout the world. I was so impressed by these beautiful international pages that I just had to share them with you!

**5 layouts from *across* the globe**

## HOKKAIDO, JAPAN

**How We Spent Our Summer Vacation** *by Reiko Tsuchida.* **Supplies** *Cardstock:* Bazzill Basics Paper; *Patterned paper:* Creative Imaginations, Daisy D's Paper Co., Jenni Bowlin Studio and Making Memories; *Stickers:* 7gypsies, Heidi Swapp for Advantus and Making Memories; *Button:* Autumn Leaves; *Flower:* Heidi Swapp for Advantus; *Other:* Tag.

Besides being on a design team for an Australian scrapbook store, Reiko enjoys photography. She definitely captured the joy and excitement of her daughter in the photos she used on this page! It may be a common tip, but Reiko benefited from taking lots of quick photos at different angles. This allowed her to tell a story by using multiple photos from the same event.

CK creative editor Britney Mellen fell in love with Reiko's style while attending CKU–Japan. When Britney returned to the office, we asked to see more of Reiko's work and knew that we had to share this layout with you.

### YOU CAN DO THIS!
Add four 4" x 6" photos to the background with this easy design configuration.

**BY JOANNIE MCBRIDE**

**CAPE TOWN, SOUTH AFRICA**

**Juicy Fruit** by Kim Watson. **Supplies** *Patterned paper:* Making Memories, Provo Craft and WorldWin; *Letter stickers:* Making Memories; *Rub-on letters:* Die Cuts With a View; *Chipboard bird:* me & my BIG ideas; *Tab:* KI Memories; *Brads:* Heidi Swapp for Advantus; *Paper frills:* Doodlebug Design; *Circle cutter:* Coluzzle, Provo Craft; *Adhesives:* Mono Adhesive, Tombow; E-Z Runner, Scrapbook Adhesives by 3L; *Pen:* Zig Millennium, EK Success; *Other:* Cardstock, ribbon, tag, thread and embroidery floss.

Kim has been involved in the fashion industry for many years, and it's no wonder that her passion for color and design has translated to her scrapbook pages. I love her use of circles mimicking the shape of the melon. The bright colors convey the feeling of summer, and the photos would make anyone long for these warm, carefree days! Kim submitted this page to our call for layouts from international readers.

### YOU CAN DO THIS!

To create a look similar to Kim's:

❶ Stitch a circle onto cardstock as a background.

❷ Cut a scalloped-edge strip and a small circle from patterned paper; adhere to page.

❸ Attach two cardstock blocks, then add ribbon strips and photos.

❹ Stitch several buttons onto the page, add a tab to one photo and journal on a tag.

❺ Add rub-on and letter stickers for the title, and finish with a paper frill.

**SOLINGEN, GERMANY**

**So You** by Janine Langer. **Supplies** *Cardstock:* Bazzill Basics Paper; *Patterned paper and flowers and collage sheets:* Prima; *Stickers:* 7gypsies; *Paper ribbon:* K&Company; *Chipboard letters:* BasicGrey; *Font:* Kozuka, Adobe; *Other:* Twine.

As a stay-at-home mom, Janine can spend a lot of time with her family. One thing that's especially important to her is being able to capture the everyday photos of her family's life. In this layout, she wanted to show her son's movement and fun during a recent soccer practice. To obtain this feel on her page, Janine used bright colors and lots of circles. She submitted this page to a call for layouts from international readers, and we requested it two weeks later.

### YOU CAN DO THIS!

To create a design like Janine's:

❶ Draw a large shape (the artisan label here) onto patterned paper with a pencil and cut it out.

❷ Cut a large paper block to fit inside the shape, then cut or punch the circles and add them to the layered block.

❸ Adhere several page accents with dimensional adhesive to add dimension.

❹ Cover chipboard letters with paper for your title, then distress them and ink the edges.

❺ Complete the page by stitching around the large shape if desired.

STRÄNGNÄS, SWEDEN

**GREAT IDEA!**

Anna created a cool flower on her album cover by layering tulle, a felt circle and a button, then hand-stitching the stem and leaf with embroidery floss.

**Favorites 2007** *by Anna Bjorklund.*
**Supplies** *Stickers:* American Crafts; *Bird:* Prima; *Ink:* ColorBox Fluid Chalk, Clearsnap; *Labels:* Dymo; *Wire:* Bind-it-All, Zutter Innovative Products; *Buttons:* Doodlebug Design (green) and unknown (black); *Other:* Felt, tulle and embroidery floss.

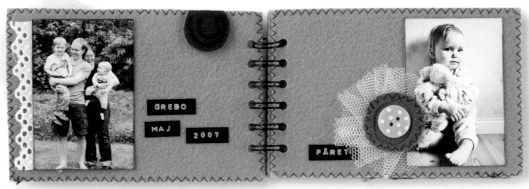

Anna created this fun felt album to showcase some favorite photos from 2007. It was simple enough that she was able to re-create similar albums to pass out as gifts. Says Anna, "Hand stitching small embellishments using felt and embroidery floss is both fun and easy. The stitching doesn't have to be perfect—the result is cute anyway."

**YOU CAN DO THIS!**

To make your own felt album:

❶ Cut album pages from thick felt in your desired size. Machine stitch around the edges and make holes for wire binding.
*Note:* Anna wasn't sure if her Bind-it-All machine would punch through the felt, so she created a paper template and used an eyelet setter to make the holes for the binding.

❷ Decorate the pages with photos, lace and other embellishments.

❸ Bind the album pages together, using a machine such as the Bind-it-All.

METRO MANILA, PHILIPPINES

**japanese again**

Having Japanese food three times in one week? Makes me think I went to Tokyo instead of Vancouver. Nevertheless, it was great hanging out with Car, Oa, Chris, Sam, Marty and James. Can't wait to go back to Vancouver! AUG 2007

With Christine's degree in history, it wasn't much of a stretch to understand the importance of creating memories not only for herself but for her family as well. By choosing colors that complement her photos rather than drown them out, she was able to balance out the not-so-perfect photos. What was most important to Christine was documenting the event rather than worrying about using perfect photos. Remember: It really is okay to use those not-so-perfect photos. The memory remains the same, regardless of how the pictures turn out.

**GREAT IDEA!**

This layout uses 4" x 6" photos, so it was easy to create! Crop some height from your photos as desired, then line them up on your layout. Add a large accent on the other side of the page to balance the photos.

**Japanese Again** by Christine Herrin. **Supplies** Cardstock: Bazzill Basics Paper; Patterned paper: Scenic Route; Chipboard letters and pen: American Crafts; Other: Paint and staples.

## 2 READER TRENDS

What's popular right now? I spotted the following trends on readers' submissions:

■ **Shapes.** Combining shapes of different sizes (whether as an accent or as an actual page) continues to be a big trend. Check out these great products from Queen & Co. (www.queenandcompany. com) and Close To My Heart (www. closetomy-heart.com) to get your inspiration going.

■ **Bright colors.** These continue to create a hip and funky feel and convey a fun sense of emotion. Don't be afraid to reach for that bright sheet of cardstock or patterned paper. It's probably exactly what you need to make a memory come to life.!

# {  *happiness* is  }

There's something to be said for watching a beautiful sunset, snuggling in bed with a good book or enjoying that last piece of homemade pie. With all life offers, I challenge you to snap some photos of whatever it is that makes you smile and scrapbook them. I'd love to see what you come up with! E-mail your page to *editorial@creatingkeepsakes.com*.

**scrap what *makes* you smile!**

**My Job** *by Pamela Young.* **Supplies** *Patterned paper:* American Crafts, Crate Paper and Pink Paislee; *Stamps:* Unity Stamp Company; *Ink and embossing powder:* Stampin' Up!; *Frame pieces:* Love, Elsie for KI Memories; *Eyelets:* The Paper Company; *Foam letters:* American Crafts; *Font:* American Typewriter; *Adhesive:* Mono Adhesive, Tombow.

*Pamela* Young is a stay-at-home mom who loves spending time with her family. She enjoys visiting her parents every Sunday, playing games with her family and quilting. Pamela's secret desire is to write a book someday.

### YOU CAN DO THIS!

❶ Stamp two borders with circles, and place a row of photos on top to make a scalloped border. Add two paper strips.

❷ Stamp an image in the corner, and add a title and journaling.

❸ Add various embellishments.

**BY JOANNIE McBRIDE**

**Annette** Pixley submitted this page as a general submission, and I requested it just one week later. This mother of three is a preschool teacher and enjoys scrapbooking, reading and riding motorcycles.

### YOU CAN DO THIS!

❶ Cut photos into 2" x 2" squares.

❷ Cut patterned paper into 2" x 2" squares. Adhere photos and patterned paper in a grid pattern, leaving some squares blank.

❸ Add a title and journaling.

**Beauty and the Beast** by Annette Pixley. **Supplies** *Cardstock:* Bazzill Basics Paper; *Patterned paper:* Crate Paper, KI Memories, Luxe Designs and Making Memories; *Die cuts:* Bazzill Basics Paper and Chatterbox; *Chipboard:* Heidi Swapp for Advantus and Maya Road; *Mickey Mouse embellishment:* EK Success; *Punch:* Fiskars Americas; *Brad:* Making Memories; *Stickers and pen:* American Crafts; *Adhesive:* 3M.

**Kim** Moreno took these photos of her daughter just for fun, but they fit perfectly with the story she wanted to tell about her daughter, who made goals for herself this year and reached them all! To create the large star, Kim cut the shape from patterned paper, backed it with cardstock and adhered it to the page using dimensional adhesive.

### YOU CAN DO THIS!

❶ Print wallet-size photos, and then back them with white cardstock.

❷ Arrange photos on layout as shown. Print journaling on cardstock and embellish. Add a title.

❸ Cut stars from patterned paper, layer the paper along the right side of the layout and add embellishments.

**Reach 4 the Stars** by Kim Moreno. **Supplies** *Cardstock:* Core'dinations; *Patterned paper, ribbon, journaling spots and stickers:* Jillibean Soup; *Brads:* American Crafts; *Punch:* EK Success; *Adhesive:* Therm O Web.

**Million-Dollar View** *by Cathy Pascual.* **Supplies** *Software:* Adobe Photoshop CS2; *Patterned paper:* Altered Ego by Paislee Press; *Frame:* Baroque Clipping Masks by Paislee Press; *Date stamp:* Presslines No. 3 by Paislee Press; *Photo action:* Pioneer Woman Photography; *Fonts:* Amelie and New Circle.

*Cathy* Pascual is a stay-at-home mom who loves photography and all forms of scrapbooking. Spending time with her family, watching movies, hiking the trails around her neighborhood and editing the school newsletter for her daughter's preschool are just a few of the activities Cathy enjoys doing.

**YOU CAN DO THIS!**

❶ Add a photo action to or colored transparency over your picture to give it a retro look. Enlarge the photo to 8¼" x 7", and add a frame around it.

❷ For the title, choose two contrasting fonts. Choose font colors by sampling colors from the photo itself—just use the eyedropper tool in a photo-editing program to click on the colors of your choice in the photo.

❸ For the journaling, create a text box on the right-hand side of the page. Add a large date at the end of the journaling block—it will serve as a resting point for the eye.

**I Adore You** by Jennifer Arble. **Supplies** Cardstock: Canson; Patterned paper: Cactus Pink and me & my BIG ideas; Punch and chipboard word and hearts: EK Success; Journaling spot: Making Memories; Journaling paper: Scenic Route; Metal accents: Marcella by K&Company; Photo corners: Heidi Swapp for Advantus; Transparencies: Heidi Swapp for Advantus and My Mind's Eye; Rub-ons: Marcella by K&Company and me & my BIG ideas; Adhesive: Elmer's and Kokuyo.

*Jennifer* Arble is an organization junkie—she spends hours organizing and reorganizing. She also works full-time and enjoys camping with her family, kayaking and reading. Jennifer created most of this page on an outing while she had a little downtime. She added her journaling and embellishments once she returned home.

**YOU CAN DO THIS!**

❶ Adhere a 6" x 8" piece of patterned paper 2" from the left and top sides of your page. Adhere a 3" x 8" piece of journaling paper 1" from the right and top sides, adding a ¾" x 11" strip across the center of the page.

❷ Adhere two 4" x 4" pictures at an angle, and tuck one photo under the paper strip.

❸ Add a title and embellishments.

# 2-page layouts to *inspire* you!

We all have photos of a special event or even of everyday life that we need to scrapbook. It doesn't have to be complicated to get these pictures out of our photo boxes or off our computers and into our scrapbooks. Check out these five creative layouts for quick, effective ways to document some of your favorite moments.

**5 quick and *easy* projects**

**Time** by Laurel Moser. **Supplies** *Patterned paper:* Crate Paper, KI Memories and My Mind's Eye; *Brads:* Bo-Bunny Press; *Clip and ribbon:* Making Memories; *Tag:* BasicGrey; *Chipboard:* Provo Craft; *Metal frame:* Forever in Time; *Rub-on:* Daisy D's Paper Co.; *Sentiment sticker:* EK Success.

For Fresh Face Laurel Moser, finding time to scrapbook hasn't been easy. She's a stay-at-home mom to four sons. Now that her youngest son, Jude, is two, Laurel can start dabbling in scrapbooking again. This layout is the first she's created of her youngest son, and she is thrilled to share it with all of you.

### YOU CAN DO THIS!

❶ Print out one large (6½" x 8") black-and-white photo for your main focal picture and a 5" x 7" horizontal picture, plus three or four smaller photos that you can crop to flow with your curved border on the second page.

❷ Create a curved border along the bottom of the pages and place the title and journaling on the curve on the left-hand page.

❸ Add embellishments and sentiments as desired.

**BY JOANNIE McBRIDE**

**Palace of Fine Arts** by Barbara Dalton. **Supplies** *Cardstock:* Bazzill Basics Paper; *Patterned paper:* My Mind's Eye (red dot) and Stampin' Up! (green); *Letter stickers:* Doodlebug Design; *Rub-ons:* Adornit - Carolee's Creations; *Flowers:* Prima; *Buttons:* Stampin' Up!; *Font:* Arial, Microsoft.

This layout started as a challenge for *Barbara* Dalton, who was inspired by a friend who creates multiphoto travel pages. Barbara wanted to do the same thing, and I'd say she accomplished just that with this beautiful layout. Notice how she captured the splendor of this magnificent building through photos taken at multiple angles around its perimeter.

**YOU CAN DO THIS!**

❶ Choose photos that offer different perspectives of the same image or scene.

❷ Decide on a title that can be easily spread across two pages and makes visual and semantic sense.

❸ Use two contrasting patterned papers and embellishments to provide uniformity and create visual appeal.

**City Girl** by Gretchen McElveen. **Supplies** *Patterned paper:* Provo Craft; *Rub-on letters:* American Crafts and Junkitz; *Acrylic stars and decorative tape:* Heidi Swapp for Advantus; *Chipboard embellishment:* Scenic Route; *Large mailbox letters:* The Home Depot.

*Gretchen* McElveen works as a physical therapist and enjoys many things, from Mexican food to NASCAR! The layout here tells the story of how she prefers her small hometown to the big city. Gretchen is fond of visiting new places—she just prefers coming home to the comforts that her small town provides. Her layout explains why.

**YOU CAN DO THIS!**

❶ Line up five vertical pictures across the two-page layout, starting from the left.

❷ Add strips of patterned paper along the bottom of the photos.

❸ Add your title to the right of the pictures and strips of journaling along the left-hand side of the layout.

**in no particular order...**

**top 5s from the seriously noncommittal**

Best soda from fast food places within one mile of work: Arby's · Chipotle · Qdoba · Taco Bell · McDonald's

Favorite "affordable" sit down restaurants: Rockne's · Applebee's · IHOP · Don Ramon's · Winking Lizard

Best ways to spend rare and precious free time: Surfing the internet · Taking pictures of goofy stuff (see above) · scrapbooking · Hanging out at the pool · Playing Scrabble/Cards/Dominos · Best Blogs: Strobist · Post Secret

Cathy Zielski · Karen Russell · Jessica Claire Photography · Favorite foods that clog my arteries and make my ass big: Cheesesteak · Cheesecake · Sausage · Macaroni · Cookies · Favorite Cookies (this one is in order!):

Snickerdoodle · Sugar · Homemade Oatmeal Raisin · Peanut Butter · White Chocolate Chip and Macadamia Nut · Foods that have redeeming qualities: Fuji or Jonagold Apples · Watermelon · Guacamole (hey! it's good fat!)

Honeydew Melon · Carrots · Favorite Female Artists: Dido · Imogen Heap · Regina Spektor · Suzanne Vega · Gwen Stephani · Best Male Singers: Paul Simon · Mike Doughty · Beck · Jack Johnson (ack!) · Johnny Cash

Favorite Groups: Soul Coughing · Modest Mouse · They Might Be Giants · Sublime · The Ditty Bops · Pink Martini · The Bare Naked Ladies · Hot Chip · Blink 182 · Green Day · The Vince Guaraldi Trio · Boys from the County Hell

**Top Five** *by Caroline Davis.* **Supplies** *Patterned paper:* K&Company; *Lettering dies:* Diesel, Vixen and Moxie SkinniMini, QuickKutz; *Circle punch:* Family Treasures; *Font:* Advantage, Internet.

*Caroline* Davis gets to spend her time doing two things she loves. First, she works as an assistant manager in a camera/scrapbook store. Second, as demonstrated on this layout, she enjoys taking pictures of goofy stuff! Normally she wouldn't scrap these random photos, but they fit perfectly on this clever layout.

YOU CAN DO THIS!

❶ Create your title using various fonts and colored cardstock.

❷ Arrange an assortment of photos printed at the same height into a strip.

❸ Print your journaling in lists on colored cardstock, leaving plenty of space for cutting and making sure that two lines of each color are printed in a row.

**Sticky Hot** *by Ashley Gailey.* **Supplies** *Cardstock:* Bazzill Basics Paper; *Patterned paper:* Autumn Leaves, Chatterbox, KI Memories and Rusty Pickle, *Chipboard letters:* Heidi Swapp for Advantus; *Buttons:* 7gypsies; *Font:* Stone Sans, Internet.

Sometimes even the hottest, most miserable days can bring fun memories. Here, *Ashley* Gailey created a layout using photos she took in her backyard on a really hot and humid day. Looking at these photos, it's clear that her son and daughter know how to make the best of a sticky, hot situation!

YOU CAN DO THIS!

❶ Combine one 8" x 11¼" photo, three 4" x 6" photos and two 2" x 6" photos on your background paper.

❷ Cut 1" strips of various types of coordinating patterned paper and adhere them to the background paper in an eye-pleasing pattern.

❸ Add journaling, title and button embellishments. Ashley stitched star outlines for a subtle but decorative look.

# pages from
## *readers* like you

I love finding new ideas for creating! Whether I'm in my kitchen trying out a fast-and-easy recipe or in my scrap space finding innovative ways to add personal flair to my pages, I can't get enough inspiration. That's why I want to share five pages with you from readers that showcase fabulous techniques.

*10 more tips* **for creating great pages!**

**My Life Is Wonderful** *by Lydia Jackson.* **Supplies** *Cardstock:* Core'dinations; *Patterned paper:* Cosmo Cricket and Scenic Route; *Buttons:* Autumn Leaves; *Rub-ons:* American Crafts; *Adhesive:* Zig, EK Success; *Other:* Fonts, date stamp, ink and thread.

Fresh Face *Lydia* Jackson has been scrapbooking for 11 years and loves all things action. The softer side of her loves to paint, sew, dream or curl up with a good book.

**❶ Straighter Stitches**
To achieve perfectly straight stitching on her page, Lydia created a cardstock guide by folding a piece of cardstock in half (approximately 3" x 2") and temporarily adhering it to her sewing machine at the desired distance to use as a guide while sewing on her layout.

**❷ Straighter Rub-Ons**
Follow the lines on patterned paper as a guide when adding rub-ons for your title.

**BY JOANNIE McBRIDE**

**No Coffee for Me, Mom** by Joscelyne Cutchens. **Supplies** *Patterned paper, label, stitches and "hilarious" brush:* Color My World by Karla Dudley Designs; *Dot brush and "life" tag:* Spring '09 Extras by Karla Dudley Designs; *Fonts:* Cafe Rojo; *Other:* Stamp frames and journaling card.

## Joscelyne

Cutchens lives in Honolulu, Hawaii— she grew up there, and her husband is currently stationed on a ship there. She loves technology, the world of blogging, computers, web design and social media.

**❸ Dotted Chipboard Letters**

Update solid-colored chipboard letters by using a white-opaque pen to create dots on them.

**❹ Split Journaling**

Break up your journaling over two journaling spots, and tuck each of them under your photos.

## Laura

Vegas works full time as a daycare provider. She has scrapbooked for over 14 years and enjoys photography. She loves organizing her scrapbook supplies as well as other items in her home.

**❺ Unexpected Colors**

Try using unexpected colors on a themed page, just as Laura did here with her Halloween photos. Instead of using dark colors, she chose to use bright, primary colors.

**❻ Stapled Tags**

Get creative when you attach tags to your pages. Remove the string from the holes in the tags and attach each tag to the layout with a staple through each hole.

**Ketchup** by Laura Vegas. **Supplies** *Patterned paper:* KI Memories; *Cork paper:* Karen Foster Design; *Acrylic letters:* Heidi Swapp for Advantus; *Ribbon, tag and brad:* Making Memories; *Silver accents:* Michaels; *Font:* AL Old Remington; *Adhesive:* Herma, EK Success; Glue Dots International; *Other:* Staples and clip.

**Father of the Bride** by Lisa Pate. **Supplies** *Software:* Adobe Photoshop Elements 6.0; *Patterned paper:* Pina - Designer Papers + Elements by Andrea Victoria; *Distressing effect:* Worn Page Edges by Lynn Grieveson; *Tags:* Groceria Words ("My Girl") and Date Spots ("June 04") by Katie Pertiet; *Clock:* Clock Parts No. 02 Clock Face Collection by Katie Pertiet; *Felt heart:* Have a Heart Felts No. 02 by Pattie Knox; *Clip:* Metal Clip Assortment by Katie Pertiet; *Stitching:* Stitched by Anna No. 02 by Anna Aspnes; *Photo collage template:* Photo Clusters No. 14 by Katie Pertiet; *Decorative pin:* Pin-Its by Pattie Knox; *Phrase brushes:* Wedding No. 02 Hand Drawn Brushes and Hello Life Title + Journal Block by Ali Edwards; *Font:* VT Portable Remington.

Fresh Face *Lisa* Pate is a junior-high math teacher who is obsessed with cupcakes and everything pink! She submitted her page at the end of April, and it was selected for publication a couple weeks later.

**❼ Polaroid Papers**

Sometimes we think the Polaroid look is only for photos, but Lisa shows how great it can be with blocks of patterned paper.

**❽ Photo and Paper Layering**

Papers don't always need to be layered underneath photos. Notice how the far-left and bottom-right paper squares are layered over small portions of the photos on Lisa's layout. And in case you want to re-create this page yourself, you'll be glad to know that the photo sizes are 2" x 2" and 2" x 4".

*Iris* Babao Uy is part of an event management group that specializes in mall events. She's also a very active person who frequents the gym and enjoys running.

**❾ Shape Contrast**

To break up the long strips of patterned paper in her sunburst design, Iris added one button to each strip. The contrast in the shape and size between the two elements adds a playful, appealing feel.

**❿ Photo Motion**

Notice how the photo sizes on the layout increase from left to right? It's a subtle way to reflect how Iris's daughter gets larger in perspective as she swings toward her, so the page viewer gets a sense of the swinging motion as well. Clever!

**Higher, Daddy!** by Iris Babao Uy. **Supplies** *Cardstock:* Bazzill Basics Paper; *Patterned paper:* Hambly Screen Prints and October Afternoon; *Felt:* Fancy Pants Designs; *Brads:* We R Memory Keepers; *Buttons:* Autumn Leaves; *Letter stickers:* October Afternoon; *Transparency overlay:* Hambly Screen Prints; *Chipboard and pen:* American Crafts; *Adhesive:* Uhu.

# *reader* gallery

BY JOANNIE McBRIDE

**WHETHER YOU'RE RECORDING** memories about your favorite hobbies, a special date, or even your everyday moments, we've got great ideas that will help you get those photos into your scrapbooks! So if it's solutions you're looking for—keep reading. You'll find tips for journaling your stories, using fun accents, and creating quick pages.

helpful *tips* from readers like you

**Craft Day** *by Laina Lamb.* **Supplies:** *Cardstock:* Archiver's and Bazzill Basics Paper; *Patterned paper, chipboard, and stickers:* October Afternoon; *Rub-ons:* 3Birds Design; *Ink:* Ranger Industries; *Decorative scissors and punch:* EK Success; *Pen:* American Crafts; *Adhesive:* 3M and Plaid Enterprises.

**Laina Lamb** saves time by storing her leftover papers by color. Laina's favorite way to use left-over striped patterned paper is to cut the paper against the direction of the stripe, just like she did with her border strip here.

**DESIGN TIP:**
Laina used punched images, ribbon, and patterned paper to dress up a plain journaling spot.

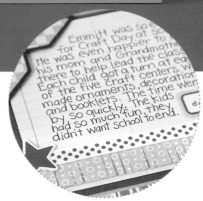

Readers' Pick winner **Jana Morton** is a stay-at-home mom who loves to design her pages with digital embellishments like clips, pins, and tags to make her layouts pop. To create a similar look traditionally, group small embellishments around cropped photos.

**DESIGN TIP:**

Cluster smaller photos and embellishments to complement a larger focal photo.

**Boots On** by Jana Morton. **Digital Supplies:** *Software:* Adobe; *Paper:* Jesse Edwards, Katie Pertiet, and Lynne Grieveson; *Frame:* Katie Pertiet; *Brushes:* Anna Aspnes and Katie Pertiet; *Overlay:* Anna Aspnes; *Clip, numbers, postmarks, stamps and word label:* Katie Pertiet; *Other:* Pin and staples.

**Linda Sobolewski** enjoys playing with and cutting up patterned paper just to see what creative results pop up. Patterned paper can be used for many things on your layouts including page accents, photo mats, titles, border strips, or to dress up a journaling spot.

**TECHNIQUE TIP:**

Create your own volleyball accent simply by using a circle punch and some embroidery floss or string.

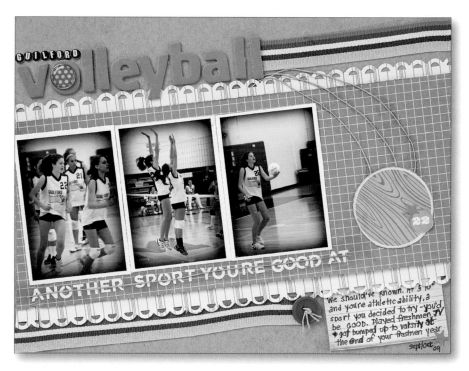

**Volleyball** by Linda Sobolewski. **Supplies:** *Cardstock:* Bazzill Basics Paper; *Patterned paper:* Cosmo Cricket, Jillibean Soup, and Studio Calico; *Punches:* Fiskars Americas and Martha Stewart Crafts; *Stickers:* American Crafts and Jenni Bowlin Studio; *Brads:* My Mind's Eye; *Note card:* Jenni Bowlin Studio; *Twine:* Karen Foster Design; *Pen:* American Crafts; *Adhesive:* 3M.

**Kindergarten** by Julie DeGuia. **Digital Supplies:** *Software:* Adobe; *Cardstock and epoxy accent:* Katie Portict; *Page template:* Michelle Martin; *Heart pebbles, felt, and letters.* Pattie Knox; *Stitching:* Anna Aspnes; *Name plate and bus:* Lynn Grieveson; *Twill tape:* Ali Edwards; *Fonts:* Schoolhouse Printed A and Rockwell.

**Julie DeGuia** created this school page in a snap by using a photo grid and minimal elements. To get this same look traditionally, place your photos in a grid, then add stitching or use a pen to create an outline. Add embellishments to finish your look.

DESIGN TIP:

Slightly overlap title letters to create a dimensional feel to your layout.

**1st Day** *by Amy Peterman.* **Supplies:** *Cardstock:* Die Cuts with a View; *Patterned paper, brads, chipboard, journaling spot, and ribbon:* Fancy Pants Designs; *Stickers:* Fancy Pants Designs, Little Yellow Bicycle, and Making Memories; *Embossed chipboard and spray ink:* Tattered Angels; *Paint:* Ranger Industries; *Ink:* Clearsnap; *Pen:* American Crafts; *Adhesive:* Scrapbook Adhesives by 3L.

**Amy Peterman** loves to take lots of photos. She chooses to scrap the photos that best tell the story and capture the moment. It's perfectly okay for you to not scrapbook all the photos you take—organize those photos in albums using sheet protectors specifically made for un-cropped 4" x 6" photos.

**TECHNIQUE TIP:**

To create a background like Amy's, use various chipboard numbers and lay them on some cardstock. Spray over numbers with spray ink.

# 5 fantastic
# reader pages

I'm so grateful for the chance to work for a magazine I love and for being able to showcase wonderful reader pages. The best part is that there are so many unique styles to choose from! As you look through the pages this month, remember to embrace your unique style. Whether you enjoy a well-embellished page or a more streamlined look, celebrate who you are as an artist.

**fall in**
*love*
**with your style**

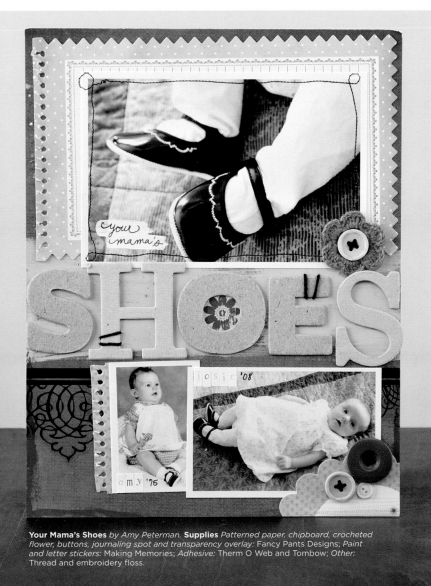

**Your Mama's Shoes** by Amy Peterman. **Supplies** *Patterned paper, chipboard, crocheted flower, buttons, journaling spot and transparency overlay:* Fancy Pants Designs; *Paint and letter stickers:* Making Memories; *Adhesive:* Therm O Web and Tombow; *Other:* Thread and embroidery floss.

*Amy* Peterman is a stay-at-home mom who enjoys knitting, reading and camping. She loves the process of scrapbooking—finding the photos and reminiscing about the memories, picking out the product and creating the layout. On this page she wanted to showcase how both she and her daughter wore the same shoes. She highlighted the shoes in a large photo and added smaller photos of both wearing the Mary Janes.

**PRODUCT TIP:**
Amy generally paints her chipboard letters, but she wanted to leave them raw for this page. A few of the letters were pre-coated, so to get a raw effect on them she simply peeled off the top layer of the chipboard.

**BY JOANNIE MCBRIDE**

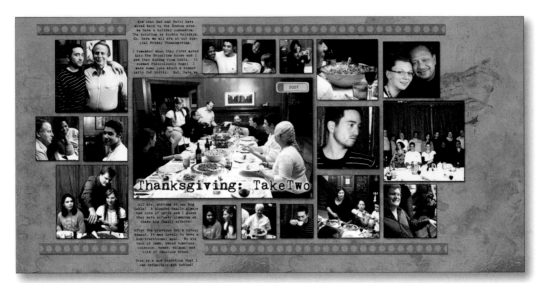

**Thanksgiving: Take Two** by Julie Fei-Fan Balzer. **Supplies** Patterned paper: Aja Abney; Ribbon: Lauren Reid; Label: Audrey Neal; Font: Kingthings Typewriter; Software: Adobe Photoshop CS3.

*Julie* Fei-Fan Balzer loves living in New York City, where she works as an artistic director. She recently purchased a vintage 1930s typewriter. Everything she creates now has type all over it because she loves the vintage look. To get out of a scrapbooking rut, Julie believes that a layout, no matter how unfinished, can be saved by adding a little paint (or a lot of it).

**PHOTO CROPPING TIP:** Place an uncropped photo in the center of your layout as a focal point, and then arrange 16 cropped photos around it to complete the look. Many of the smaller photos can be trimmed from the same photo if you crop carefully!

**Birthday Cake & a Cookie** by Christine Hertel. **Supplies** Cardstock: Bazzill Basics Paper; Patterned paper, flower transparency, owl, journaling spot and circle tag: My Little Shoebox; Number stickers: Making Memories; Lettering template: Silhouette, QuicKutz; Fonts: Fling and Pharmacy; Adhesive: Glue Glider Pro Max, GlueArts; Therm O Web; Other: Pen.

Fresh Face *Christine* Hertel's time-saving strategy for scrapbooking faster is having a plan. She likes to sketch out what she's doing. Christine has a degree in visual communication and a minor in illustration, so it's no wonder she likes to have a blueprint!

**DESIGN TIP:** On this layout, Christine downloaded an image of the patterned paper from the manufacturer's website and used it to lay out her pages on the computer, which helped her see how all the photos and papers were going to look before doing any of the actual cutting.

*Sue* Mylde is another Fresh Face this month! She was born in Singapore and has lived in Italy, England, Hong Kong, Canada, Norway and Scotland. She married her high-school sweetheart, and together they have a four-year-old daughter. Sue's daughter loves traveling just as much as Sue and her husband. In fact, this page is about her daughter's love for traveling, discovering cool places and meeting new people.

**BUDGET-SAVING TIP:** To maximize your paper, don't use the entire sheet if you're only going to see the outside border. On this layout, Sue cut out the middle of the red paper and saved it for another layout.

**Travel Bug** *by Sue Mylde.* **Supplies** *Cardstock:* Bazzill Basics Paper; *Patterned paper:* Graphic 45 and Pink Paislee; *Rub-ons:* Marah Johnson for Creative Imaginations; *Letter stickers:* American Crafts and Heidi Swapp for Advantus; *Font:* Rough Typewriter.

*Christi* Spadoni is a big-time Red Sox fan. She absolutely loves summer. And she's a newly married woman. *(Congratulations, Christi!)* Christi fit three small photos on a 4" x 6" print, and she used the extra space on the print for her title.

**JOURNALING TIP:** There's no time like the present to record your thoughts. So if you're waiting for others to finish Thanksgiving dinner, use a paper napkin or place card to jot down your thoughts until you can transfer them to your layout.

**Auntie Sheila's China** *by Christi Spadoni.* **Supplies** *Cardstock:* Bazzill Basics Paper (brown, crimson and kraft) and KI Memories (orange); *Epoxy sticker:* KI Memories; *Lettering template:* Silhouette, QuickKutz; *Corner-rounder punch:* Creative Memories; *Ink:* Clearsnap; *Pen:* Slick Writers, American Crafts; *Adhesive:* Scotch ATG, 3M.

# { colorful & spunky }

Nothing says delightful like the five pages highlighted here. They're colorful, playful and full of spunk. They showcase the artists' passion for the people, places and things they love. Can't you just feel the energy coming from the pages?!

check out these *reader* layouts!

**KATHIE LINK,** who originally submitted her page to the Australian version of *Creating Keepsakes*, is a "Fresh Face" whose page I couldn't resist showcasing. Kathie and her husband enjoy renovating houses and are currently on their fourth project. She is mom to a little boy and works part-time as an occupational health and safety adviser. Note how Kathie has captured her son's love of trucks on this layout—in particular, his love for "Scoop" (or "Koop" as he calls him) from the *Bob the Builder* series.

Trucks *by Kathie Link.* **Supplies** *Patterned paper:* Daisy D's Paper Co., K&Company and Mustard Moon; *Letter stickers:* American Crafts; *Stickers:* Daisy D's Paper Co.; *Scalloped chipboard border:* Creative Imaginations; *Ribbon:* Prima; *Flower:* My Mind's Eye; *Brads:* 7gypsies; *Pen:* Pigment Liner, Staedtler.

**BY JOANNIE McBRIDE**

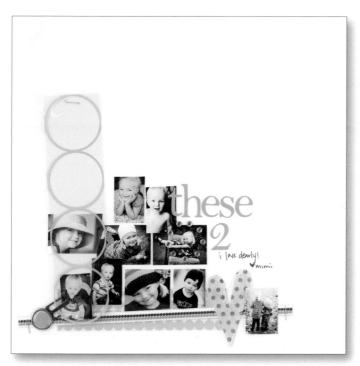

*These 2 by Meg Barker.* **Supplies** *Cardstock:* Bazzill Basics Paper; *Patterned paper:* Sweetwater; *Pebble clip:* Making Memories; *Ribbon:* American Crafts; *Overlay:* Hambly Studios; *Letters:* Heidi Grace Designs; *Rhinestones:* K&Company; *Other:* Staples.

What I loved most about *Meg* Barker's page is that she used so many small photos (10!). What's even more fun is that she cut her photos with scissors rather than a cutter. The results are imperfect and her photos differ in size, but that's what gives the page a more handmade feel. Meg was a "Standout Reader" in our June 2008 issue. She began submitting more pages to the "Fresh Face" call, and within a week of her submitting this adorable page, we contacted her to request it for publication.

**YOU CAN DO THIS!**

❶ Print out fun small pictures in different sizes.

❷ Find some of your favorite elements to add to your page! They don't all have to match.

❸ Cluster the elements to make a fun, easy-to-finish, beautiful layout! Overlay some of the pictures to add a little dimension.

*Susan* Dupre submitted this page in the "Defining Moments in Your Life" contest held last May at CKC–Manchester. What a fun, bright page! I love how it's so full of life. The journaling is cleverly tucked behind a photo, which doubles as a pocket. Once an interior designer, Susan is now a stay-at-home mom who spends a lot of time playing games and watching cartoons. She has fond memories of her time living in London, including the birth of her son and the many friendships she created while living abroad.

**YOU CAN DO THIS!**

❶ Lay four photos out in the design shown here.

❷ Scatter hand-cut clouds or other embellishments around your photos.

❸ Add lace and ribbon near the bottom of the layout to anchor the design, placing your title on the top. Tuck hidden journaling on a tag behind one of the photos.

*My London by Susan Dupre.* **Supplies** *Patterned paper:* Pink Paislee and Sassafras; *Ribbon:* Jo-Ann Stores and Making Memories; *Letters:* Sassafras; *Ink:* Ranger Industries; *Other:* Tag.

*Carey* Bridges was featured in "Our Faves, Your Faves" in our December 2007 issue, but this is her first time having a page featured in the magazine. The larger photo on her layout is one of her husband's favorites, and I can see why. Sweet expression! The smaller photo is equally expressive, and I love how Carey captured the concentration on her son's face while he worked on a dot-to-dot activity. This page is the first layout in a book Carey is creating for and about her son. I'd say she's off to a great start!

**Amazing** by Carey Bridges. **Supplies** *Software:* Adobe Photoshop Elements 6.0; *Digital patterned paper, frame, stars, brads, rickrack, staples and letters:* Snazzy Boy Kit by Mandy McQuillis, *www.mandymystiques.wordpress.com*; *Digital journaling stamp:* Carina Gardner, *www.diginirvana.com*; *Digital swirl brushes:* Obsidian Dawn, *www.brushes.obsidiandawn.com*; *Digital scallop paper cutters:* www.digiscrap.ch; *Font:* Peamissy, Internet.

I love how *Amy* Peterman created dimension with felt accents, popped-up photos and chipboard title letters. To create the picture of her daughter riding the dinosaur, Amy had her daughter sit facing backward on a barstool while holding onto the backrest. She then printed the photo to scale and cut around her daughter's silhouette. The result is simply delightful!

**Dino Girl** by Amy Peterman. **Supplies** *Patterned paper, chipboard, die cuts, felt, ribbon and transparency:* Fancy Pants Designs; *Paint:* Making Memories; *Pen:* American Crafts; *Other:* Embroidery floss.

# photos in a *series*

No matter the event, I am the designated family historian when it comes to capturing the moments of our lives on film. Since I'd rather take photos than write about them, I try to let the photos themselves tell the bulk of the story. A photo series provides the perfect method as you'll see on the following layouts. I hope they'll inspire you to use a series of photos on your next page.

let the *photos* tell your story

*The Official Taste Tester by Stacy Cohen.* **Supplies** *Cardstock:* Bazzill Basics Paper; *Patterned paper and die cuts:* Cosmo Cricket; *Letter stickers:* BasicGrey and Making Memories; *Cookie-cutter accent:* Melissa Frances; *Embroidery floss, rhinestones and hemp:* Darice; *Adhesive:* Fabri-tac, Beacon Adhesives; Tombow; *Other:* Buttons.

*Stacy* Cohen, a Fresh Face, loves to scour estate sales and the local flea market for vintage treasures that she often incorporates onto her pages. Stacy's favorite aspect of scrapbooking is that she's leaving a legacy for her daughters.

TECHNIQUE TIP:
To achieve straight lines when hand-stitching, use a paper piercer and a ruler to punch your holes before you stitch onto your layout.

BY JOANNIE McBRIDE

**Balloon Pets and Silly Lilly** *by Davinie Fiero.* **Supplies** *Cardstock:* American Crafts (cream), Bazzill Basics Paper (white embossed and yellow) and WorldWin (kraft); *Patterned paper:* American Crafts (circle), My Mind's Eye (red dot), Pebbles Inc. (yellow) and Scenic Route (green balloon); *Letter stickers:* American Crafts (blue), Heidi Swapp for Advantus (gray) and Making Memories (green); *Stickers:* KI Memories (border) and Sassafras (flowers); *Stamps:* Studio Calico; *Font:* Arial; *Other:* Embroidery floss and paint.

*Davinie* Fiero enjoys looking at photos of her loved ones while creating. She finds that keeping her children on a schedule makes it easy for her to scrapbook in the evenings once the children are in bed.

**TECHNIQUE TIP:** For a fun technique, trace shapes onto your layout using objects in your home. Davinie traced a salad plate for the patterned-paper circle on her layout.

**Sunshine, Lollipops and Rainbows, Too** *by Nicole Pomeroy.* **Supplies** *Cardstock:* Bazzill Basics Paper; *Patterned paper and flowers:* Prima and Sassafras; *Letter stickers:* American Crafts (white), Doodlebug Design (green), Making Memories (cream block) and Pink Paislee (orange); *Stickers:* American Crafts and Prima; *Journaling spot:* Shabby Chic Crafts; *Chipboard:* Creative Imaginations (bird, birdhouse and grass) and Making Memories (glitter bracket frame); *Buttons:* KI Memories, Kittyrobot and Such Sweet Tierney; *Brads:* BasicGrey and Prima; *Rub-on:* BasicGrey; *Paint:* Making Memories and Twinkling H2Os, LuminArte; *Ink:* VersaColor, Tsukineko; *Other:* Ribbon, felt, thread and feathers.

*Nicole* Pomeroy lives in Australia and enjoys the creative side of scrapbooking. She loves using different products and textures on her pages. Nicole has been published in the Australian edition of *Creating Keepsakes*, but this is her first publication in the U.S.-based edition.

**TECHNIQUE TIP:**

Ink the edges of your photos to create an instant frame.

**Thank You for . . .** *by Amy Ballard.* **Supplies** *Patterned paper and transparency overlay:* Fancy Pants Designs; *Stamps:* BasicGrey ("thank"), Fiskars Americas ("i am grateful"), Heidi Swapp for Advantus ("for"), Papertrey Ink (background text and "happy Father's Day") and Technique Tuesday ("you" and "you are amazing"); *Ink:* Close To My Heart (red), Papertrey Ink (light brown), Ranger Industries (brown) and Tsukineko (dark brown); *Paper strips:* Cloud 9 Design, Fiskars Americas; *Adhesive:* 3-D Foam Squares, Close To My Heart; Cheetah Runner and Create-a-Sticker, Xyron.

*Amy* Ballard, a Fresh Face, has been scrapbooking since she was six years old, when she received her first Barbie scrapbook. Of course her style has evolved with the hobby, but her desire to save and record her memories remains.

TECHNIQUE TIP: Amy added depth to her layout by placing some page elements over a 12″ x 12″ transparency and some underneath it. You'll find photos and stamped images on both sides, and she added her journaling strips and title letters to the top.

Congratulations to *Kayleigh* Wiles for creating this month's Readers' Pick page! Kayleigh is the mother of two young children and a fan of using templates and sketches to get a jump-start on her pages. She often shrinks or rotates the templates to make them work for her creativity and her photos.

TECHNIQUE TIP: Choose three photos that show various perspectives of the event you're scrapbooking to help tell the story.

**Roll with It** *by Kayleigh Wiles.* **Supplies** *Software:* Adobe Photoshop CS4; *Cardstock, patterned paper and letters:* O.M.G. PageSet by Anna Aspnes; *Page template:* Stitched Layered Template No. 02 by Katie Pertiet; *Journaling tags:* Receipt of Memories No. 01, Worn and Torn Journalers and Tailed by Katie Pertiet; *Clouds, sun and bee:* Felt Board Friends: In the Woods - Gear and In the Woods - Critters by Pattie Knox; *Word art, yarn, airplane and arrows:* Going Away Collection by Katie Pertiet; *Twill:* Basic Twills: Summertime by Katie Pertiet; *Stitching:* Flossy Stitches: Yellow by Katie Pertiet; *Brushes:* Dripped Stains No. 04 BrushSet and CircleIT Basix No. 01 BrushSet by Anna Aspnes; *Word art ("the meaning of life"):* Love Sentiment Strips by Ali Edwards.

# *sharing* the big and the small

Whether you're celebrating the arrival of a little one, a festive holiday or simply life itself, you are not alone in wanting to savor every minute of it. We've all been given many opportunities to observe the wonder of life and all it encompasses. Don't let the moments you want to remember slip away. Document the people, the places and the things that define and complete you. You are the storyteller of your life. If it's important to you, it's important enough to record.

live well and *document* along the way

**Coming from Afar** by Paula Barber. **Supplies** *Patterned paper:* BasicGrey (brown solid), Cosmo Cricket (cream with red swirls), My Mind's Eye (stripe and green dot) and Scenic Route (red flower); *Chipboard:* BasicGrey; *Transparency overlay:* My Mind's Eye; *Cardstock stickers:* Cosmo Cricket; *Buttons:* Autumn Leaves; *Vintage rickrack:* Paper Salon; *Twine:* Martha Stewart Crafts (stripe) and DMC (cream); *Ink:* Stampin' Up!; *Font:* High Fiber, www.dafont.com.

*Paula* Barber's "Coming from Afar" layout was originally submitted in her 2007 Scrapbooker of the Year entry. She resubmitted the layout for a call several months back, and I fell in love with it!

The journaling on this layout talks about family traditions and why her family carries on this tradition from year to year. It was fun to read about the nativity set and why the Wise Men are kept in a separate room. As the holiday draws closer, the Wise Men are moved little by little until they are finally reunited with the rest of the nativity set. What family traditions do you have for special holidays? Scrapbook them today!

**YOU CAN DO THIS!**

❶ Trace a curve.

❷ Cut it out.

❸ Repeat!

**BY JOANNIE McBRIDE**

For *Ashley* Kennedy and her husband, this page represents more than just the joy they felt the first time they met their new son. It signifies the start of a new life together. Although their beautiful boy was born half a world away, the moment Ashley held him in her arms she knew he was meant for her.

When I viewed Ashley's pages online, I sensed her love for her family and for this hobby. She has been scrapbooking since high school. This is her first time having a layout published in *Creating Keepsakes*. Congratulations, Ashley!

**YOU CAN DO THIS!**

❶ To help tell your story, use two photos that complement each other.

❷ For a fun twist, type out your journaling and cut it into strips.

**First Family Photo** *by Ashley Kennedy.* **Supplies** *Software:* Adobe Photoshop CS3; *Brown stitching, ticketed journaling, stapled words and journaling strip masks:* Katie Pertiet; *Frames:* Stacked Vintage Frames No. 02 and Little Vintage Frames by Katie Pertiet; *Digital elements:* Staple Its!, Shimmer Me Tidbits and Have a Heart Felt by Pattie Knox; 12 X 12 Zig Zag Stitched Frames - Brown, Distressed ToolSet and Torn n Tattered Paper Templates by Anna Aspnes; Groovy Boy Kit by Mindy Terasawa; April Picnic Solids Paper Pack by Jesse Edwards; *Font:* Typewriter Old Style, Internet. All digital elements downloaded from *www. designerdigitals.com.*

When *Julie* Fei-Fan Balzer's husband is asked what she does, he answers, "Julie lives a creative life." It's very true! Her job is in the theatre, and she scrapbooks, quilts and makes jewelry. Julie calls herself the "mad scientist of crafting," pushing her supplies to their limits.

Frustrated by the lack of Judaica images, Julie decided to create her own. For this page, she used a Wacom tablet to draw the border, dots, stars and menorah. Her home is full of all the little things she's collected over a lifetime. Julie wants to scrapbook each and document why it matters to her. What a wonderful gift to give herself as well as her family.

**YOU CAN DO THIS!**

❶ Drag cropped photos onto your background paper.

❷ Create a path for your journaling and tell your story!

❸ Add embellishments.

**Menorah of My Own** *by Julie Fei-Fan Balzer.* **Supplies** *Software:* Adobe Photoshop CS3; *Digital elements:* Balzer Designs, *www.balzerdesigns.-typepad.com; Fonts:* CK Ali's Handwriting, *www.creatingkeepsakes.com;* Graphic Attitude and Kingthings Typewriter, Internet.

*Denise* Pavone-Brooks is a single mom to three sons. This page is about her autistic son and a trip they took to the Smithsonian's Udvar-Hazy museum. Denise works for a company that launches commercial satellites, and since that's typically not a very creative outlet, Denise converted her bedroom's walk-in closet into her scrap space. Because a puzzle piece is the symbol for autism, Denise includes one on each layout about her son.

### YOU CAN DO THIS!

❶ Choose patterned papers according to the mood you want to convey.

❷ Trim the inner square of your background to 9⅛" x 8⅝". Trim the photo to 5" x 5⅛" (cut down from a 5" x 7" print).

❸ Fit your pieces together like a puzzle.

**Autism** by Denise Pavone-Brooks. **Supplies** *Patterned paper and chipboard:* Cosmo Cricket; *Puzzle piece punch:* EK Success; *Brads, corner-rounder punch and pen.* Stampin' Up!; *Ribbon:* Top Line Creations; *Lettering template:* Opposites Attract Cartridge, Cricut, Provo Craft.

**Snow in Central Park** by SeowYin Goh. **Supplies** *Software:* Adobe Photoshop CS2; *Digital paper: www.weedsandwildflowersdesign.com;* *Foil and brown paper snowflakes:* Rachel Young, *www.scrapbookgraphics.com;* *Word strips and tags: www.peppermintcreative.com;* *Stamped letters:* Lemonaid Lucy, *www.divinedigital.com;* *Tree accents:* Candy Cane Trees by Heidi Larsen, *www.littledreamerdesigns.com;* *Frame template: www.yindesigns.blogspot.com;* *Font:* Attic, Internet.

*SeowYin* Goh is a wife and a mom, and she works part-time at a bank. She teaches Sunday school, has a fascination for cocktail rings, enjoys family travels and scrapbooks. The photos on this layout were taken the second day SeowYin's family was in New York. They had never seen real snow before, so you can imagine the excitement they felt and the fun they had playing in it.

When creating layouts, SeowYin spends the most time arranging her photos. Once she is happy with the placement of the pictures, the elements, papers, title and journaling are easy for her to complete!

### YOU CAN DO THIS!

❶ For multiphoto layouts, use interesting but non-patterned background paper and add a white border to your photos. Add elements around and behind the photos.

❷ When using multiple photos, try pulling them together in a strip similar to photo-booth style prints.

❸ Vary the sizes of photos and tilt them at different angles, overlapping the edges for interest.

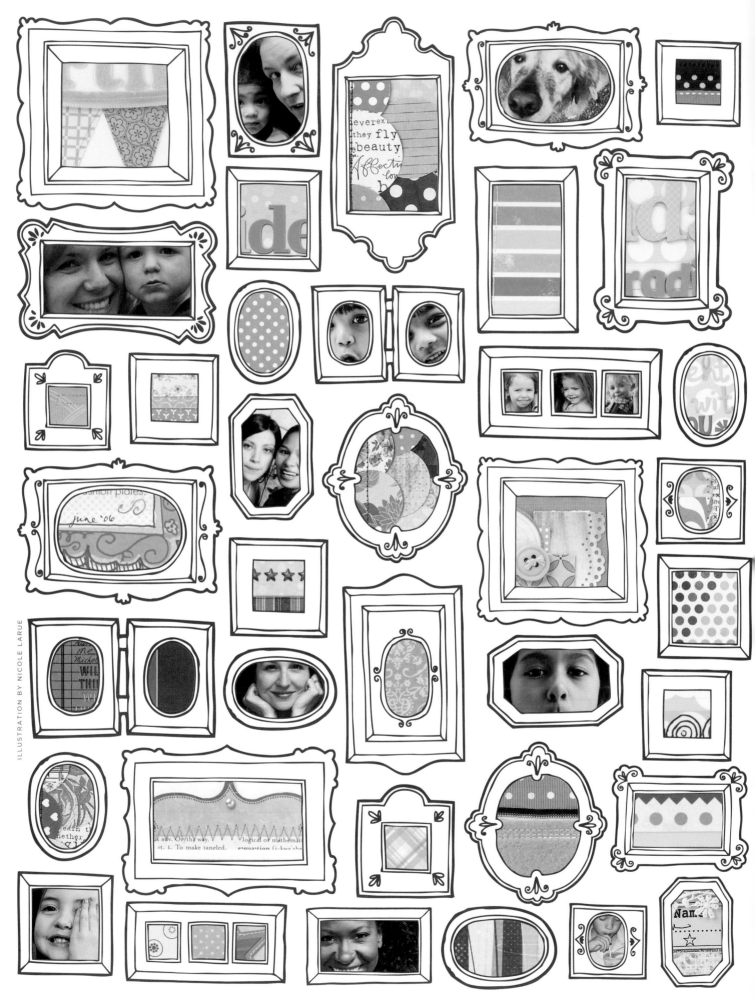

# SCRAPBOOK YOUR LIFE

## SHARE THE EVERYDAY & THE EXTRAORDINARY IN THIS GALLERY OF 100+ IDEAS

During an episode of *The Wonder Years* sitcom, character Kevin Arnold remarked, "Memory is a way of holding onto the things you love, the things you are, the things you never want to lose." "Profound," I thought, "and I'm profoundly in trouble. My memory is getting worse all the time."

The thought was a not-so-subtle reminder that now is the time to scrapbook my life. Sure, I've been sharing tidbits with family and friends via Facebook, but those messages (albeit fun) are short-lived. Who knows how long they'll last? I suspect not very long.

Scrapbook your life with me, and I guarantee we'll leave a mark we won't regret. Our family and friends will gain a tangible, more complete look at our rituals, our loves, and our traditions. Following is an idea gallery of 30 layouts selected for their go-to ideas. Let's get started!

BY JANA LILLIE

WHAT YOU DO EACH DAY   THE TRADITIONS YOU EMBRACE
THE RELATIONSHIPS YOU TREASURE   THE MILESTONES YOU CELEBRATED
THE FUN YOU CAN'T RESIST

# WHAT YOU DO EACH DAY

REFLECT for a moment on the routines that make up your day. Do you wake up early or late? Exercise? Call friends? Commute to work? Tend to your little ones? We all have our little rituals—the repeated acts that bring order and familiarity to each day. They bring comfort as, bit by bit, they define our lives. What do your routines say about you? Record these pieces of your day on a scrapbook page—years from now, you'll enjoy reflecting back on what has and hasn't changed.

## SCRAPBOOK
YOUR BEAUTY ROUTINE, MEALS, DOMESTIC TASKS, COMPUTER TIME, SHOPPING, SCHOOL & JOB.

DESCRIBE YOUR DAILY ROUTINE, WHETHER IT'S DRAB OR DAUNTING. LIST TYPICAL EXPERIENCES HOUR BY HOUR TO COMMUNICATE THE "EBB & FLOW" OF YOUR LIFE.

**What We Do** by Laura Vegas.
**Supplies** *Patterned paper:* Fancy Pants Design; *Letter stickers:* Jillibean Soup; *Rub-ons and stickers:* Heidi Grace Designs; *Punch:* Stampin' Up!; *Pen:* American Crafts; *Font:* Old Remington; *Adhesive:* Creative Memories (pop dots) and Scrapbook Adhesives by 3L (tape runner).

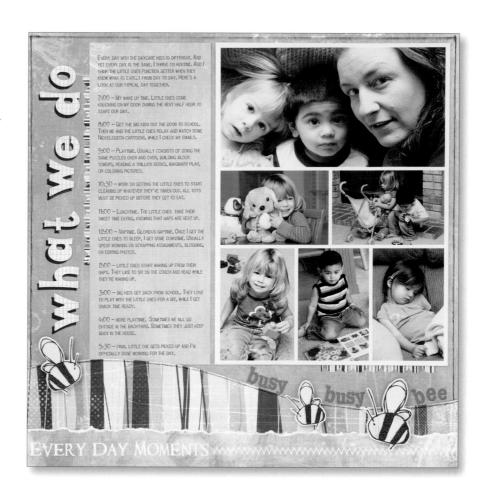

{ DESIGN TIP TO ADD OOMPH }
AND COLOR TO A TITLE

1. Select the same style of letter stickers in two colors.

2. Layer the sticker sets, adhering one sticker on top and slightly left for a shadow effect.

3. Adhere letters to layout.

{ HERE'S ANOTHER QUICK TRICK }

If a phrase rub-on won't fit existing space, simply cut apart each word, keeping the protective backing in place. Position your words as desired, remove their protective backing, and rub away, as Laura Vegas did with the phrase, "Busy, busy bee" on her layout shown above.

**Ride and Play** by Julie DeGuia. **Supplies** *Software:* Adobe; *Digital patterned paper:* Little Explorer kit by Mindy Terasawa and Classic Cardstock and Naturally Krafty series by Katie Pertiet; *Letters:* Bare Chipboard Alpha (DIY series) by Pattie Knox and Stitched Alpha set by Anna Aspnes; *Digital frames:* Vintage Photo Frames No. 16 and Matte Black Vintage Frames by Katie Pertiet; *Stars:* TNT Star Templates by Anna Aspnes; *Star brad:* US of A Page Set by Anna Aspnes; *Brass screw:* Fasten Its! by Pattie Knox; *Brass staple:* Staple Its! by Pattie Knox; *Journal strips:* Krafty Journal Strips (recolored); *"Laugh" element:* Zipper Pulls; *Hanging tag:* Lil Bit Tags; *Circle stitching holes:* Stamped-n-Frames Template No. 6; *Blank bookplate:* Bookplate Notes by Katie Pertiet; *Fonts:* American Typewriter, Angelina and SU! Jodyola.

## { PLAY WITH THESE EASY DESIGN TIPS }

### TO ADD EXTRA VISUAL INTEREST TO YOUR PAGE:

WOW with a bracketed title, white-on-black text or a "surprise" dangling tag.

REINFORCE the sense of motion with subtle, decorative circles.

SHARE THE ADVENTURES EXPERIENCED ON YOUR STREET OR AT A LOCAL PARK. DON'T FORGET TO DOCUMENT YOUR KIDS' FIRST WOBBLY BIKE RIDES WITHOUT TRAINING WHEELS!

SHOW THE GOOD, THE BAD & THE UGLY OF YOUR DOMESTIC REALITY. DON'T BE SHY—YOU DEAL WITH LAUNDRY, DISHES, CARPETS, TOYS & TRASH TO MAKE HOME BETTER FOR THOSE YOU LOVE.

**Every Day** by Heather Lough. **Supplies** *Cardstock:* Bazzill Basics Paper; *Patterned paper:* Jenni Bowlin Studio; *Letter stickers:* Jenni Bowlin Studio (large) and Making Memories (small); *Chipboard swirls:* Bo-Bunny Press; *Ink:* Clearsnap.

## { CAPTURE THE "WHIRL" WITH A SWIRL }

LEAD the eye to a certain photo.

ADD a circular look to soften the photos' rectangular pattern.

EXPLAIN HOW YOU GOT YOUR
JOB & HOW YOU FEEL ABOUT IT.
SHARE HOW YOUR LIFE HAS BEEN
CHANGED THANKS TO THE PEOPLE
& EXPERIENCES THERE.

**My Night Job** by Grace Tolman. **Supplies** *Patterned paper:* Making Memories; *Flowers:* Petaloo (white) and Prima (pink); *Letter stickers:* Making Memories; *Copper spray ink:* Tattered Angels; *Pen:* EK Success; *Rhinestone:* Kaiser Craft; *Other:* Button.

{ CELEBRATE YOUR ACHIEVEMENTS IN STYLE }

SPRAY paper butterflies with Glimmer Mist, fold them slightly. Adhere the charming creations to your page.

BIG on fashion and retail? Mimic fabric by sewing around the edges of decorative paper blocks.

USE a company promotional piece to house journaling.

**Happy Daily Walk** by Heidi Sonboul. **Supplies** *Patterned paper and chipboard:* Cosmo Cricket; *Stamps:* Nikki Silvis; *Pen:* American Crafts; *Adhesive:* 3M.

TELL WHAT BRINGS YOU JOY
WHEN YOU'RE OUT & ABOUT.
DESCRIBE WHAT YOU DO, WHERE
YOU GO, & WHETHER YOU'RE
ACCOMPANIED BY A PAL OR NOT.

{ CREATE A WHIMSICAL SETTING }

PENCIL in a scallop design on the backside of patterned paper, trim the rounded edges with a craft knife.

DRAW small, curvy "v" shapes in your sky to mimic birds.

RAISE cloud shapes with foam tape for a 3-D effect.

that's **my boy**

Each morning, when the big boys are settled doing something and James is strapped in his high chair eating cereal, I grab whatever book I happen to be reading and spend ten minutes or so oblivious to everything but my story and my Raisin Nut Bran. Honestly, the house could fall down, and I probably wouldn't notice until debris obscured the words. Although I'm pretty sure I'd notice a choking baby... Anyway, this morning I looked up from my book and saw Carter, perched on the counter, still in his jammies, eatng Cinnamon Toast Crunch, totally absorbed in the second Magic Treehouse book. Oblivious. He didn't even look up until I snapped the the fifth picture. Cereal and a good book: that's my boy.

Carter 10.7.09

**That's My Boy** *by Autumn Baldwin.* **Supplies** *Software:* Adobe Photoshop Elements 6; *Patterned paper:* Yes and Colorchallenge 02May09 kits by Anna Aspnes and Cotton Easter Red by Katie Pertiet; *Tag:* Sing for Spring kit by Liv E; *Stitching holes:* Best Friends kit by Katie Pertiet; *Brushes:* Painted Circle Splatz by Anna Aspnes; *Letter:* Basic White Paper Alpha by Katie Pertiet; *Font:* Cochin.

DIVULGE HOW ANOTHER FAMILY MEMBER IS LIKE YOU. (WE ALL LOVE A SENSE OF CONNECTION.) DON'T BE AFRAID TO POINT OUT THE GOOD & THE NOT-SO-GOOD!

{ TO BOOST YOUR TITLE'S IMPACT }

CHANGE the title color with a photo filter. The deep-yellow filter used here turned white letters a creamy yellow.

STYLIZE the look with a showy circle brush or two.

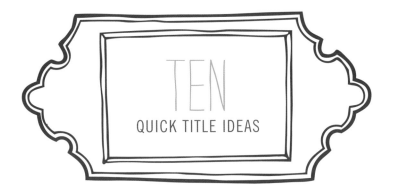

TEN
QUICK TITLE IDEAS

1. 100% DRIVEN
2. ALL ABOARD!
3. BUSY HANDS, HAPPY HEARTS
4. HOW TIME DOES FLY
5. JUST ONE DAY WITH YOU
6. LOOK WHAT I DID
7. SPLISH, SPLASH
8. SWEET DREAMS
9. THE CIRCLE OF LIFE
10. WALK WITH ME

## THE TRADITIONS YOU EMBRACE

LIFE is full of change, and it's easy to feel disconnected. Enter family traditions! They endure from year to year, and they help family connect the past and the present. Best of all, people can count on them, and that's always welcome. What traditions enrich your life? Scrapbook them to help you remember how much you enjoy observing your yearly events. Learn what other scrapbookers enjoy in the examples that follow.

## SCRAPBOOK
YOUR HOLIDAYS, CELEBRATIONS, GIFT EXCHANGES, VACATION PLANS & SEASON-SPECIFIC TASKS.

We love driving up to the state park on a sunday afternoon to feed the ducks, play on the... slides and just be together. •June '09

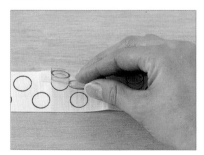

**Our Sunday Tradition** by Wendy Sue Anderson. **Supplies** *Cardstock:* Bazzill Basics Paper; *Patterned paper, letter stickers, rub-ons and pen:* American Crafts; *Journaling block:* Cosmo Cricket; *Ribbon:* C.M. Offray & Son; *Stamp:* Papertrey Ink; *Ink:* Tsukineko; *Other:* Thread.

# SHOWCASE A FAMILY OUTING THAT'S SO RELAXING & FUN IT'S BECOME A REPEAT PERFORMANCE. THINK PICNICS, SUMMER CONCERTS OR SIMPLY FEEDING DUCKS AT THE PARK.

## { CAPTIVATE WITH A FRESH }
### RIBBON TWIST

1. Stamp circles on ribbon.

2. Position a rub-on in the center of each circle.

3. Knot one end of a wide grosgrain ribbon.

## { HERE'S ANOTHER QUICK TRICK }

Use random words or phrases from rub-on sheets to create a decorative journaling block. (See left-hand side of layout.) Fill in and complete journaling with letter rub-ons.

LOVE TO VISIT DISCOVERY PARKS & MUSEUMS? NOT ONLY ARE THEY PACKED WITH FUN, THEY OFFER INTRIGUING SIGHTS TO PHOTO-GRAPH. HIGHLIGHT A HANDS-ON EXPERIENCE YOU ENJOYED WITH YOUR FAMILY.

We are a family that loves museums, and if they are a "hands on" museum it's even better! We couldn't pass up spending a day at this one in Cleveland when we were there with Grandma. You loved this outdoor area and had fun playing in the water. I think Grandma liked playing in the water too!

Great Lakes Science Center

**Hands On** *by Cindy Tobey.* **Supplies** *Patterned paper:* American Crafts (clouds), Luxe Designs (red and blue rules), October Afternoon (yellow) and We R Memory Keepers (rainbow dots); *Cardstock:* Bazzill Basics Paper; *Stickers:* American Crafts (tab), Colorbök (red circles), EK Success (pebbles) and KI Memories (black border); *Chipboard:* American Crafts (hand and star) and CherryArte (arrow); *Brad:* Queen & Co.; *Ribbon:* We R Memory Keepers; *Paper frill:* Doodlebug Design; *Punch:* EK Success; *Rub-ons:* Luxe Designs; *Badge and pen:* American Crafts; *Font:* Century Gothic; *Adhesive:* 3M, Glue Dots International and Tombow.

{NOT FULLY DIGITAL?}

DUPLICATE the cool border edge with a wide rub-on instead.

{TREAT YOURSELF TO A HOT TREND IN TITLES}

TYPE your title in one font. Select different weights, such as book, demi or medium, for different text portions.

NO ONE PAMPERS A CHILD QUITE LIKE GRANDMA OR GRANDPA. SNAP PICTURES TO CAPTURE THE SWEET RELATIONSHIP & THE OUTINGS MEANT TO SPOIL. SHOW BOTH GENERATIONS HOLDING HANDS, HUGGING & ENJOYING PRECIOUS, ONE-ON-ONE MOMENTS.

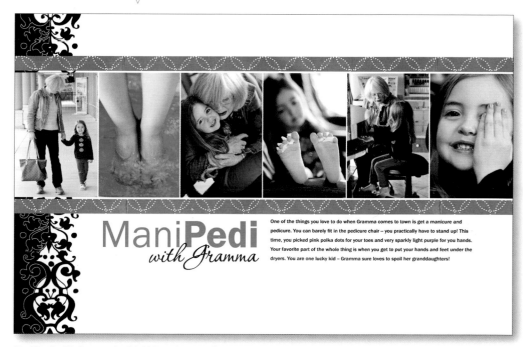

**Mani**Pedi *with Gramma*

One of the things you love to do when Gramma comes to town is get a manicure and pedicure. You can barely fit in the pedicure chair -- you practically have to stand up! This time, you picked pink polka dots for your toes and very sparkly light purple for your hands. Your favorite part of the whole thing is when you get to put your hands and feet under the dryers. You are one lucky kid – Gramma sure loves to spoil her granddaughters!

**Mani Pedi with Gramma** *by Brigid Gonzalez.* **Supplies** *Software:* CS3, Adobe; *Patterned paper:* Certainly Fresh kit by Cori Gammon; *Die cut:* Border Edge Die Cuts by Katie Pertiet; *Fonts:* Franklin Gothic Book and Franklin Gothic Demi (title), Franklin Gothic Medium (journaling) and P22Corinthia (subtitle).

WHAT TASKS DO YOU TYPICALLY TACKLE EACH SPRING, SUMMER, FALL AND WINTER? RECORD HOW YOU ACCOMPLISH THEM & THE SATISFACTION YOU FEEL.

**Spring Car Cleaning** *by Cindy Tobey.* **Supplies** *Cardstock:* Bazzill Basics Paper; *Patterned paper and chipboard:* Cosmo Cricket; *Ribbon:* Cosmo Cricket (velvet), SEI (red dot) and We R Memory Keepers (red crochet and blue grosgrain); *Stickers:* Doodlebug Design; *Paint:* Heidi Swapp for Advantus; *Rub-on:* Love, Elsie for KI Memories; *Brad:* Queen & Co.; *Button:* My Mind's Eye; *Ink:* Clearsnap; *Font:* Century Gothic; *Adhesive:* Glue Dots International and Tombow; *Other:* Thread.

{ SPRUCE UP YOUR PAGE }

MACHINE-STITCH bright-colored frames on black-and-white photos.

COVER a chipboard shape with patterned paper. Paint portions of it to add additional details (see the windows on Cindy's car).

LOVE TO SPEND LEISURE TIME WITH GAL PALS? JOIN THE CLUB! WHETHER YOU CROPPED, SHOPPED, EXERCISED OR ATE OUT, DIVULGE THE JUICY DETAILS NEXT TIME YOU SCRAPBOOK.

{ STREAMLINE YOUR PAGE CREATION }

POSITION two 2" x 3" photos side-by-side and print them on 4" x 6" photo paper. (Lisa Kisch created a quick photo collage in Picasa.)

DRAW a text box, add a title, and select the perfect background color from your color menu.

**Ladies Who Brunch** *by Lisa Kisch.* **Supplies** *Software:* Photoshop Elements 5, Adobe; *Cardstock:* Creative Memories; *Patterned paper:* BasicGrey and Creative Memories; *Flowers and pen:* Creative Memories; *Stickers:* Jenni Bowlin Studio; *Chipboard:* Scenic Route; *Punch:* Fiskars; *Americas Brads:* American Crafts; *Jewel:* Provo Craft; *Paint:* Maya Road; *Font:* Ripe.

**Lemonade @ Grandma's** by Brenda Hurd. **Supplies** *Patterned paper:* BasicGrey (yellow floral), Creative Imaginations (lined) and Crate Paper (yellow circle); *Chipboard accents and letters:* BasicGrey; *Corrugated letters:* Jillibean Soup; *Index card:* Adornit - Carolee's Creations; *Brads:* BasicGrey (lemon) and Making Memories (glitter); *Lined sticker:* American Crafts; *Pom-pom ribbon:* Fancy Pants Designs; *Paint:* Ceramcoat, Delta Creative; *Pigment spray:* Maya Road; *Font:* Arial Narrow; *Adhesive:* Adhesive Technologies, Inc.

NOTHING QUITE COMPARES WITH A HOMEMADE TREAT, ESPECIALLY ONE PREPARED WITH PAINSTAKING CARE. SNAP PICTURES OF THE CHEF IN ACTION—HE OR SHE COULD BE THE NEXT EMERIL OR RACHAEL RAY!

{ SWEETEN YOUR LAYOUT }

MAT your photos instantly by printing them with borders.

INTENSIFY a color or add shimmer with spray ink.

PAINT over corrugated letters for quick pizzazz.

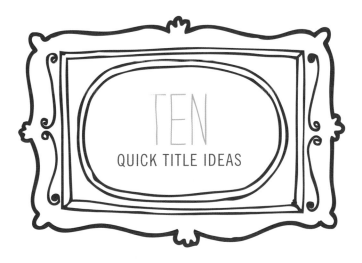

TEN
QUICK TITLE IDEAS

1. A SEASON FOR GIVING
2. HERE WE GO AGAIN
3. HOW WE . . .
4. LET'S EAT!
5. MEMORIES IN THE MAKING
6. ONE BIG, HAPPY FAMILY
7. SATURDAY AT THE PARK
8. WE ARE BLESSED
9. WE DID IT OUR WAY
10. WE GATHER TOGETHER

# THE RELATIONSHIPS YOU TREASURE

IDENTIFY who touches your heart and makes you feel valued. Think of who inspires your dedication and loyalty. This could be a spouse, a friend, a parent, a child or teacher. It could even be your pet begging for a scratch behind the ears. Check out the layouts that follow, then express your appreciation for those who share your life by including them in your scrapbooks.

## SCRAPBOOK:
FAMILY, FRIENDS, ONLINE PALS, TEACHERS, CO-WORKERS, PETS, MENTORS & NEIGHBORS.

**More Than Just a Dog** *by Sara Winnick.* **Supplies** *Patterned paper:* Pebbles Inc.; *Chipboard:* Darice (paw print) and Maya Road (heart); *Border stickers:* Doodlebug Design; *Rub-ons:* American Crafts; *Corrugated letters:* Jillibean Soup; *Paint:* Delta Creative; *Dimensional glaze:* Diamond Glaze, JudiKins; *Font:* Calibri; *Adhesive:* Scrapbook Adhesives by 3L.

PRAISE YOUR PET'S DEVOTION ON A SCRAPBOOK PAGE. POINT OUT EXAMPLES, SUCH AS HOW YOUR FURRY FRIEND GREETS YOU AT THE DOOR OR CURLS UP IN YOUR LAP.

{ SHARE THE LOVE WITH A GLOSSY HEART }

1. Paint a chipboard heart red.

2. Add a rub-on to the center.

3. Apply a clear coat of glaze.

INTRODUCE THE DEAR FRIENDS YOU'VE MADE ONLINE. CELEBRATE YOUR TREASURED CONNECTION, & SHARE THE NICKNAMES YOU'VE GIVEN EACH OTHER.

**They Call Me Panda** by Jing-Jing Nickel. **Supplies** *Cardstock:* Prism Papers; *Patterned paper, chipboard elements and rub-on:* Imaginisce; *Letters:* American Crafts, Collage Press and Jenni Bowlin Studio; *Journaling spot:* Maya Road; *Punch and pen:* EK Success; *Font:* Myriad Web Pro Condensed; *Adhesive:* Glue Arts.

{ TONE DOWN COMPLEX PATTERNS }

WHEN layering patterned papers, simplify the look by matting the top sheet with cardstock.

MAT with neutral colors to keep the transitions low-key. Note how Jing-Jing Nickel chose panda colors: black and white.

SHOW HOW YOUR FAMILY LOVES TO WORK & PLAY TOGETHER. START WITH A GROUP SHOT (GET IN CLOSE!), THEN INCLUDE PHOTOS OF FAMILY MEMBERS IN ACTION.

**Our Family . . . Everyday Life** by Shelly Jaquet. *Supplies Patterned paper:* Cosmo Cricket, October Afternoon and Studio Calico; *Die cut:* Collage Press; *Stickers:* American Crafts (letter) and October Afternoon (label); *Pearls:* BasicGrey; *Other:* Thread.

{ SHORT ON SPACE FOR CAPTIONS? }

WRITE them directly on your photos.

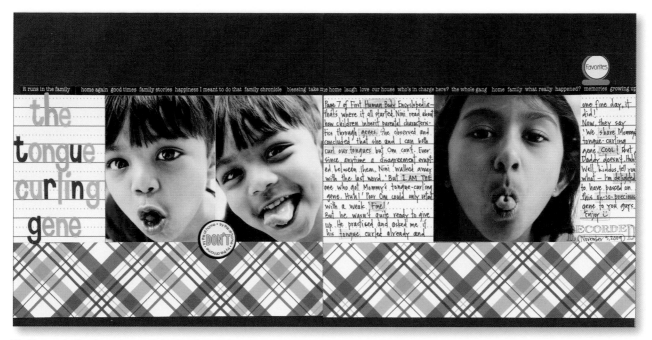

The Tongue-Curling Game *by Mou Saha.* **Supplies** *Cardstock:* Die Cuts With a View; *Patterned paper:* Piggy Tales; *Stickers:* 7gypsies (cardstock) and Piggy Tales (title); *Stamp:* Autumn Leaves; *Ink:* Tsukineko; *Colored pencils:* Faber-Castell; *Pen:* American Crafts; *Adhesive:* 3M.

DON'T miss more "family connections" pages by Mou Saha in our May/June 2010 issue.

JOURNALING looking long and blasé? Add bursts of color to words with colored pencils.

AH, GENETICS. THANKS TO THEM YOU CAN ROLL YOUR TONGUE OR WIGGLE YOUR EARS—OR NOT. RECORD YOUR FINDINGS IN A QUICK FAMILY COMPARISON. WHO KNEW?

ACKNOWLEDGE HOW AN "ANGEL" IN YOUR HOUSE- HOLD RESCUES YOU WHEN YOU NEED HELP. SHOW THIS PERSON PITCHING IN TO PICK UP THE SLACK.

She Saves Me *by Revlie Schuit.* **Supplies** *Cardstock:* Bazzill Basics Paper; *Vinyl letters and foam hearts:* American Crafts; *Chipboard wings and sheer journaling spots:* Maya Road; *Ink:* Clearsnap; *Font:* Type Right!; *Other:* Adhesive.

{ DELIGHT WITH EXTRA DIMENSIONS }

HANDWRITE, cut and ink the edges on all or part of your title. Elevate with foam dots.

APPLY white acrylic paint in a thick layer on chipboard wings. Press the brush firmly to mimic the look of real feathers.

My sister said to me the other day (after watching a movie about Julia Child): "I want a purpose in life--like cooking was for Julia." I joked: "You procreate. That's your purpose." I certainly didn't mean that a woman's entire purpose in life is to have kids. But for me, during these short years before the boys grow up and move away, loving them and teaching them and being their mom really *is* my purpose right now. I like it. And I'm good at it-- (most of the time). I may not be Julia, but I am Mom.

*they call me*

# mom

**They Call Me Mom** *by Autumn Baldwin.* **Supplies** *Software:* Adobe Photoshop Elements 6.0; *Patterned paper:* Zippy Hippy kit by Paislee Press; *Letter:* Basic Paper Alpha by Katie Pertiet; *Stamp:* Ninascraps Grids and Dots; *Flourish:* melgendesign decoflowerstamps2; *Font:* Optima.

BEING A PARENT CAN BE ROUGH (THINK DIAPERS, TEMPER TANTRUMS & DRIVER'S ED)—BUT IT'S REWARDING, TOO. SHARE WHAT MAKES PARENTHOOD WORTHWHILE FOR YOU.

TEN
TENDER
TITLE IDEAS

1. #1 DAD
2. A MOTHER'S LOVE
3. ALL IN THE FAMILY
4. FOREVER & EVER
5. HEART TO HEART
6. HELPING HANDS
7. HOME IS WHERE THE HEART IS
8. JUST YOU AND ME
9. S.W.A.K.
10. WE ARE FAMILY

{ TRY THIS FAST }
BOX TECHNIQUE

1. Create different sized boxes to cover two-thirds of a page.

2. Fill some boxes with photos and others with patterned paper.

3. Finish off your page with journaling, title and embellishments.

# THE MILESTONES YOU CELEBRATED

CONGRATULATIONS! From the moment you were a babe in your mother's tummy, your life has been marked by one big milestone after another. These events are your passage through life, in a sense, and they signify your personal growth. Be sure to scrapbook your birthday, baptism, bat mitzvah, graduation, first job or any event that shows you evolving and changing. Here's how others captured these events.

## SCRAPBOOK
### BIRTHDAYS, WEDDINGS, ANNIVERSARIES, GRADUATIONS, RELIGIOUS CEREMONIES & BUSINESS SUCCESS.

**Happy Birthday**
*by Maggie Holmes.* **Supplies**
*Cardstock:* Making Memories; *Patterned paper:* October Afternoon (pink), Sassafras (pink), Scenic Route (green) and Studio Calico (blue and yellow); *Letter stickers:* American Crafts (pink), BasicGrey (green) and Heidi Swapp for Advantus (gray); *Ribbon, buttons, crown and green tag:* Making Memories; *Flowers:* Heidi Swapp for Advantus (tissue) and Making Memories (paper); *Photo corner and leaves:* Anna Griffin; *Stickers and stamps:* Studio Calico; *Ink:* Tsukineko; *Pen:* Sakura; *Other:* Metal clip.

BIRTHDAYS ARE A JOYOUS CELEBRATION OF LIFE. PARTY WITH GLEE & PHOTOGRAPH THE SUBJECT, FOOD & FESTIVITY WITH ABANDON. SCRAPBOOKING THE FUN AFTERWARD IS THE ICING ON THE CAKE!

{ HELP YOUR COLLAGE LOOK ITS BEST }

1. Avoid scattering accents all over your page. Instead, group them for a unified look.

2. Layer and overlap the clustered items for texture and dimension.

3. Use items in contrasting colors—they'll stand out more.

{ HERE'S ANOTHER QUICK TRICK }

Love the playful banner on Maggie Holmes' page? To duplicate the look, create a triangle template and trace triangles on patterned-paper scraps. Position the triangles across your page, and sew ribbon across the top of the banner.

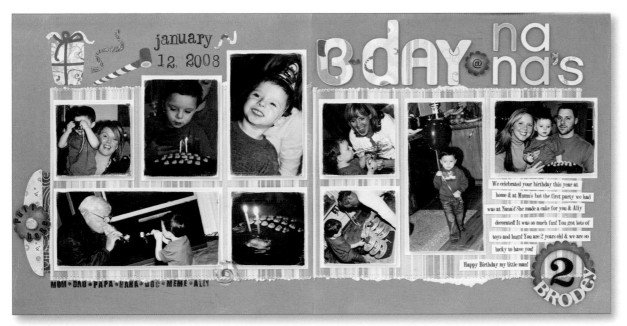

B-day @ Nana's by April Massad. **Supplies** *Cardstock:* Prism Papers; *Patterned paper and stickers:* BasicGrey; *Scalloped chipboard, letter stamps and brads:* Technique Tuesday; *Paint:* Ranger Industries; *Font:* CK Newsprint.

{ SNEAK IN A FEW MORE PHOTOS }

CREATE a photo pocket by adhering patterned paper (leave the left-hand side open) to your page background.

ADHERE three photos to a paper strip; cover them with laminate to help the strip slide easily from the pocket.

CREATE a pull tab for the photo strip by covering a piece of chipboard with patterned paper. Secure the tab elements with a brad, stamp "Pull Here" on the tab.

IF YOU CELEBRATED A BIRTHDAY AWAY FROM HOME, RECOGNIZE THE EXTENDED FAMILY OR FRIENDS WHO BRIGHTENED THE FESTIVITIES. SHOW THEM INTER-ACTING WITH THE BIRTHDAY GUEST.

HONOR A SACRED RELIGIOUS EXPERIENCE WITH A LOVELY TREATMENT THAT CAPTURES ITS BEAUTY & SIGNIFICANCE.

First Communion by Kristie Coleman. **Supplies** *Patterned paper:* Making Memories; *Calendar:* Jenni Bowlin Studio; *Tickets:* Tim Holtz for Advantus; *Vine and packaging:* Prima; *Buttons:* Favorite Findings; *Pen:* American Crafts; *Embroidery floss:* DMC; *Font:* Storybook, Cricut.

{ ILLUMINATE YOUR SUBJECT }

POSITION him or her under or next to a light source (think skylight, window or doorway).

SELECT white clothing, lettering and flower accents to soften the look.

**Our Special Day** by Piradee Talvanna. **Supplies** *Cardstock and chipboard letters:* American Crafts; *Patterned paper, flowers, leaves and pearl swirls:* Prima; *Butterfly stamp:* Purple Onion Design; *Trinket pins:* Maya Road; *Dimensional glitter paint:* Ranger Industries; *Adhesive:* EK Success and Glue Dots International.

# THINK BACK ON YOUR WEDDING DAY WITH ITS JOY & JITTERS, PROMISE & SPLENDOR. CAPTURE THE BEAUTY OF THE DAY THROUGH YOUR PHOTOS & DESIGNS.

## { CONVEY THE ELEGANCE }
### OF THE OCCASION

INK and distress the edges of patterned-paper rectangles.

ADD sparkle to stamped butterflies with dimensional glitter paint.

ACCENT the page with flowers, leaves and pearl swirls.

## { NEED TO FIT A LOT ON }
### TWO PAGES?

OVERLAP photos but keep important elements (like faces) in view.

PLACE caption strips in open photo spaces.

# RECALL A TIME WHEN YOU WERE FOOTLOOSE & FANCY-FREE WITH FRIENDS. WHERE DID YOU TRAVEL? WHAT DID YOU DO? WHAT MEMORIES WILL YOU SAVOR?

**Grand Ole Opry** by Gretchen McElveen. **Supplies** *Cardstock:* KI Memories (yellow) and Prism Papers (white); *Patterned paper:* KI Memories; *Chipboard letters:* Cosmo Cricket; *Bling:* Heidi Swapp for Advantus.

*san diego state university*
# GRADUATION

5.23.09

art school graduates!

WHAT I REMEMBER MO...

john & I are now alumni of SDSU! our college years were a crazy, busy, stressful, interesting whirlwind that we will never forget!

09

YOU DID IT—YOU SURVIVED THE RIGORS OF COLLEGE & EARNED THAT IMPORTANT DEGREE. SHOWCASE YOUR GRADUATION ON A CELEBRATION PAGE.

**Graduation** *by Ann-Marie Morris.* **Supplies** *Cardstock:* Bazzill Basics Paper; *Patterned paper:* American Crafts (yellow dot), Cosmo Cricket (cream), October Afternoon (blue-green) and Sassafras (blue); *Stamps:* Prima (graph) and Studio G (label); *Letter stickers:* American Crafts; *Ruler die cut:* K&Company; *Punches:* Fiskars Americas (corner rounder, quote bubble and scalloped border) and Martha Stewart Crafts (lace border); *Rhinestones:* Darice; *Brad:* Making Memories; *Ink:* Tsukineko; *Other:* Buttons.

{ DEMONSTRATE YOUR }
## YOUR DESIGN SMARTS

CUT boldly into decorative patterned paper and use bits and pieces as embellishments.

SEPARATE photos with a decorative paper strip (see the punched lace border here).

USE paper punches to add dimension and texture minus the bulk.

TEN
"EVENT-FUL" TITLE IDEAS

1. 50 YEARS & GOING STRONG
2. A NIGHT TO REMEMBER
3. A STAR IS BORN
4. BELIEVE IN YOURSELF
5. CELEBRATE!
6. DORM SWEET DORM
7. EXTRA! EXTRA!
8. IN LOVING MEMORY
9. LOOK WHO'S [INSERT AGE]
10. YOU DID IT!

# THE FUN YOU CAN'T RESIST

CONTEMPLATE what brings you passion and makes you feel most alive. What consumes your spare—and not so spare—time? What speaks to your personal interests and talents? Perhaps it's music, travel, home decor or sports. Perhaps it's a favorite TV show. Perhaps it's even scrapbooking. (No surprise there.) Enjoy the examples that follow, then scrapbook what you personally find most rewarding.

## SCRAPBOOK
### FAVORITE GETAWAYS, HOBBIES, ACTIVITIES, TALENTS, TV PROGRAMS, SPORTS & SECRET INDULGENCES.

WHAT'S YOUR ESCAPE WHEN YOU FIND AN UNEXPECTED POCKET OF TIME? A GOOD BOOK? A SOAK IN THE TUB? REVEAL YOUR GUILTY PLEASURE.

**My Other Passion** by Jen Jockisch. **Supplies** *Cardstock and rhinestone brad:* American Crafts; *Patterned paper:* 7gypsies, BasicGrey, Hambly Studios, Jillibean Soup, Making Memories, Pink Paislee, Prima, Sassafras, Scenic Route and SEI; *Corrugated letters:* Jillibean Soup; *Letter stickers:* American Crafts; *Velvet flower:* Maya Road; *Tag:* Jenni Bowlin Studio; *Lace, flower and leaf:* Prima; *Punches:* EK Success (circle), Fiskars (border) and We R Memory Keepers (corner rounder); *Other:* Cardboard.

{ NO FOAM ADHESIVE FOR A LARGE ELEMENT? }
USE CARDBOARD

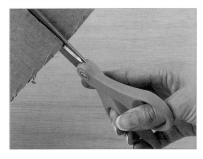

1. Cut the cardboard ½" smaller on all sides than the element to be raised. Piece sections as needed—no one will see them.

2. Adhere the cardboard to your base and apply adhesive to the top edge.

3. Position the element on top and press slightly.

{ HERE'S ANOTHER QUICK TRICK }
Punch circles from patterned-paper scraps and group them.

**Wii Get Out of Control** by Pamela Young. **Supplies** *Software:* Adobe Photoshop CS2; *Cardstock:* Core'dinations; *Patterned paper and letter stickers:* Rusty Pickle; *Embroidery floss:* DMC; *Pen:* Newell Rubbermaid; *Adhesive:* Tombow.

'FESS UP. TELL HOW A HOBBY OR PASTIME KEEPS YOU COMING BACK FOR MORE. VOICE WHAT DRAWS YOU BACK AGAIN & AGAIN.

## {BREAK AWAY FROM THE NORM}

DESIGN your layout so it's "lopsided" (a little asymmetry never hurt anyone!).

DEVOTE extra time to hand-cutting intricate page accents—they're cool.

SET off your photos with dynamic digital frames.

**Ballgame** by Laina Lamb. **Supplies** *Software:* SureCutsALot (SCAL), Adobe Illustrator; *Cardstock:* Bazzill Basics Paper; *Patterned paper:* Adornit - Carolee's Creations (blue star), CherryArte (white and blue stars), Cosmo Cricket (yellow dot), Creative Imaginations (red notebook), Fiskars Americas (blue dot), KI Memories (stripe) and Scenic Route (red dot and red graph); *Stickers:* American Crafts (blue/red star), EK Success (shirt) and Karen Foster Design (baseball); *Rub-on:* 7gypsies; *Brad:* 3Birds; *Vinyl:* Orcal 631; *Embroidery floss:* DMC; *Circle punches:* EK Success; *Pen:* American Crafts; *Fonts:* Athletic and Myriad.

WHAT'S YOUR SPORTS SCORE? WHETHER YOU'RE A FAN OR A PLAYER, KEEP TRACK OF THE SPORTS MEMORIES YOU LOVE MOST— EVERYTHING FROM BIG PLAYS TO PERSONAL BESTS.

## {PLAY UP YOUR BALLGAME THEME}

PUNCH patterned-paper circles and line them up above your title.

MARK paper with light pencil lines and pierce paper for baseball hand stitching.

DRAW dashes with pen to suggest the bounce of the balls.

**Fashion Plates** *by Cindy Tobey.* **Supplies** *Cardstock:* Bazzill Basics Paper; *Patterned paper, letter stickers and rub-ons:* American Crafts; *Journaling tag:* Bam Pop; *Chipboard:* We R Memory Keepers; *Ribbon:* Making Memories; *Felt and buttons:* Fancy Pants Designs; *Brads:* Making Memories (flowers) and Queen & Co. (all other); *Pen:* Sakura; *Font:* Function LH; *Adhesive:* 3M, Glue Dots International and Kokuyo; *Other:* Fibers and thread.

LET YOUR ARTISTIC SPIRIT FLY & CREATE A PAGE THAT'S AS FUNKY & FUN AS YOUR TALENT. PLAY WITH TEXTURE & COLOR—PEOPLE WILL LOVE YOUR FRESH TAKE ON MATERIALS.

{ ADD FLAIR WITH FABULOUS "FRINGE" }

1. Cut fibers an equal length and secure them with machine stitching.

2. Add a glue dot to a larger button. Push fiber into the glue dot.

3. Add a glue dot to a smaller button. Place the button on top of the larger button, sandwiching the fiber between.

DESCRIBE WHAT HAPPENS WHEN YOU CHALLENGE FAMILY MEMBERS TO A GAME LIKE SCRABBLE OR SEQUENCE. WHO'S THE BEST SPORT—OR NOT?

**IFOON Is Not a Word!** *by Terri Davenport.* **Supplies** *Software:* Adobe Photoshop CS2; *Cardstock:* Classic Cardstock: Cleansing by Katie Pertiet; *Template:* CZ Template No. 8; *Patterned paper:* Miranda Paper Pack by Michelle Martin and Spookable Kit by Mindy Terasawa; *Brushes:* Loop Da Loop Art Strokes by Anna Aspnes.

CONGRATULATIONS TO TERRI FOR WINNING OUR "THE FUNNEST SCRAPBOOKER EVER" CONTEST. WE LOVE HOW HER COMEDIC TALENT SHINES THROUGH IN THE JOURNALING ON THIS PAGE.

# LEGO

**ONE** Brandon and Daddy would sit for hours making up Star Wars fighter ships. Here we have two "X-wing fighters!"

**TWO** Now, Brandon makes them on his own! This is a gunner ship. A clone trooper is driving and Anikan is shooting at the bad guys! And it's called a T-wing fighter.

**THREE** This one is a space police ship driven by a droid. The person laying down in the back is an alien robber being taken to jail.

**FOUR** Here we have an M-wing fighter (name made up by Brandon because it looks like an "M.") It's also being driven by a droid and has a rocket under the ship.

**FIVE** This one is so cool. It's another space police ship made out of a fire chief's truck. This one is driven by a clone trooper!

**SIX** This is called the Voyager III. It is a bad guy ship that is driven by a storm trooper and shoots guns from the front and the back.

# CREATIONS

YOUR HARD WORK PAID OFF—YOU'VE MASTERED YOUR FAVORITE HOBBY! SHOWCASE YOUR MOST SPECTACULAR CREATIONS.

**Lego Creations** by *Julie DeGuia.* **Supplies** *Software:* Adobe Photoshop CS2; *Paper:* Art Warehouse, Candles and Cakes Solids Paper Pack by Danelle Johnson (blue strips) and Mon Petit Ballon Bleu Solids Paper Pack by Katie Pertiet (white); *Stamps:* Numbers by Katie Pertiet; *Elements:* Between the Lines Borders by Katie Pertiet and Staple Its! by Pattie Knox; *Fonts:* Bernard MT Condensed and Skia.

---

## {LEAD THE WAY}
### WITH NUMBERS

SPELL out numbers to introduce descriptions.

INCLUDE a boxed number by each photo to help connect related items.

TEN
PLAYFUL
TITLE IDEAS

1. #1 FAN
2. [INSERT WORD] MANIA
3. CATCH OF THE DAY
4. GUILTY AS CHARGED
5. I SEE A PATTERN HERE
6. MADE WITH LOVE
7. V-I-C-T-O-R-Y
8. WELCOME ABOARD
9. YES, I'M HOOKED!
10. LET THE GAMES BEGIN

# the inside *story*

It's tempting to bemoan the short days and lack of sunshine in January. But let's resolve instead to focus on all the fun activities we can only experience inside the comfort of our homes. Whether you're scrapping occasional pursuits, funny family rituals or everyday pastimes, you're sure to actually enjoy cabin fever with these terrific reader ideas!

**terrific**
*tips*
for scrapbooking indoor-play pages

**Bakin' Cookies** *by Stacy Cohen.* **Supplies** *Cardstock: Bazzill Basics Paper; Patterned paper and die cuts: Cosmo Cricket; Chipboard letters: BasicGrey; Charms: Karen Foster Design; Rhinestones and cord: Darice; Pen: American Crafts; Adhesive: 3D-Dots, EK Success; Fabri-tac, Beacon Adhesives; Glue Lines, Tombow; Other: Burlap, cheesecloth, eyelets and ribbon.*

**DESIGN TIP**

Stacy Cohen created a homespun look on her page about baking. To prevent her photos from getting lost on this appetizing layout, she printed them with a white mat and incorporated a piece of cheesecloth in a dark, solid tone behind them. Always be sure—no matter how adorable your papers and accents—that your photos get the attention they deserve.

To color cheesecloth, let it soak in ink from an inkpad refill, use a sponge dauber to sponge ink onto it in fun patterns or spritz it with a color spray.

BY BETH OPEL

### EMBELLISHMENT TIP

If you're looking for accents that won't break the budget, incorporate game or toy pieces right on a page, like Andrea Friebus did here. Hopefully her son won't notice that his Lego stash has been raided! When the found embellishments are this bright, consider enlarging your focal-point photo so it isn't overshadowed by the toys.

**Lego Love** *by Andrea Friebus.* **Supplies** *Cardstock:* American Crafts (black, red and white) and Bazzill Basics Paper (kraft); *Patterned paper:* Cosmo Cricket; *Chipboard accents:* Li'l Davis Designs; *Die-cutting machine:* Slice, Making Memories; *Font:* Candara; *Adhesive:* Mounting Squares and Zips, Therm O Web; *Other:* Lego blocks and pen.

### JOURNALING TIP

You've got a photo like this somewhere—what seems to be a very ordinary-looking household scene belies a beautiful backstory. It's time to tell yours, so look carefully at the shot in your photo stash, and remember exactly how you were feeling the moment it was taken. If it helps, follow Kristin Rutten's example and write as if you're actually speaking to someone to make your page powerful and personal.

**Wonderful Story** *by Kristin Rutten.* **Supplies** *Software:* Adobe Photoshop 7.0; *Patterned paper:* 2nd Hand Memories Kit by Katie Pertiet (cream) and Bohemian Garden Kit by Mindy Terasawa (green, recolored); *Frames:* Vintage Photo Frames No. 07 by Katie Pertiet; *Staples:* Mega Tag Pack by Katie Pertiet; *Date strip:* Date Strips No. 01 (altered) by Katie Pertiet; *Heart:* Have a Heart Felts No. 02 by Pattie Knox; *Tag:* Christmas Dreams Kit by Mindy Terasawa; *Stitches:* HeartStitched by Anna White No. 01 by Anna Aspnes (recolored) and Apple Bites Kit by Katie Pertiet (recolored); *Script words:* Photography Word Art by Ali Edwards; *Clipping mask:* Worn Page Edges No. 02 by Lynn Grieveson; *Fonts:* CK Ali's Handwriting and Traveling Typewriter.

**Playing Dress Up** *by Mou Saha.* **Supplies** *Patterned paper, letter die cuts, sticker and brad:* Anna Griffin; *Punches:* EK Success and Fiskars Americas; *Embroidery floss:* DMC; *Pen:* American Crafts; *Adhesive:* Scotch, 3M.

## PHOTOGRAPHY TIP

Turn your camera sideways and take several related photos of someone you love engaged in a favorite indoor activity. Then arrange the pictures in a line on your layout. Crop off edges, like Mou Saha did, to fit even more photos on your layout. Grab your camera and snap some vertical shots today to replicate this smart, easy design.

## BORDER TECHNIQUE

Visually tie a series of photos together with paper strips. Mou punched the edges of some papers and tore others for added interest. She then stitched them down to her layout, leaving room for her title and journaling.

## EMBELLISHMENT TIP

Create a custom journaling spot using text boxes and shapes in Microsoft Word. Leigh Penner's retro television set, which she printed on cream cardstock and cut out by hand, lends a unique charm to her layout. Experiment with shapes and dingbat fonts to make one-of-a-kind accents.

**The Saturday Morning Stare** *by Leigh Penner.* **Supplies** *Cardstock:* Bazzill Basics Paper; *Patterned paper:* Bo-Bunny Press (floral), Fancy Pants Designs (stripe), Pink Paislee (pink) and Scenic Route (ledger); *Flowers:* Stampin' Up!; *Buttons:* BasicGrey; *Corner-rounder punch:* Creative Memories; *Font:* Splendid 66; *Adhesive:* Dot 'n' Roller, Kokuyo.

**Mr. Monopoly** *by Laina Lamb.* **Supplies**
*Cardstock:* WorldWin (blue) and
The Paper Company (black, white
and green); *Patterned paper:* Jenni
Bowlin Studio (yellow ledger) and KI
Memories (red and stripe); *Paper border:*
Doodlebug Design; *Chipboard dollar
sign:* Scenic Route; *Letter stickers:*
American Crafts ("Mr."), SEI ("go") and
EK Success (white block); *Punches:* EK
Success (circle) and Fiskars Americas
(arrow); *Sketch:* Vicki Boutin; *Software:*
Adobe Illustrator; *Font:* Century Gothic;
*Adhesive:* Scotch ATG Gold Tape,
3M; Pop Dots, All Night Media, Plaid
Enterprises; *Other:* Thread.

## SUPPLY TIP

Why spend time searching your supplies
to support a theme when it's already
been done for you? Scan icons from a
game box and replicate them for a perfectly specific execution of a game-night
theme. Laina Lamb made the scanned-
and-printed game pieces stand out by
matting them with circle punches and
using foam tape for dimension.

## JOURNALING TIP

To make the journaling card mimic a
real game piece, Laina used Adobe
Illustrator to draw the shape and set
her type. You could also use an actual
game piece and cover the bottom with
a cardstock block filled with your own
journaling.

# cozy colors

If you're looking for some pretty palettes for your pages, check
out these sensational picks for January:

**Citron, Burgundy, Boysenberry**
Wausau Paper
*WausauPaper.com*

**Papaya Puree Medium, White
Prismatic, Gray Prismatic**
Prism Papers
*PrismPapers.com*

**Aqua, Blue Calypso, Atlantic**
Bazzill Basics Paper
*BazzillBasics.com*

# january
## *jubilation*

With the winter months upon us, you'll find plenty of activities to participate in. Is your weather so cold that you stay indoors most of the time this month? Or is your summer heat so unbearable that the winter months finally give you a chance to play outdoors? Either way, find time to document the everyday activities of the month. Just use some of the techniques, products, journaling ideas or quotes featured on the following pages to get you started!

**15 ideas for scrapbooking *January* memories**

### WINTER TECHNIQUE:

**1**

If the bright letters you want to use seem a little too bold against your winter-themed layout, tone down the color by sanding a little color from the top. This technique works on both chipboard letters and letter stickers. Sand letter stickers before removing them from the sticker sheet. **>>**

**Winter** *by Shaunte Wadley.* **Supplies** *Patterned paper:* Bo-Bunny Press and Crayola (silver); *Brads and chipboard:* Bo-Bunny Press; *Paint (for snow texture):* Ornamental Snow-Tex, DecoArt; *Snowflake die cut:* QuicKutz; *Font:* Times New Roman.

**BY BRITTANY BEATTIE**

## WINTER TECHNIQUE:

Add a frosted look to your page accents by layering paint over select portions to create a winter snowdrift. In her layout on page 133, Shaunte Wadley used this cool technique on her chipboard letters and flourishes. Make the snow-like appearance even more realistic by using Ornamental Snow-Tex from DecoArt.

**He Is All Boy** by Cindy Tobey. **Supplies** Cardstock: Bazzill Basics Paper; Patterned paper: KI Memories (blue stripe) and We R Memory Keepers (blue); Lace paper: KI Memories; Brads: Fancy Pants Designs; Letter stickers and badge: American Crafts; Chipboard: American Crafts (arrow and letters) and Scenic Route (calendar); Acrylic accent: Heidi Swapp for Advantus; Thread: Gutermann; Font: Arial Narrow; Other: Felt and twill.

## WINTER TECHNIQUE:

Cut "hills of snow" from white felt—they'll bring a nice, cozy feel that re-creates the look of real snow on your layout. To enhance the technique, stitch a border or two near the edges to reflect the dimension and gradual slope of real snowbanks. Top off the look by adding glitter that's reminiscent of the sparkling, white, powder snow.

## WINTER TECHNIQUE:

Layer clear snowflakes over your photos and page elements to resemble the softness of actual snowflakes falling from the sky.

### GO BLUE

Blue accents like those Shaunte Wadley used or blue patterned papers like Cindy Tobey used help bring a feeling of crisp winter weather to your layouts.

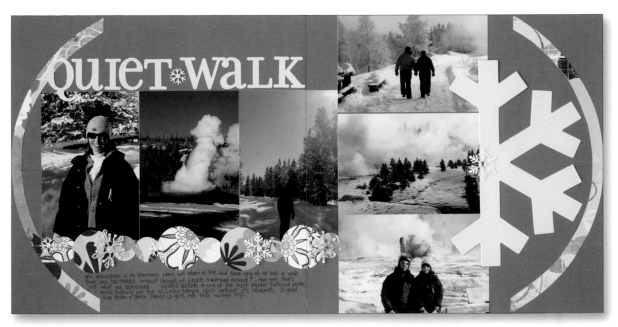

**A Quiet Walk** *by Natalie Call.* **Supplies** *Cardstock:* WorldWin; *Patterned paper:* American Crafts (cream) and BasicGrey (floral); *Letter stickers:* Making Memories; *Dimensional snowflake stickers:* Jolee's Boutique, EK Success; *Circle punches:* EK Success (large) and Marvy Uchida (small); *Large snowflake die cut:* Ellison; *Pen:* American Crafts.

## WINTER TECHNIQUE:

Layer half of a large snowflake over your photos. Try Natalie Call's cool twist: she left the forked pieces of the snowflake's center intact instead of cutting the shape exactly in half.

## WINTER TECHNIQUE:

If you're wishing that you had a snowflake accent you could trace, check out your kitchen before heading to the store. You may already have a cookie cutter that would work as a tracing template.

## COLOR ME JANUARY

Your winter pages don't have to be filled with cold colors like blue. Instead, try one of these colorful palettes to break out of the winter doldrums on your January layouts.

**Wasuau Paper:** Bright White, King's Gold and Mustard     **Prism Papers:** Mountain Rose, Starburst and Spring Larc

**Bazzill Basics Paper:** Stormy, Blackberry and Wisteria

*It's a Good Day by Emily Anderson. Photography by Allyson Cheney for Dimensionals Photography.* **Supplies** *Cardstock:* Prism Papers; *Patterned paper and flower die cut:* Fancy Pants Designs; *Brads:* Making Memories; *Letter stickers:* American Crafts; *Punches:* Marvy Uchida and Stampin' Up!; *Pen:* Signo, Newell Rubbermaid; *Font:* Prissy Frat Boy.

## COLOR TIP FROM EMILY:

"Use color! January can be such a 'down' month. Winter is still here, but the holidays are over. I find that if I just use some bright colors on my layouts, it makes the month feel really fun and fulfilling."

## JOURNALING IDEA:

If you always catch a cold at the same time each year, capture the "tradition" (however unpleasant) on a layout. Heidi Sonboul created this layout to showcase the reality that she gets bronchitis every year and has to stay in bed the whole time. Whether you get sick in January or during another month of the year, take time to record the details on a layout. Another cool thing about Heidi's page? Her five-year-old son took the photos of her while she was sick.

**Under the Weather** *by Heidi Sonboul.* **Supplies** *Cardstock:* Bazzill Basics Paper; *Patterned paper:* American Crafts; *Rub-ons:* Scenic Route; *Brads and paint:* Making Memories; *Letter stickers:* Marcella by K, K&Company.

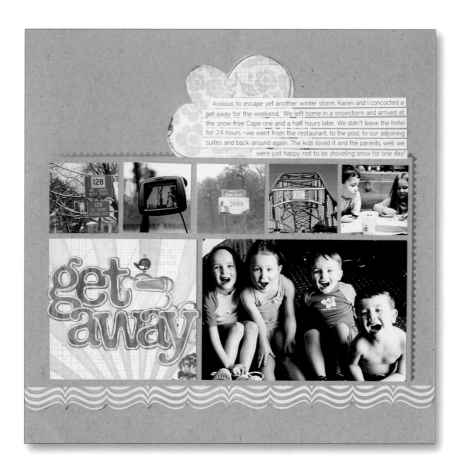

The journaling reads:

Anxious to escape yet another winter storm, Karen and I concocted a get-away for the weekend. We left home in a snowstorm and arrived at the snow-free Cape one and a half hours later. We didn't leave the hotel for 24 hours –we went from the restaurant, to the pool, to our adjoining suites and back around again. The kids loved it and the parents, well, we were just happy not to be shoveling snow for one day!

**JOURNALING IDEA:**

When you need a break from the cold weather, what do you and your family do to cheer up? Jot down your thoughts in a single paragraph, then turn the journaling into a layout.

**Getaway** *by Paula Gilarde.* **Supplies** *Cardstock:* Bazzill Basics Paper (yellow) and Stampin' Up! (kraft); *Patterned paper and letter stickers:* Sassafras; *Rub-ons:* Jenni Bowlin Studio; *Font:* District Thin.

**Banana Bread** *by Emilie Ahern.* **Supplies** *Software:* Adobe Photoshop CS2; *Cardstock, patterned paper, brads and ribbon:* Jack-O-Lantern by Oscraps Collab; *Stitches:* Ultimate Stitches Vol. 1 by Lisa Whitney; *Staples:* Nancie Rowe Janitz; *Font:* Century Gothic.

**JOURNALING IDEA:**

When you have lots of time on a winter day, use it to document the step-by-step process of an activity your family enjoys participating in together. It could be baking bread like Emilie Ahern's family, or maybe it includes playing games, putting on a puppet show or acting out a story from a favorite book.

**MORE JOURNALING IDEAS**

In addition to the ideas listed on this page and pages 136 and 137, consider journaling about one of these items this month:

- What is your favorite winter memory from childhood years?

- How long does it take to gear up for outside play on a cold day?

- How do you feel about driving in the snow or during ice storms?

- Who in your family is most excited to play in the snow? Who is least excited?

- How long do you wait before taking down the holiday decorations from December?

- If you live in a warm-weather climate, what activities do you do in the "winter" that you don't normally participate in during the summer months?

- If you could change one aspect of winter, what would it be and why? And likewise, if you could keep one aspect what would it be and why?

- If you've moved between states that have different winter climates, what was the biggest change you experienced about this season after moving to the new climate?

## 5 QUICK QUOTES

Looking for the perfect accent to finish up a winter layout? Try adding one of these delightful quotes to your page.

snowflakes are ONE OF NATURE'S MOST FRAGILE THINGS, but just look what they DO WHEN THEY STICK TOGETHER.

—verna m. kelly

Silently, like thoughts that *come and go*, the snowflakes fall, each one a gem.

—WILLIAM HAMILTON GIBSON

When the bold *branches* bid farewell to rainbow leaves— *welcome* wool sweaters.

—B. Cybrill

*you* CAN'T GET TOO MUCH WINTER IN THE *winter*.

—ROBERT FROST

*winter* is the time for comfort, for good food and *warmth*, for the touch of a friendly *hand* and for a talk beside the fire: it is the time for *home*.

—edith sitwell

# { winterize! }

This month, throw a snowball, enjoy an extra-long run, take a few deep breaths, warm yourself by the fire, bundle up in your softest mittens, renew your spirit with a quick trip to the beach and scrapbook—with one of these many solutions for all your January adventures.

Stay *inspired* with these January ideas

**The Beach in January** *by Suzy Plantamura.* **Supplies** *Patterned paper:* My Mind's Eye; *Ink:* Tsukineko; *Chipboard letters:* Li'l Davis Designs; *Markers:* EK Success (red) and Uni-ball Signo, Sanford (white); *Other:* Ribbon.

**BY BRITTANY BEATTIE**

## heed the designer

"Once you lay your photos down for placement, think of an idea that will make your page more interesting—always push the limits a little. Adding interesting design techniques makes an average layout an excellent layout. Every time I make a scrapbook page, I ask myself: 'How can I make this layout more interesting?' That question helps me come up with a better design. In this case, the wave design adds interest and supports the beach theme without overwhelming the layout."

—SUZY PLANTAMURA

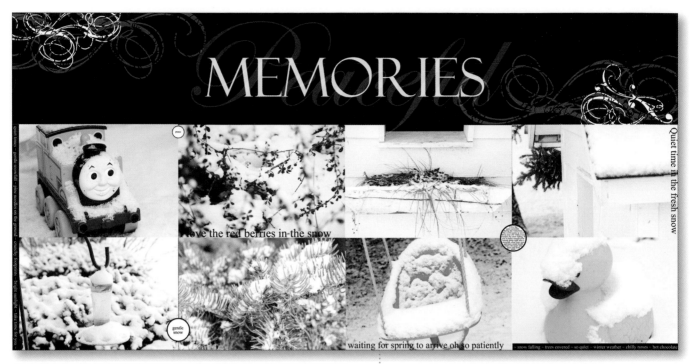

Peaceful Memories *by Stephanie Vetne.* **Supplies** *Patterned paper:* 2Peas New Year Paper by Rhonna Farrer, *www.twopeasinabucket.com; Text strips and circular embellishments:* Stephanie's own designs; *Fonts:* Felix Titling, downloaded from the Internet; Edwardian Script and Times New Roman, Microsoft Word.

# relieve
# the stress

Feeling a little stressed out after the holidays? Indulge in some quiet solitude *just for you.* That's what Stephanie Vetne did, camera in tow to take some pictures along the way to create this layout. Now the layout serves as a reminder of those peaceful moments of downtime she made for herself one blissful winter day.

## finish it quick

This layout is created with eight horizontal 4" x 6" photos along the bottom of a 12" x 12" spread—easy!

PHOTO BY LAURA POLY

### STAND HERE—
### WITH PATIENCE

Heading to the ski slopes? You'll capture a unique photo if you stand about 20–30 feet beyond the entry to the ski lifts, nearest the mountainside, then aim upward.

**The Hat** *by Cindy Tobey.* **Supplies** *Cardstock:* Bazzill Basics Paper; *Patterned paper:* Autumn Leaves (black) and KI Memories (yellow); *Stamps and acrylic letters:* Heidi Swapp for Advantus; *Ink:* Clearsnap; *Ribbon:* Michaels (diagonal stripe) and KI Memories (other); *Brads:* Queen & Co.; *Letter stickers:* KI Memories; *Chipboard star:* American Crafts; *Label stickers:* Li'l Davis Designs; *Buttons:* My Mind's Eye; *Felt flames and stars:* Cindy's own design; *Font:* Futura, Microsoft Word; *Other:* Craft felt, staples and thread.

# hip-notize your frames

Play with leftover strips of ribbon to create edgy frames near page borders.

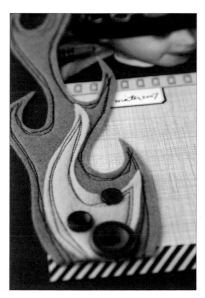

### SAVE YOUR BUDGET

Felt accents can get pricey, and the colors or designs may not be an exact match for your page. For an inexpensive option, buy sheets of craft felt and hand cut your own designs, backing them with paper for extra stability. A simple pass through the sewing machine gives the handmade embellishments even greater appeal.

### INTENSIFY WITH TEXTURE

Repetition of elements is a basic design principle. But adding various textures to the rule bumps your pages up a notch. Check out how Cindy used four textures for stars on this page: patterned paper (background), chipboard (white), hand-painted star on a transparency (yellow outline) and felt (yellow on blue).

**Cutie Pie** *by Suzy Plantamura.* **Supplies** *Cardstock:* Bazzill Basics Paper; *Patterned paper, ribbon, letter stickers, flower stickers and chipboard buttons:* Love, Elsie for KI Memories; *Buttons:* Autumn Leaves; *Embroidery floss:* DMC; *White pen:* Sakura; *Other:* Thread.

# picture this

When you have a lot of "white space" in your photo—whether from solid-colored coats, fields of snow or blue skies—use it to your advantage. Instead of letting the eye get stuck there, embellish the space with journaling (use pens designed for slick surfaces), strips of ribbon or other accents. This works best when the photo subject has a strong focal point.

## make it monochromatic

When selecting color schemes for your page, try selecting patterned papers with a background that's a shade *lighter* than your photo subjects (here, a light pink). Select accents in the same intensity as your photos (here, a bright pink). The monochromatic combination will help keep the focus in the right spot. For added contrast, add a neutral color, like black or white, to the background.

## pull a flower "flake out"

Use funky flowers as "snowflakes" for a winter page.

PHOTO BY MELINDA ALEXANDER

### LANDSCAPES: TURN DREARY INTO CHEERY

Dead trees got your photos down? Simply blur them by using the portrait mode on your camera or using a shallow depth of field. You'll get the forest appearance without the lifeless branches.

# *organize* your pages

I love thumbing through the pages of Creating Keepsakes magazine to be inspired by all the layouts. It makes me want to hurry to my scrap space to create. And so often, it leaves me thinking, "How did the designer do that?" or "How did she come up with that great idea?" So in honor of this month's "organization" issue, I asked these eight designers how they came up with and organized the ideas on their layouts to create such eye-catching designs. I'm excited to share their tips with you!

designer *tips* for March layouts

**HELEN'S TIPS:**

- I wanted the layout to be colorful and fun without being "overdone." I like that this design is so simple yet eye-catching.

- Except for the background cardstock, I used scraps of paper for all the elements on this layout.

**Kiss Me, I'm Irish** *by Helen Croft.* **Supplies** *Cardstock:* WorldWin; *Patterned paper:* Die Cuts With a View, Imaginisce and Scenic Route; *Letter stickers:* EK Success (letters) and SEI (exclamation point); *Chipboard letters:* Scenic Route; *Rub-ons:* Daisy D's Paper Co.; *Photo turn:* 7gypsies; *Paint, epoxy flowers and brads:* Making Memories; *Gloss:* Close To My Heart; *Pen:* American Crafts.

**BY BRITTANY BEATTIE**

**Herndon Festival** *by Dawn Hagewood.* **Supplies** *Cardstock:* Bazzill Basics Paper; *Patterned paper:* Tinkering Ink; *Letter stickers and chipboard:* Scenic Route; *Font:* SP You've Got Mail.

**DAWN'S TIPS:**

■ For events like this festival, I think the more pictures, the better! I kept a large white border around the layout to group the elements and keep it from being too busy.

■ The little butterflies were actually cut from patterned paper—they make a great handmade embellishment that's also low cost.

■ For the word "festival," I didn't have any t's left in that alphabet, so I used an L with two dots from i's. I actually like it better than if I had used a t!

**DEBBY'S TIPS:**

■ The birds and wildlife are just coming back this year, waking up and getting active. So put on a sweater, get out your tripod and camera, and settle in with some patience to photograph the awesome nature found in your backyard.

■ Think texture! Rip, tear and fold those edges. Don't be afraid. Get messy. Roll the edges. . . . You might like how it looks.

**House Guests** *by Debby Visser.* **Supplies** *Cardstock:* Bazzill Basics Paper; *Patterned paper and flower accents (cut out from paper):* Cloud 9 Design, Fiskars; *Chipboard:* Maya Road (scallop frames) and Scenic Route (letters); *Heart punch:* EK Success; *Ink:* Stampin' Up!; *Pens:* Zig, EK Success; Stampin' Up! (gel).

**At Play** *by Mary MacAskill.* **Supplies** *Cardstock:* Bazzill Basics Paper; *Patterned paper:* Making Memories; *Vellum:* The Paper Company; *Stamps:* Hero Arts; *Ink:* Impressions; *Stickers:* American Crafts (letter) and Making Memories (definition); *Chipboard:* September 2008 Kit, KitoftheMonth.com (star) and Scenic Route (photo corner); *Decorative paper strips:* Doodlebug Design; *Paper edge:* Making Memories; *Photo turn and brads:* American Crafts; *Button:* Autumn Leaves; *Punches:* Fiskars (scallop) and Marvy Uchida (corner rounder); *Font:* Arial.

## MARY'S TIPS:

- Take a lot of photos and worry later about whether they are usable! To squeeze lots of photos onto your layout, use a photo strip. It keeps the layout uncluttered and helps you tell your story with more images.

- I pulled my color scheme directly from the red, yellow and blue playground equipment in my photos!

- I started this layout with the "play" word photo strip, and I matched the title font as closely as I could to keep the design unified.

- I took 43 photos of our playtime at the park, but it was easy to narrow them down. Sadie is a typical toddler, so she was on the move and a lot of the photos were blurry. I chose the photos that were in focus and also communicated the fun that she (and we) had exploring at the park. I tried to select photos that showed her playing on different pieces of the playground equipment, which also helped to show how quickly Sadie moves from one item to the next!

**VIVIAN'S TIPS:**

■ I made the focal-point photo stand out more by adhering it with Pop Dots on the page.

■ I added black brads and pen-drawn lines to help move the viewer's eye around the layout.

**Trike** by Vivian Masket. **Supplies** Patterned paper: American Crafts (purple) and October Afternoon (yellow); Letter stickers and brads: American Crafts; Rubber bird charm: October Afternoon; Sticker: KI Memories; Chipboard heart and pen: American Crafts; Dimensional adhesive: Plaid Enterprises.

**DAWN'S TIPS:**

■ I probably took a dozen photos of this activity. I chose one picture to show the slide, and I printed the others as close-ups to focus in on how much fun my son was having.

■ These papers are actually from a birthday collection of papers. Sometimes I like using themed papers for fun, everyday layouts.

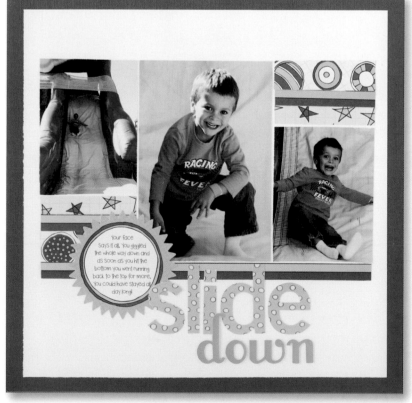

**Slide Down** by Dawn Hagewood. **Supplies** Cardstock: Bazzill Basics Paper; Patterned paper and die cuts: Scenic Route; Letter stickers: American Crafts; Font: SP You've Got Mail.

**Adequately Charmed** by Linda Harrison. **Supplies** Cardstock: Bazzill Basics Paper; Patterned paper: Scenic Route; Chipboard: Technique Tuesday (journaling border), EK Success (scallop circle) and Heidi Swapp for Advantus (bookplate); Stamps: Inkadinkado; Ink: Tsukineko; Letter stickers: Adornit - Carloee's Creations; Number stickers: Doodlebug Design; Brads: Doodlebug Design (red) and Queen & Co. (shamrock); Letter die cuts: QuicKutz; Embroidery floss: DMC; Pen: Newell Rubbermaid; Font: Incognitype.

**LINDA'S TIPS:**

■ I wanted the photos to be the main focus since they pretty much speak for themselves on this memory. I kept the background clean and light with just a few touches of additional color to help the photos shine.

■ By layering elements, hand-stitching, tearing paper and adding chipboard accents, the layout became more dimensional without looking cluttered or bulky.

■ Bigger isn't always better. I *love* using oversized shapes on my layouts, but on this particular layout one little shamrock was just the right size to complement and not overpower the photos.

■ Swirls don't always have to be paired with girls and flowers. I used some hand-stitched swirls on this page to create a sense of movement and texture.

■ If you don't have papers with shamrocks or pots of gold on them for St. Patrick's Day, just gather papers from your stash with colors that create a feel for the holiday. It's amazing how an ordinary green patterned paper turns into the perfect sheet of St. Patrick's Day green once it's paired with your holiday photos on the page.

**Every Boy Needs a Tree Swing** by Lisa Truesdell. **Supplies** *Cardstock:* Bazzill Basics Paper; *Patterned paper:* Daisy D's Paper Co. (green), Making Memories (ledger) and October Afternoon (cloud, wood grain, green floral, yellow dot, red, orange dot and yellow floral); *Chipboard:* Maya Road; *Letter stickers:* Making Memories; *Ribbon:* American Crafts; *Buttons:* Autumn Leaves; *Butterflies:* Mellette Berezoski by Design; *Jewels:* Heidi Swapp for Advantus; *Decorative scissors:* Fiskars.

**LISA'S TIPS:**

■ The red door and red buttons create a visual triangle to help draw the eye through the layout.

■ Every time I come home, I love seeing the tree swing that's in our front yard. This fun, whimsical layout with a picture of my son swinging captures that feeling.

■ I appreciate that the photo is the star of the layout despite all of the other things going on.

■ I added jewels to the text-paper butterflies to give them a little more presence on the layout.

■ When selecting papers for my page, I pulled together a bunch of floral and dot patterns in bright colors that made me think of spring. Seeing them with my photo made it easier to choose which ones I wanted to use.

# easter
## *extravaganza*

Whether you're celebrating Easter, Passover or simply life's joys this month, record the memories in your scrapbooks. Then, spend an afternoon making a project to showcase in your home—you can enjoy the celebration all month long even when your scrapbooks are closed on your shelves. Keeping handmade reminders of life's joys around the home is worth every minute spent creating them!

Brighten your *home* with these cheerful ideas

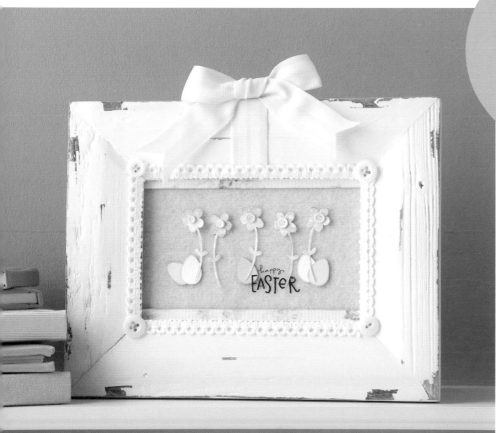

**Happy Easter** *by Melissa Phillips.* **Supplies** *Cardstock:* Bazzill Basics Paper (purple) and WorldWin (green); *Patterned paper, trim, buttons and rub-ons:* Melissa Frances; *Ink:* Ranger Industries; *Mini button brads:* Making Memories; *Die-cut machine (for flowers):* Cuttlebug, Provo Craft; *Ribbon:* Li'l Davis Designs; *Glitter:* Ranger Industries; *Felt eggs (used as template for cardstock eggs):* American Crafts; *Other:* Frame and felt from craft store.

### FRAME HOW-TO:

❶ Distress frame and remove glass.

❷ Fill frame interior with felt, then add a thin border of patterned paper.

❸ Die cut or punch five flowers and five eggs from patterned paper. Arrange on felt.

❹ Cover five mini button brads with glitter to create flower centers. Add to flowers.

❺ Add title with rub-ons—they work even on felt!

❻ Surround frame center with trim on all four sides and a button over each corner. Top with a bow along the top side of the frame.

**BY BRITTANY BEATTIE**

**Thanks, Easter Bunny!** *by Connie Tomasula.* **Supplies** *Patterned paper:* Rusty Pickle; *Rub-ons:* Doodlebug Design; *Ribbon:* May Arts; *Brads:* Lasting Impressions for Paper; *Fonts:* DW Dingbats (bunny clip art), *www.twopeasinabucket.com*; Hot Chocolate (text), Internet; *Other:* Vellum.

**Well Done** *by Marci Lambert.* **Supplies** *Cardstock:* Bazzill Basics Paper; *Patterned paper and chipboard accent:* Scenic Route; *Journaling stamp:* Technique Tuesday; *Ink:* ColorBox, Clearsnap; *Chipboard letter stickers:* Heidi Swapp for Advantus; *Pen:* Pilot; *Font:* Bulky Refuse Type, *www.dafont.com*; *Other:* Buttons, embroidery floss, brads and metal frame.

## ‸wrapped text made easy

Getting your journaling to wrap around an accent can be frustrating. I know I've printed try after try before achieving a journaling box that's just right. That's why I love Connie's layout. The Easter Bunny accent is actually a dingbat she printed onto white cardstock and cut out. Here's how to simplify your journaling wraps:

1. Type your text.

2. Add a dingbat accent in your text document and use the text wrap feature for a perfect fit.

3. Print the dingbat onto a separate sheet of cardstock. Cut the image out, then adhere it over the dingbat on the journaling block for nice dimension.

## ‹ nontraditonal photo frames

To highlight this photo, Marci created a "frame" of her own—using patterned paper combined with three accents in a visual triangle (the chipboard circle, the bookplate and the button).

**Easter Egg Hunt** *by Natalie Call.* **Supplies** *Cardstock:* WorldWin; *Patterned paper:* Rusty Pickle; *Rub-ons:* Doodlebug Design; *Brads:* Bazzill Basics Paper; *Flower, letter stickers, velvet stickers and journaling paper:* Making Memories; *Journaling spots:* Heidi Swapp for Advantus.

## ^ not just for journaling anymore

Two made-for-journaling accents on this layout aren't used for journaling. Spot one is behind the Easter title—it makes a great title block. Spot two is the pink egg in the trio at the bottom—it's a circle journaling spot cut in half to look like part of an egg.

### MAKE IT MEANINGFUL

Here's how Natalie did it:

1. First, she decided to show how much her mother-in-law put into the events so the kids would have fun and good memories.

2. The patterned-paper zigzag at the bottom mimics the Easter baskets Grandma cut (see the photo on the left side).

3. The photo of Grandma with the bunny ears shows that she "sacrificed a little embarrassment to make it more fun for the kids—because she is not a silly person."

### DON'T FORGET

Says Natalie, "Remember to get photos of the older teen cousins at family events. Sometimes I forget to do this because I'm focused on getting good shots of my children, but I'm so glad that this layout focuses on our extended family. It will be nice to remember them at this age."

**Easter Egg Garland** *by Julie Boardman.* **Supplies** *Cardstock:* Bazzill Basics Paper; *Patterned paper:* BasicGrey and unknown; *Ribbon:* AC Moore, Cosmo Cricket, Making Memories and May Arts; *Brads:* Making Memories; *Flowers:* Prima; *Letter die cuts:* Opposites Attract, Cricut, Provo Craft; *Wooden eggs:* AC Moore; *Pen:* Sharpie, Newell Rubbermaid; *Dimensional adhesive:* Mod Podge, Plaid Enterprises; *Other:* Acrylic paint.

## egg garland

Turn wooden football accents into an egg garland! Here's how:

1. Add paper to the eggs with Mod Podge and sand the edges.

2. Use a Crop-A-Dile or heavy-duty hole punch to punch a hole on each long side of each egg.

3. Cut several short pieces of assorted ribbon and use them to tie the eggs together. Add a looped ribbon to each end of the garland for hanging.

4. Add letters to spell "Happy Easter" and embellish to create chick and bunny faces.

**Easter Egg Scramble** *by Lea Lawson.* **Supplies** *Cardstock:* Bazzill Basics Paper; *Patterned paper:* Chatterbox; *Rub-ons:* Autumn Leaves; *Ink:* ColorBox, Clearsnap; *Letter stickers:* Making Memories; *Rhinestones;* Westrim Crafts; *Chipboard letters:* Scenic Route; *Font:* Century Gothic, Microsoft; *Die-cut machine (for scallop borders):* Cricut, Provo Craft.

## organized chaos

Lea's family participates in a "scramble" instead of a hunt. She wanted to achieve that "scramble" feeling without sacrificing her page elements' sense of unity. Here's how she did it:

1 Lea adhered her title letters at different heights while keeping the word easily readable as a single unit from left to right.

2 She included gems along the border just below the photos. It reinforces the eggs covering the ground in all the photos, yet they're all in a single line to avoid drawing too much attention.

### PHOTO ENHANCEMENT: EASY CROPS

Lea's great advice for achieving this layout with photos that tell her story? "Look closely at your photos to find what your layout needs. Many of the detail-oriented photos here, like the basket of candy and of the eggs, came from a photo with a lot of unnecessary background. Those items caught my eye, so I cropped down to only what I needed from the photo."

## think outside
## the easter box

Look through the four Easter layouts in this column and you won't find any Easter-specific patterned papers. In fact, two layouts used girl-themed papers! Sometimes picking universal patterns make paper easier to work with—you don't have to worry about seeing only half of a bunny or not being able to recognize an egg. Focus on color and see what Easter layouts you can use with papers already in your stash.

# springtime and *easter*

The arrival of springtime brings renewed energy and playfulness into my life—and my scrapooking. During spring, I can't wait to scrapbook in a more creative way because of the inspiration I receive for my pages from the beautiful world around me. Ready to get creative yourself? Scraplift an idea—whether it's an entire page, a photo angle, a color scheme or a cool accent idea—from one of the following amazing layouts about spring and Easter!

enjoy a bouquet of *fresh* looks

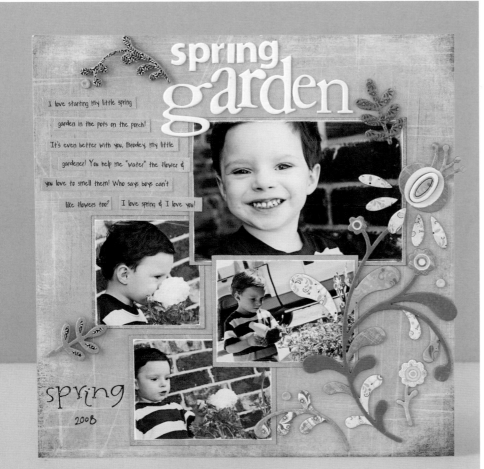

**Spring Garden** by April Massad. **Supplies** Patterned paper, chipboard letters and chipboard accents: BasicGrey; Stamps: Heidi Swapp for Advantus ("2008") and Wordsworth (letter); Ink: StazOn, Tsukineko; Font: CK Study Hall.

**SCRAPLIFTABLE IDEAS:**

- Create a flower garden on your pages with flower die-cut shapes or accents.

- Arrange your photos into an asymmetrical photo collage, then use the space around it to include your journaling and creative embellishing.

- Chipboard is already dimensional, but you can increase the effect by adding dimensional adhesive under some of the pieces on your page.

**BY BRITTANY BEATTIE**

**Sweetie Pie** *by Brenda Hurd.* **Supplies** *Patterned paper:* BasicGrey (blue and butterfly) and Scenic Route (white); *Rub-ons:* BasicGrey ("Sugar & Spice") and Scenic Route ("Sweetie Pie"); *Ribbon:* American Crafts; *Buttons:* BasicGrey; *Die cuts:* BasicGrey (bee and vine) and Bazzill Basics Paper (scalloped border); *Glitter spray:* Tattered Angels; *Pen:* Zig Writer, EK Success.

**SCRAPLIFTABLE IDEAS:**

- If a patterned paper is too busy for the look you want to create, use a craft knife to cut out only one or two shapes from the pattern, then use them as individual elements on your layout.

- If you don't have a lot of time to spend creating title letters, look through your rub-on stash to see if any phrases would fit as a title.

- As your child eats her Easter candy, snap photos on the continuous mode on your camera (often in the same menu as the self-timer mode). Brenda Hurd used this mode to "capture the intensity on [her] daughter's face when she unwrapped the candy. Going across the layout with the photos was the perfect solution to portray the story."

**SCRAPLIFTABLE IDEAS:**

- Photo collage grids don't always need to contain photos of equal size. Here, Ruth Dealey included three sizes of photos in her collage.

- Add an accent overlapping the corners of two photos or papers to break up the solid lines.

- This grid paper was actually cut from only one piece of patterned paper, even though it appears to span more than half the layout.

**A Walk with Nature** *by Ruth Dealey.* **Supplies** *Cardstock:* Bazzill Basics Paper; *Patterned paper:* Fancy Pants Designs (grid and green) and Scenic Route (stripe); *Letter stickers:* BasicGrey; *Chipboard circles:* Scenic Route; *Punch:* Stampin' Up!; *Pen:* Pilot Corp.

**SCRAPLIFTABLE IDEAS:**

- Joscelyne Cutchens used a series of long, thin pictures to show her son running to find Easter eggs. Her creative cutting let her crop out distracting items. Says Joscelyne: "I considered using one large picture of Jordan running, but I couldn't decide which one was the best. That's when I decided to use long strips in a row. They still give the same effect as the whole lawn covered in colorful eggs but have the added benefit of seeing Jordan run."

- The labels on this page started as black-and-white images. Joscelyne colored them in with blue and green to give them a new look.

- Joscelyne balanced the journaling block by using a second block (turned on its side) as a tab in the page's top-right corner. The blue title in the lower-left corner of the layout helps complete the visual triangle of blue accents.

- Add unity to your page by overlapping all elements (even if just slightly) on your layout.

**Easter Egg Hunt** *by Joscelyne Cutchens.* **Supplies** *Software:* Adobe Photoshop Elements 6.0; *Tablet:* Wacom; *Patterned paper:* Rainbow Joy by Miss Mint; *Letters:* Fat Plastic Alphabet by Miss Mint; *Bunny:* Cutesy Doodle Doo - April by Miss Mint; *Label, frame and glitter strip (color added):* Kooky Spooky Elements by Miss Mint; *Font:* Century Gothic.

**Easter Sunday . . . Remember** *by Greta Hammond.* **Supplies** *Cardstock:* Bazzill Basics Paper; *Patterned paper, ribbon, buttons and brads:* Fancy Pants Designs; *Rub-ons:* Fancy Pants Designs ("circa 1974") and Scenic Route ("Easter Sunday"); *Ink:* ColorBox, Clearsnap; *Paper clips:* EK Success; *Chipboard:* BasicGrey; *Digital photo overlays and frames:* Rhonna Farrer; *Font:* Times New Roman; *Other:* Tag and thread.

**SCRAPLIFTABLE IDEAS:**

■ Create "Easter eggs" from oval punches and a few scrapbooking supplies—Greta Hammond used paper, lace and brads. To add extra appeal to one of the eggs, try embossing it to add texture (see the pink egg on the layout).

■ Take time this month to scrapbook memories of your childhood Easter celebrations. Comments Greta: "My kids love to look at photos of me when I was a child. And with the descriptive journaling, my kids will have a glimpse into my childhood."

■ Add a vintage feel to photos by matting them on white or black cardstock to create a "Polaroid" look.

■ Use stitching, lace and inked edges to enhance a vintage theme on your layout.

■ If most elements on your page are linear, try tilting your photos to add a homey feel.

**Easter** by Kim Watson. **Supplies** Patterned paper: Autumn Leaves, Bazzill Basics Paper, Creative Imaginations and Making Memories; Flowers, buttons, epoxy brads, letter stickers, ribbon, journaling tag and metal-rimmed tags: Making Memories; Corner-rounder punch: EK Success; Embroidery floss: Karen Foster Design; Pen: Zig Millennium, EK Success; Adhesive: Mono Adhesive, Tombow; Other: Thread and butterfly from greeting card.

### SCRAPLIFTABLE IDEAS:

- Turn your journaling block into a decorated "Easter egg" by trimming it into an oval shape and tying a ribbon around part of it.

- Add a cohesive feel by facing any stripe patterns or paper strips the same direction. On the "Easter" page above, Kim Watson chose to have everything face a horizontal direction.

- Kim cut the blue-dot scallop shape from a block of patterned paper to add interest to a paper she'd had in her collection for a while.

**SCRAPLIFTABLE IDEAS:**

- To add interest to a solid-colored background cardstock (especially if it's a neutral color), add a light coat of bright-colored paint around your photographs and behind your journaling and title.

- If you want to visually "ground" a busy patterned paper to your layout's background, add a solid-colored ribbon across the strip.

- Layer a button on a felt circle for a new twist on your design.

**Spring Has Sprung** *by Brenda Hurd.* **Supplies** *Patterned paper, chipboard letters and rub-ons:* BasicGrey; *Ribbon and flower:* Making Memories; *Buttons:* BasicGrey and Making Memories (felt); *Jewel:* Creative Imaginations; *Letter stickers:* American Crafts; *Paint:* Ceramcoat, Delta Creative; *Embroidery floss:* DMC; *Font:* Bell MT.

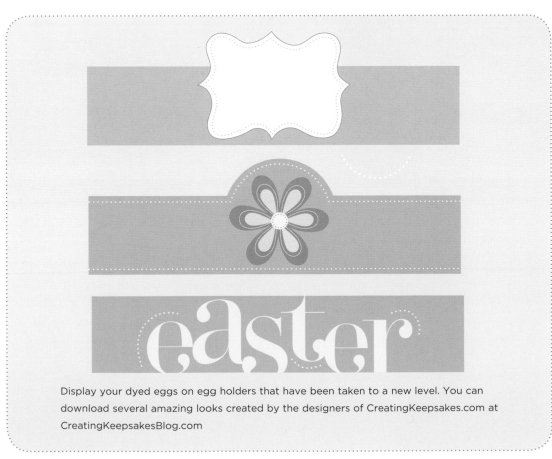

Display your dyed eggs on egg holders that have been taken to a new level. You can download several amazing looks created by the designers of CreatingKeepsakes.com at CreatingKeepsakesBlog.com

# { nature's *majesty* }

No matter where I go, there's always something remarkable to look at—majestic mountains, rolling hills, luscious green foliage or beautiful red rock. In fact, the abundance of unique natural creations is one of the main reasons I love to travel so much. I always stand in awe at the many sights to see. But even when I don't travel, there's still so much in nature to inspire me.

Celebrate the *beauties of nature* today

This month, I'm going to let nature inspire me to:

- Photograph a color scheme from flowers to use as the palette for a layout.

- Head to a park, canyon or garden with notebook in hand, then take time to journal my thoughts on what nature means to me. (I may use the journaling on a layout—if not, I'll at least print it and include it in my album.)

- Stamp with flowers or leaves that grow in my yard.

- Find 10 favorite nature photos I've taken (I have over 1,000 of them!) and compile them onto a layout to hang in my home.

**Meet Bob** by Paula Barber. **Supplies** *Cardstock:* Prism Papers (brown metallic) and The Paper Company (kraft); *Patterned paper:* Love, Elsie for KI Memories (fabric houses and green scribbles), Making Memories (shaped dot) and Scenic Route (leaf); *Ink:* Stampin' Up!; *Twine:* Martha Stewart Crafts (striped) and Stampin' Up! (red); *Dimensional glitter paint:* Stickles, Ranger Industries; *Chipboard heart:* Heidi Swapp for Advantus; *Die-cutting cartridges and machine:* Cricut Expression, Provo Craft; *Pen:* Faber-Castell.

**BY BRITTANY BEATTIE**

## swirls & snails

To create this incredible snail accent, Paula Barber used a swirl die cut as her base, then embellished it to fit her needs. Check out *your* stash to see what products could be turned into accents of nature's wonders.

### ACCENTS THAT TELL A STORY

When choosing accents for your pages, pick items that represent the story behind the layout, like Paula did. She says, "Noah was just fascinated with snails and the fact that they haul their houses around everywhere they go. I added the houses from the Love, Elsie fabric paper as a little visual play to that effect."

## buttons & butterflies

Add dimension to stamped butterflies (and dip into your stash of supplies at the same time!) for extraordinary accents with a personal touch. Simply add two buttons over the butterfly to serve as the body. This idea works great if you're working with sticker, rub-on, die-cut or hand-cut butterflies as well!

**A Secret Oasis** by Summer Fullerton. **Supplies** *Cardstock:* Bazzill Basics Paper; *Patterned paper:* 7gypsies, BasicGrey and Hot Off The Press; *Stamps:* Inque Boutique; *Ink:* StazOn, Tsukineko; *Letter stickers:* American Crafts; *Buttons:* foof-a-La, Autumn Leaves; *Chipboard:* Déjà Views by The C-Thru Ruler Co.; *Decorative border:* Doodlebug Design; *Font:* Typenoksidi, Internet.

# landscape backgrounds

While I don't usually enlarge my photos, I make an exception for layouts about nature. I think there's something special about enlarging a favorite landscape photo for the base of a page. Plus, it makes it easy to complete the layout quickly—just add a title block and journaling and it's done! Layouts like these make great displays for home decor, where I can appreciate the natural beauty of the outside world even when I'm indoors.

"I want my kids to always appreciate the beauty and awe of nature. There's nothing more breathtaking than the sight of something created by the hand of God, and nature is so pure, so beautiful, that nothing our human hands create could ever improve it. For that reason, I added only my title and journaling so the photo—and the beauty of nature—would remain the focal point. By making the photo full page and embellishing it sparingly, I was able to let the beauty of nature stand on its own and take center stage."

—DEENA WUEST

{God's} *beauty*

Kansas wheat fields. We see them every single day. We admire their beauty and marvel as they turn from brilliant green to golden brown. And every year we stop, walk through them, smell the kernels and run our hands over the stalks. It's a beauty straight from God. A beauty that the human hand could never match. A beauty that makes us stand in awe of our creator.

**God's Beauty** *by Deena Wuest.* **Supplies** *Software:* Adobe Photoshop Elements 4.0, Adobe Systems; *Template (revised for the layout):* Tortuga Template No. 57 by Kellie Mize, *www.designerdigitals.com; Fonts:* Avant Garde and Impact, *www.fonts.com;* Hannibal Lecter, Internet.

PHOTOGRAPH BY ALLISON ORTHNER

### SUNSET SILHOUETTES

When you want to focus on the beauty of a sunset but still capture your family in the photo, go for a silhouette shot. By positioning your family members between the sunset and yourself and turning the flash off, you'll get an instant silhouette photo.

To get the perfect shot here, Allison snapped around 50 photos during a 10-minute period while the sun was setting. Admittedly, you may need to spend some time to capture your best picture, but those 10 minutes will be worth it when you get to hang the final photo on your wall or put it in your scrapbook.

*Note:* As Allison reminds, "Be very careful about aiming your camera into direct sunlight because it can cause 'lens flare' on your photo and even damage your camera's light sensor. For sunset photos, it's best to wait until the sun is low on the horizon and not quite so bright."

**Little Hands, Big Finds** *by Jennifer Armentrout.* **Supplies** *Cardstock:* Bazzill Basics Paper and The Paper Company; *Patterned paper:* Lazar StudioWERX; *Chipboard letters:* American Crafts; *Rub-on letters and paint:* Making Memories; *Rub-ons:* Chatterbox; *Photo turns:* 7gypsies; *Transparency:* 3M; *Pen:* Sakura.

## *handy* ideas

Incorporating hands into your layouts can add a personal touch and also some perspective. For example, check out the two great uses of hands on Jennifer's layout:

**❶** When photographing objects from nature, hold them in your hands to provide a point of reference for others to know how large the items or insects actually are.

**❷** For pages of childhood adventures, have your children stamp their handprints with paint once a year to capture their growth from year to year. For a fun twist on mud-themed pages, try stamping with brown paint.

PHOTOGRAPH BY ALANNAH JURGENSMEYER

### THE PERFECT COLORS

Wondering how to capture the beauty of nature in its truest colors? Alannah Jurgensmeyer has some great tips. "Nature photos," she says, "are always more visually appealing when you really draw out the colors that you see. To help the colors in the photos pop, I try to not take photos with sunlight directly overhead. A mildly cloudy day, early-morning light or light at sunset are all great photo-taking times that help nature's best colors really shine through in the photographs."

Notes Alannah, "Sometimes it's hard to control location at specific times of day when traveling, though. If I have nature pictures that seem a bit washed out from direct sunlight, I will increase the color saturation in Photoshop to pump the colors up in the shots."

# on being a *mother*

Motherhood is an important part of your life! But have you recorded your feelings in your scrapbook yet? This month, you've got help! Here's how:

❶ Look through the layouts in this column—they'll show you many creative approaches to scrapbooking this topic.

❷ Read the journaling on the layouts. Let it inspire thoughts for *your* journaling. Take a moment to jot down some things you want to say about being a mom. These notes won't be your final draft of the journaling—they'll just get you started.

**scrapbook your thoughts on being a *mother***

*the hardest job I'll ever love*

So many people told me that staying home with my son could be a rough transition. I never thought it would be hard. I had dreamed all my life of getting to stay home and raise my children. Before finding out I was pregnant I was a teacher and I loved my job! I even thought I may return to teach even after having children...boy was I wrong! I have been staying home with Ethan now for 11 months and I wouldn't trade a minute of it for any job or any amount of money! It has been a rough transition for me at times, but it is by far the best job I will ever have...the job of being Ethan's 'mama'!
-November 2008-

*\*mama*

**Mama** *by Rebecca Shogren.* **Supplies** *Cardstock:* Bazzill Basics Paper; *Patterned paper (including cutout butterfly and leaf accents):* BasicGrey; *Letter stickers:* American Crafts; *Chipboard:* Making Memories; *Pen:* Gelly Roll, Sakura; *Font:* CK Classical; *Other:* Jewels.

❸ Check out the "Scrapbooking This Layout" text that accompanies each page. The text will provide more approaches for your layout, help you develop your ideas into a page and spark ideas to record.

❹ Now you can start your layout and experience the joy of having recorded one of the best parts of your life in your album. >>

**BY BRITTANY BEATTIE**

## ON SCRAPBOOKING THIS LAYOUT

- I created this layout (see page 163) when my son was eleven months old. He had just started walking, and my job as a mom was taking on a whole new dimension! I wanted to create a page that symbolized my feelings as a mom at that moment—I made sure to create room for a lot of journaling so my son would always know how important he is to me.

- For me, scrapbooking is a form of therapy just as much as it is about preserving memories. This time in my life was one that was bittersweet. My son learned to walk, which was exciting but also a bit sad because he wasn't my baby anymore. He was now a toddler. Creating this page was therapeutic because it gave me a chance to remember those moments of babyhood before moving forward into toddlerhood.

- I think it's important to take time to scrapbook about your thoughts and feelings. Your kids will love reading about and seeing more of you in the years to come!

- When you're on a tight budget, get creative with what you've got. For example, the butterfly embellishments on this page are cut from a piece of patterned paper.

—REBECCA SHOGREN

## ON SCRAPBOOKING THIS LAYOUT

- For the photo, I simply placed a camera on books stacked on the floor, set the timer and ran to pose on the floor with my boys. Immediately when I saw the photo on my computer, it reminded me how lucky I am to be able to stay home with my boys every day. I used the house chipboard shapes to emphasize the stay-at-home-mom theme.

- Don't be afraid to take photos of yourself with your children. The time while they're young is so fleeting, so don't put it off. Most cameras have timers, which makes it easy to set up fun shots with your kids.

- When creating a page about myself, I think about how much I would have loved to see my mom create a page like this for me. I think about how much I love seeing photos of us together when I was young. I want my boys to know how much I truly treasure them and the joy of staying home with them.

—KELLY NOEL

**@ Home** by Kelly Noel. **Supplies** Cardstock: Bazzill Basics Paper; Patterned paper: Making Memories; Chipboard: American Crafts (letters) and Maya Road (shapes); Flowers, ribbon and brads: American Crafts; Paint: Plaid Enterprises; Embroidery floss: DMC; Dimensional adhesive: Glossy Accents, Ranger Industries; Font: Kayleigh.

**Love-** One of the best examples of love I can give is that of a parent to a child. I truly did not understand such love until I became a parent myself. I was overwhelmed with the physical pain I felt, with the total sacrifice of any sleep or time alone, and with the thought that I was saddled with this for a lifetime. I kept thinking- "This is hard!" "Why do we even do this?" "How did my parents do this?" Slowly, I learned the answer. It is love. We sacrifice our time, money and efforts. We hurt physically and emotionally at times. We smile at the smallest accomplishment. We pray and hope and do it again and again. All because we love each other. And in return, we are blessed with a family of people who do the same for us.

**On Motherhood** *by Emily Higbee.* **Supplies** *Cardstock:* Making Memories; *Patterned paper:* American Crafts (black) and Imaginisce (green); *Letter stickers:* American Crafts and Doodlebug Design; *"Smitten" sticker:* Scenic Route; *Circle accent and chipboard arrow:* American Crafts; *Felt border:* Li'l Davis Designs; *Chipboard heart:* Heidi Swapp for Advantus; *Journaling spot:* Elle's Studio; *Other:* Binder clip.

## ON SCRAPBOOKING THIS LAYOUT

- After I had my third child, I was a little overwhelmed and asked my mom, "How did you do this?" She gave me a vague look and said, "I don't remember!" We laughed, and I made a mental note to do a layout for my daughters so that when they had the same question, they would know I felt the same way and how I dealt with it. The main message I wanted to communicate in this layout was love. I used hearts and some valentine accents to help communicate this.

- When I looked through my pictures, I tried to choose some "real" mom ones. I wanted my girls to see that I wore my hair in a ponytail a lot, that I wore some baggy clothes to hide my baby fat, and that lots of days I wore no makeup. I also wanted to show that it was still fun—I tried to use bright, cheery colors to help communicate that.

- It's hard to scrap photos of myself, especially ones with no makeup and with baby fat. I recently noticed that my scrapbooks contained a lot of photos of individuals —not relationships. I realized that I was missing a huge part of our story, so now I focus on the relationships —mother and child, husband and wife, cousins, friends, grandparents. I hope when my children look through their albums they will remember that they are surrounded by wonderful people who love them and care for them. That means I have to put some pictures of me in there!

- I think it's easier to scrapbook about yourself if you identify a specific audience. What do you want your kids, husband or friends to remember about you? Is there something specific they might not know or may wonder about in the future? Try to think of what you would like to see and hear about a specific time in your mother's or grandmother's life and scrap that for the people who love you!

—EMILY HIGBEE

**Changes** by Gabriella Biancofiore.
**Supplies** *Cardstock:* Archiver's (red) and Die Cuts With a View (tan); *Patterned paper:* BasicGrey; *Ribbon:* American Crafts (dot) and unknown; *Letter stickers:* SEI; *Buttons:* American Crafts (gold) and Dress It Up (small brown); *Flourish:* My Mind's Eye; *Glitter paint:* Stickles, Ranger Industries; *"Motherhood" sticker:* 7gypsies; *Chipboard heart and clock:* Heidi Swapp for Advantus; *Font:* Geo Sans Light.

### ON SCRAPBOOKING THIS LAYOUT

■ I created this layout after a former colleague of mine asked me if I missed working. I had taught for ten years and enjoyed it, but I am more than happy where I am as a stay-at-home mom. That's not to say life as a stay-at-home mom is perfect—there are moments when I miss the ease of my former life. Those were the things I wanted to communicate in this layout, but I wanted to stress how it's all worth it in the end.

■ I specifically chose the hearts and the clock as accents to emphasize both time and love, and I chose this photo taken on Mother's Day because I felt my expression reflected the pleasure I take in being a mom.

■ Most of my scrapbooking is a tribute to my children; however, I honestly believe that we need to include pages about ourselves, our own lives and our likes and dislikes, because while our children want to hear stories about themselves, they need to know their moms.

I personally know very little about my mom's early days as a mom, and I know nothing about my grandmother's. Wouldn't my children and grandchildren like to know who I am and what I believe and how I feel? Moms are people, too, and I believe our children would love to see proof of that in our scrapbooks.

■ While this layout is about me, at the same time it records what Emma is like at this age—her likes and dislikes. Through the journaling, I'll remember her toddler quirks.

■ This tip has been said over and over: pass that camera over to someone else so *Mom* is actually in the photo for once!

—GABRIELLA BIANCOFIORE

**Self-Renewing Gift** *by Deena Wuest.* **Supplies** *Software:* Adobe Photoshop Elements 4.0; *Template:* Today You Photobook Layered Templates by Ali Edwards; *Patterned paper:* Don't Forget Crumpled Notes by Ali Edwards (white) and Essential Bases by Lynn Grieveson (gray); *Fonts:* Avant Garde, Hannibal Lecter and Impact.

## ON SCRAPBOOKING THIS LAYOUT

■ Even though Brooklyn is our third child, she is every bit as amazing, magical and loved as our very first. *And* even though Brooklyn is our third child, my experiences as a mother are every bit as amazing, magical and loved as those I had with our firstborn. I dearly wanted her to know this, so that is how this layout originated.

■ It *is* hard to scrapbook about yourself. I'm completely guilty of putting children-featured layouts ahead of ones about me. I'm starting to realize, though, that leaving pieces of myself in my kids' albums is probably one of the greatest gifts I can give them. I don't remember much from when I was their age, so it's safe to say they probably won't either—and I don't want those memories to die with me. Even if you just create one layout per month about you or your feelings, it would be an incredible legacy to leave with your family.

■ Just like each child needs individual attention, I also believe that each child needs an individual scrapbook album. I always try to create layouts for one specific child instead of addressing all three at the same time. Each layout is created lovingly for one individual so that child will know exactly how much he or she is loved.

—DEENA WUEST

"My mom is a never-ending *song* in my *heart* of comfort, happiness and being. I may sometimes forget the words, but I always *remember* the tune."

—GRAYCIE HARMON

**ON SCRAPBOOKING THIS LAYOUT**

■ I created this page to communicate how my life revolves around my kids, using the photos, title, journaling and chipboard-people accents to do so.

■ To me, scrapbooking is a way of celebrating people and relationships. My family's everyday life might not be very glamorous, but it is special to me as the moments are mine. Layouts like this one connect the dots for me and communicate to my children why I'm recording their lives in such detail.

■ Think outside the box in choosing accents for "mom" pages and suddenly you will have more to play with. I used a travel-themed metal clip with "the big adventure" on it because it summed up my sentiments well.

—MOU SAHA

*Smitten* by Mou Saha. **Supplies** *Cardstock:* Die Cuts With a View; *Patterned paper:* Luxe Designs; *Stickers:* 7gypsies and Rusty Pickle (letters); *Tags and rhinestones:* Rusty Pickle; *Journaling cards:* 7gypsies and Teresa Collins ("This is the best"); *Bingo card:* Jenni Bowlin Studio; *Brads and metal clip:* Making Memories; *Paint:* Plaid Enterprises; *Chipboard people accents:* Maya Road; *Embroidery floss:* DMC; *Pen:* American Crafts; *Other:* Fabric and felt.

**ON SCRAPBOOKING THIS LAYOUT**

■ I want to make sure my kids will know how I felt about each of them as they look through their scrapbooks when they're older. I express that love to them individually on my layouts, but I express it more about how I felt about the moment or event—not about how I felt in general about being a mother. It felt good to get that feeling down on paper for this layout.

■ Just knowing how important it is to document our "mothers"—not just our own but documenting ourselves as "mothers"—will make our scrapbooks complete.

—BRENDA HURD

**Lucky Me** *by Brenda Hurd.* **Supplies** *Patterned paper:* Collage Press (background) and Cosmo Cricket (red); *Rub-ons (flourish and butterfly):* Crate Paper; *Journaling card, letter stickers and epoxy button:* Making Memories; *Felt flowers:* Queen & Co.; *Phrase stickers:* 7gypsies; *Chipboard:* BasicGrey (flowers) and Scenic Route ("take note" circle); *Circle punch:* Fiskars; *Font:* Tempus Sans ITC; *Other:* Buttons and thread.

# mom & me

Time spent with Mom is priceless—from childhood to adulthood, the memories will never fade because of the love that each memory represents. Every activity, every conversation, every hug and every "I love you" expressed between mother and child holds infinite value.

**7 themes** for Mother's Day layouts

Haven't recorded those precious expressions of your mother relationships on a layout yet? Now's the time with one of these seven ideas and inspirational layouts. You may have heard the ideas before, but *have you actually done them yet?* This is the month to make it happen!

**1** Find a heritage photo of you with your mother and create a decorative layout for her home.

You showed me this photo just a little while ago. I was struck by how young you were, almost a decade younger than I am now. I have Audrey now, almost the same age as I am here, and I see the same love and devotion in your eyes as I see in photos of Audrey and I. Some things never change.

august 1975

Mother

**Mother, Circa 1975** *by Lisa Kisch.* **Supplies** *Patterned paper, flowers and button:* Making Memories; *Rub-ons:* BasicGrey and FontWerks; *Ink:* ColorBox, Clearsnap; *Letter stickers:* BasicGrey and Making Memories; *Software:* Picasa.

**BY BRITTANY BEATTIE**

**Together with You** *by Mou Saha.* **Supplies** *Cardstock:* Frances Meyer; *Stamps:* Autumn Leaves; *Ink:* Ranger Industries; *Letter stickers:* Heidi Swapp for Advantus (red) and Making Memories (mini); *Card-stock phrase stickers:* 7gypsies; *Paper borders:* Doodlebug Design; *Embroidery floss:* DMC; *Printed binder clip:* Jo-Ann Stores; *Pen:* Precision Pens, American Crafts; *Fonts:* Century Gothic (journaling) and Typewriter (on photo), Internet; *Software:* Adobe Photoshop Elements 5.0, Adobe Systems.

## 2

Showcase favorite activities of the two of you together, using Mou's advice: "Focus on the relationship. Take photos that show how you enjoy each other. Even if all the photos don't turn out perfect, scrap them anyway."

**{Purr}fect Pair** *by Kim Watson.* **Supplies** *Cardstock:* Bazzill Basics Paper; *Patterned paper:* Autumn Leaves, KI Memories and Scenic Route (leaves); *Fabric label and dimensional word embellishment:* Making Memories; *Buttons:* Autumn Leaves; *Stamps:* Autumn Leaves (flourish) and Croxley (date); *Ink:* StazOn, Tsukineko; *Letters:* American Crafts; *Pen:* Zig Writer, EK Success; *Adhesive:* Scrapbook Adhesives by 3L; Mono Adhesive, Tombow; *Other:* Decorative sewing pins, crochet flower (made by Kim's grandmother) and embroidery floss.

## 3

Plan a special day just for the two of you, then scrap the photos from it as a gift for your child.

**IDEA TO NOTE:**
Kim created her own transparent layout by cutting the three-ring strip off of a page protector, placing a strip of lace cardstock inside and sewing all four sides to close the page. She then added photos and embellishments on top of the page protector for a clear layout.

**4** Thank Mom for the example she's set and the ways she's blessed your life.

**5** Express to your child *why* you do all you do for her. Journal your mother's love!

**The Mom I Want to Be** *by Deanna Misner.* **Supplies** *Cardstock:* My Mind's Eye (pink) and Prism Papers (blue); *Patterned paper:* BasicGrey and The Paper Studio (notebook); *Rub-on heart and straight pins:* Fancy Pants Designs; *Ink:* ColorBox Fluid Chalk, Clearsnap; *Flowers and buttons:* Making Memories; *Letter stickers:* American Crafts; *Scallop strip (used as a template):* Li'l Davis Designs.

**Mom & Me** *by Emilie Ahern.* **Supplies** *Cardstock:* Déjà Views by The C-Thru Ruler Co. and Die Cuts With a View; *Patterned paper:* Déjà Views by The C-Thru Ruler Co.; *Chipboard circles:* WorldWin; *Letter die cuts:* Base Camp, Cricut, Provo Craft; *Font:* Arial, Microsoft; *Software:* Photoshop CS2, Adobe Systems; *Other:* Hole punch.

**Pals** by Lovely Cutler. **Supplies** Patterned paper: BasicGrey and Scenic Route; Brads: Doodlebug Design; Paint: Li'l Davis Designs; Button: Autumn Leaves; Acetate clocks: Heidi Swapp for Advantus; Circle title block: My Mind's Eye; Journaling block: Making Memories; Pens: EK Success and Staedtler.

# 6 Take a "self-portrait" with each of your children (Lovely used a mirror for her shot) so they'll have photos of the two of you together.

# 7 Showcase the similarities you share, including physical, personality, emotional, spiritual or intellectual traits.

**Messy Hair Bun Twins** by Monica Skeels. **Supplies** Software: Adobe Photoshop, Adobe Systems; Flower, ribbon and notebook paper: July [2006] Free {Pea} Kit by Anne Langpap, www.twopeasinabucket.com; Photo "negative" frame: DigiKit—Snap Shots Selements by Rhonna Farrer, www.twopeasinabucket.com; Font: Myriad Pro, Adobe Systems.

# honoring dad

Father. He protects you. He comforts you. He teaches you. He makes you laugh. He helps you keep things in perspective when troubles arise. He loves you more than life itself. And you share that love in return, as do your children with their father. This daddy-child relationship is one of the most precious you and your family share. So if you haven't created a layout showcasing a fatherly bond in your family, make time this week to preserve your feelings for years to come.

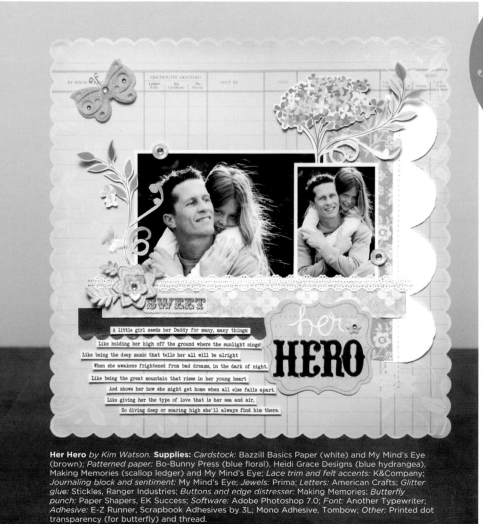

scrapbook a *fatherly* relationship

**Her Hero** *by Kim Watson.* **Supplies:** *Cardstock:* Bazzill Basics Paper (white) and My Mind's Eye (brown); *Patterned paper:* Bo-Bunny Press (blue floral), Heidi Grace Designs (blue hydrangea), Making Memories (scallop ledger) and My Mind's Eye; *Lace trim and felt accents:* K&Company; *Journaling block and sentiment:* My Mind's Eye; *Jewels:* Prima; *Letters:* American Crafts; *Glitter glue:* Stickles, Ranger Industries; *Buttons and edge distresser:* Making Memories; *Butterfly punch:* Paper Shapers, EK Success; *Software:* Adobe Photoshop 7.0; *Font:* Another Typewriter; *Adhesive:* E-Z Runner, Scrapbook Adhesives by 3L; Mono Adhesive, Tombow; *Other:* Printed dot transparency (for butterfly) and thread.

**SOMETIMES IT CAN** be hard to capture in words the thoughts and emotions you feel about a dear relationship—especially if writing has never come easy for you. And that's okay. If you have favorite photos that visually depict these emotions, simply pair them with a poem for a meaningful layout.

**BY BRITTANY BEATTIE**

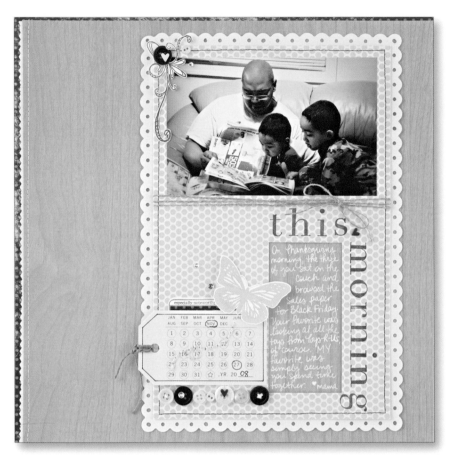

**DEDICATE A LAYOUT**

to one of the everyday activities your husband and children enjoy together on a weekend. Be sure to mention what that quality time together means to you and your family.

**This Morning** *by Jennifer Barksdale.* **Supplies** *Cardstock:* Paperbilities; *Patterned paper:* Junkitz (green), Melissa Frances (burgundy) and Scenic Route (dots and grid); *Rubons:* BasicGrey; *Stamps:* Inkadinkado (letters and swirl) and Studio G (label); *Ink:* Big and Juicy, Ranger Industries (black) and Tsukineko (brown); *Brads:* Making Memories; *Punch:* Fiskars Americas; *Buttons:* Favorite Findings (blue and burgundy) and unknown; *Gems:* Westrim Crafts; *Embroidery floss:* DMC; *Hemp:* Darice; *Pens:* Uni-ball Signo, Newell Rubbermaid (white); Zig, EK Success (black); *Software:* Adobe Photoshop CS; *Adhesive:* Scrapbook Adhesives by 3L; Zots, Therm O Web; *Other:* Thread, tag and digital brush (butterfly).

**RECORD THE STORY**

of the gifts your children give your husband this Father's Day.

**A Father's Love** *by Suzy Plantamura.* **Supplies** *Cardstock:* Bazzill Basics Paper; *Patterned paper, stickers and embellishments:* me & my BIG ideas; *Ink:* Clearsnap; *Marker:* EK Success; *Adhesive:* Herma, EK Success; *Other:* Ribbon and thread.

**DEDICATE A PAGE** to showcasing how great your husband is with your kids. For a fun journaling approach, ask your children their favorite things to do with their dad. Include their answers on the page. You could even interview Dad and jot down his perspective about the activities as well.

**He's Simply the Best** by Shannon Brouwer. **Supplies** *Cardstock:* Bazzill Basics Paper; *Patterned paper:* Heidi Swapp for Advantus; *Chipboard swirl:* Maya Road; *Chipboard letters:* Scenic Route; *Letter stickers:* American Crafts; *Ink:* ColorBox Fluid Chalk, Clearsnap; *Font:* 2Peas Quirky; *Adhesive:* Tombow.

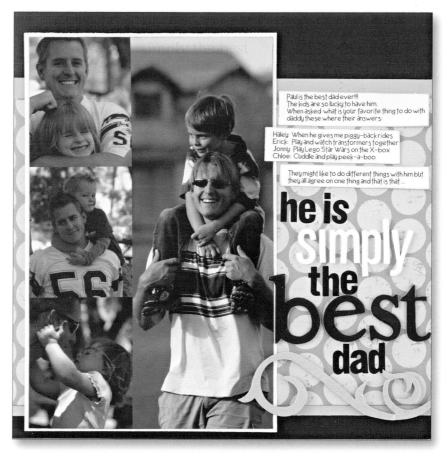

**DOES YOUR CHILD** have Daddy wrapped around her little finger? If so, jot down some thoughts on that aspect of their relationship. I love how Linda Rodriguez recorded some of the looks her husband gives her when their daughter isn't looking.

**The Parent Trap** by Linda Rodriguez. **Supplies** *Software:* Microsoft Digital Image Pro 9.0; *Patterned paper and ribbon:* Orange Crush Kit by Lynn Grieveson; *Letters:* Oversprayed Alphabet Brushes and Stamps by Katie Pertiet; *Felt letters:* Jewels Felt Alphabet Collection by Pattie Knox; *Grunge overlay:* 12 X 12 Distressed Edge Overlays No. 03 by Anna Aspnes; *Circle shape:* Torn N Tattered Circle Templates No. 01 by Anna Aspnes; *Stitching and stitched holes:* Saffron Villa PageSet by Anna Aspnes; *Staples:* Staple Its! by Pattie Knox; *Tags:* Krafty Tags: Celebrate ("Happy") and Sewn Statements No. 02 ("Playful") by Katie Pertiet; *String:* Yarn Swirls by Katie Pertiet; *Paper strips:* Journaling Strip Masks by Katie Pertiet; *Frames:* Stitched Up Frames No. 01 by Katie Pertiet; *Font:* CK Squiggle.

**IF YOU DON'T HAVE MANY PHOTOS** of the father and child together, grab your camera tonight. Simply head outdoors this evening (you'll get great lighting an hour or so before the sun sets) and take pictures from many angles as you watch the two interact while they play.

**Daddy's Girl** *by Sheri Horton.* **Supplies** *Software:* Corel Paint Shop Pro 9; *Template:* Template 18 by Simply Yin; *Orange paper and swirl brush:* Art of Play by Heather Ann Designs; *All other accents:* Parker Mega Kit by DigitalDesignEssentials.com; *Font:* Georgia.

## Masculine Color Palettes

Trying to decide how to create a page about Dad that's masculine but still works well with photos of young girls or boys? Try one of these sensational schemes.

**Arctic, Ladybug, Katydid**
Bazzill Basics Paper,
*BazzillBasics.com*

**Intense Yellow, Frosted Yellow, Intense Pink**
Prism Papers,
*PrismPapers.com*

**Ice Blue, White, King's Gold**
Wausau Paper,
*WausauPaper.com*

# pet *pages*

Like children, pets are part of the family *and* very hard to photograph! So when you do achieve the perfect shot, you want to show it off in your scrapbook. Check out the following solutions for reaching that perfect pet photo. You'll also find tips for highlighting it on a layout that's sure to be the cat's meow.

**Focus on the *photos***

**Frame the subject** of your photo with a circle accent (here, a chipboard frame) inside the boundaries of the photo. For emphasis, add jewels or other eye-catching items to the frame. A neutral frame works well to lead the eye to your subject without drawing attention from it.

*Did you notice?* Laina used an expense sheet for her dog's expenses as a page accent.

**Darling Dog** *by Laina Lamb.* **Supplies** *Cardstock:* Archiver's; *Patterned paper and ribbon:* KI Memories; *Rickrack:* Wrights; *Rub-ons:* American Crafts (flourish) and BasicGrey (utensils and dollar sign); *Brads and staples:* Making Memories; *Letter stickers:* American Crafts (foam) and EK Success (sticker); *Gems:* Darice; *Photo corner:* 7gypsies; *Chipboard:* Fancy Pants Designs; *Bird stickers:* Kamio Japan; *Pen:* Uni-ball Signo, Newell Rubbermaid; Zig, EK Success; *Other:* Vintage file folder.

**BY BRITTANY BEATTIE**

**Birdbrained** *by Deena Wuest.* **Supplies** *Software:* Adobe Photoshop Elements 4.0, Adobe Systems; *Patterned paper:* Purely Happy Paper Pack by Katie Pertiet, www. designerdigitals.com; *Brushes:* Frame It Custom Shapes by Anna Aspnes, *www.design-erdigitals.com*; *Arrows:* You Are Here Brushes-n-Stamps by Katie Pertiet, *www.design-erdigitals.com*; *Fonts:* Avant Garde, *www.fonts.com*; Establo, *www.dafont.com*.

**Enlarge a photo** and use it as the main element on a two-page spread. **Include solid cardstock** as the other papers to let the photo stand out even more. **Direct the eye** toward the photos with an arrow as well.

*Photo tip:* To help keep your pet occupied while you capture a few photos, entertain him with a toy or other object.

*Deena's photo tip:* When photographing your pets, get in close and capture the small details of their eyes, fur or feathers.

**Please?** *by Ingunn Markiewicz.* **Supplies** *Cardstock:* Bazzill Basics Paper; *Patterned paper:* BasicGrey; *Die-cut tab:* QuicKutz; *Chipboard letters:* Heidi Swapp for Advantus; *Font:* Calibri, Microsoft.

**Surround the picture** with blocks from a patterned paper that's monochromatic, then leave a lot of white space on the page.

*Photo tip:* Just as with photographing portraits, natural side lighting such as that near a window will help you capture your pet in his best light.

*Ingunn's photo tip:* Take photos of and document your pet's everyday routines. Bobby always puts on this heartbreaking face when we leave the house, so I wanted to focus on his huge, begging eyes.

## TITLE STARTERS

Searching for a title to complement the lovable photos of your pet? Let one of these animal idioms help you get started:

### Birds

a bird in the hand . . .

a little bird told me . . .

birds of a feather

for the birds

free as a bird

the early bird

### Cats

cat's got your tongue

copycats

he's a cool cat

letting the cat out of the bag

look what the cat dragged in

raining cats and dogs

simply purr-fect

the cat with nine lives

the cat's meow

when the cat's away . . .

### Dogs

a dog and pony show

dog tired

every dog has his day

in the doghouse

his bark is worse than his bite

going to the dogs

leading a dog's life

let sleeping dogs lie

puppy love

raining cats and dogs

the dog days of summer

### Fish

a big fish in a small pond

fishing for a compliment

of all the fish in the sea...

that's a fish story

there are other fish in the sea

### Rabbits

a few gray hares

neither hare nor there

quick as a rabbit

**Select a frame that matches your pet's coat or fur, add two favorite photos and display the results on your wall.**

*Pam's photo tip:* Help your animals settle down by giving them treats a few minutes before you take their picture.

**Love** *by Pam Callaghan.* **Supplies** *Frame:* Pottery Barn; *Patterned paper:* We R Memory Keepers; *Rub-ons:* Die Cuts With a View and Heidi Grace Designs; *Flowers and tag sticker:* Creative Imaginations; *Chipboard letters:* Crate Paper; *Paper frill:* Doodlebug Design; *Other:* Embroidery floss.

**Add accents over white spaces of a photo** that could otherwise become "black holes" for the eye. Francine added the circle accent over the pillow in the background and her journaling (with accompanying brackets) over the blanket in the foreground.

*Photo tip:* Taking photos of your pets in both active and quiet times will help you capture a more complete profile of their personality.

**Nap Time** *by Francine Clouden.* **Supplies** *Cardstock:* Bazzill Basics Paper; *Patterned paper:* BasicGrey (floral) and Crate Paper (dot); *Stamps:* Urban Lily; *Ink:* Tsukineko; *Foam letter stickers:* Miss Elizabeth; *Phrase stickers:* 7gypsies; *Font:* Arial Black, Microsoft; *Scalloped label:* www.everyjotandtittle.etsy.com; *Software:* Adobe Photoshop, Adobe Systems. **This page is 6" x 12".**

**Meet the Beast** *by Amy Hummel.* **Supplies** *Cardstock:* Bazzill Basics Paper; *Stamps:* Autumn Leaves; *Ink:* VersaFine, Tsukineko; *Brads:* Doodlebug Design; *Letter stickers:* American Crafts; *Paint:* Making Memories; *Chipboard letters and heart:* Heidi Swapp for Advantus; *Eyelets:* Provo Craft; *Pen:* Precision Pens, American Crafts; *Eyelet setter:* Crop-A-Dile, We R Memory Keepers; *Other:* Embroidery floss and buttons.

When you're snapping pictures to get the perfect pet photo, you're bound to have several that look quite similar. When deciding how to arrange them on the page, **a photo strip** helps unify them without making them feel unnecessary on the layout. Include the **photo with the best eye contact** as the center of your photo strip.

*Amy's photo tip:* Don't just take pictures from a standing position, with your animal looking up and your feet visible at the bottom of the picture. Get down on your pet's level! Look the animal in the eye. And try to make the photographs intimate.

# summer *traditions*

Whether you head to the pool multiple days each summer or enjoy popsicles on a hot day, you're sure to have numerous summertime traditions to capture on layouts. That's why on the following pages you'll find photo, journaling and design tips, along with the photo sizes on the layouts, to help you complete all your summer-tradition layouts in as little time as possible.

**scrapbook your *summer* traditions**

**Serious Summer Fun** *by Denine Zielinski.* **Supplies** *Cardstock:* Die Cuts With a View; *Patterned paper:* Autumn Leaves (blue) and Bo-Bunny Press (pink, stripe and yellow); *Rub-ons:* Déjà Views by The C-Thru Ruler Co. (stitching) and Wordsworth (words); *Stamps:* Autumn Leaves (swirl) and Limited Edition Rubberstamps (circle words); *Ink:* ColorBox, Clearsnap; *Ribbon:* American Crafts (blue) and C.M. Offray & Son (green); *Brads:* Making Memories and Queen & Co.; *Button:* My Mind's Eye; *Chipboard:* BasicGrey; *Software:* FotoFusion, LumaPix; *Pen:* Sakura; *Fonts:* Scrap Cursive and Times New Roman; *Adhesive:* Zig 2-Way Glue, EK Success.

**Photo sizes:** *1½" x 2" (all photos)*

## PHOTO TIP

Denine Zielinski fit 14 photos on her layout by printing them around 1½" x 2" and including them on three strips. By using this smaller photo size, you can include a large number of summer-tradition photos on a single layout.

## DESIGN TIP

Do you have even more photos you want to include? Turn this layout into a two-page spread by mirroring the image to create a left-hand page and using this layout as the right-hand page.

**BY BRITTANY BEATTIE**

**Signs of Summer** *by Kim Watson.* **Supplies** *Cardstock:* Bazzill Basics Paper; *Patterned paper, photo corners and letter stickers:* Pink Paislee; *Stamps:* Croxley Stationery; *Ink:* ColorBox, Clearsnap; *Ribbon and brads:* Making Memories; *Butterfly and tab punches:* Paper Shapers, EK Success; *Software:* Adobe Photoshop CS2; *Pens:* Pentel and Zig Photo Signature, EK Success; *Adhesive:* E-Z Runner, Scrapbook Adhesives by 3L; Mono Adhesive, Tombow; *Other:* Typewriter and thread.

*Photo sizes:* 6" x 4½", 3⅝" x 2½", 3½" x 1½" (two photos), 3⅛" x 2¼", 3⅛" x 4½", 3⅛" x 1⅞"

### JOURNALING TIP

If you want to focus on the feel or mood of the summer photos instead of the journaling, journal on thin strips of cardstock, cut them into strips, and then place them in a border near the edge of the page.

### PHOTO TIP

If you're including photos overlapping each other, consider printing or matting each one with a thin mat of the same color (Kim used white)—it will help the eye clearly distinguish between the photos.

### KIM'S DESIGN PROCESS

"In creating this page, I wanted a visual reminder that would forever remind me of the beginnings of summer. I used a collection of photos to do this: the kids in the pool, a chilled melon, sunshades, beach wraps, sandals on green grass and cool eats and drinks. The rich colors of summer are a 'feast for the eyes,' so I kept the page bright and fun to complement the rich colors in the photographs, which are the focal points of my page."

—KIM WATSON

**Small Town USA** *by Katrina Simeck.* **Supplies** *Cardstock:* WorldWin; *Patterned paper:* Scenic Route; *Brads:* American Crafts; *Letter dies and die-cutting machine:* Silhouette, QuicKutz; *Label machine:* P-Touch Labeler, Brother International Corporation; *Squeeze punch:* Fiskars; *Software:* Adobe Photoshop Elements; *Adhesive:* Scrapbook Adhesives by 3L.

**Photo sizes:** 1⅞" x 2¾" (three photos) and 3⅛" x 2⅛"

## LAYOUT TIP

Your summer-traditions layouts don't have to summarize all the events of your summer. Consider creating one page for each of your summer traditions and what they mean to you.

## KATRINA'S PHOTO TIPS

■ "It's tempting to take photos of only family, friends and people in general. I'm happy that I looked beyond just faces to capture the essence of the parade I scrapbooked here.

■ "Notice that this layout is *not* specifically about my family. Instead, it's about something that my family does together. Don't hesitate to redirect your focus sometimes. Look around! Be sure you're capturing the atmosphere surrounding your traditions, not just the people participating in them."

—KATRINA SIMECK

# Summer Color Palettes

Looking for the perfect color combos for your summer pages? Try one of these sensational schemes.

**Bumblebee, Butterfly, Marmalade**
Bazzill Basics Paper
*BazzillBasics.com*

**Celeste, Ciliegia, Butter Cream**
Prism Papers
*PrismPapers.com*

**Royal Blue, Lunar Blue, Citron**
Wausau Paper
*WausauPaper.com*

**Moves** by *Emily Pitts*. **Supplies** *Cardstock:* Bazzill Basics Paper and Stampin' Up!; *Patterned paper:* October Afternoon; *Chipboard:* Heidi Swapp for Advantus (stars) and Maya Road (letters); *Rivets:* Scrapbook Interiors; *Label maker:* Dymo; *Adhesive:* Glue Dots International and Xyron.

*Photo sizes:* 4" x 4" (all photos)

### JOURNALING TIP

As parents of young children, we may think we'll never forget the summer traditions of our little ones' childhoods. Yet, ask any parent of older children, and they'll likely tell you they don't remember all the details of the childhood days anymore. That's why it's important to capture the memories—the traditions—today.

Keep Emily Pitts's words in mind as you create layouts about your traditions: "My kids are quickly growing up, and although they still love the Slip 'n Slide, they don't beg to run around in the backyard like that anymore.

Now I hear, 'Can we go to the pool?' I wanted to have a page that showed how much fun my kids had in the backyard with the Slip 'n Slide. Now I can almost hear my son's giggles as he tried out the best ways to get down that slippery hill."

### EMILY'S DESIGN TIP

"Use bright colors for summer and put them against a neutral kraft cardstock to allow the colors and photos to shine."

—EMILY PITTS

**Pet Parade** *by Davinie Fiero.* **Supplies** *Cardstock:* Bazzill Basics Paper and Doodlebug Design (textured); *Patterned paper:* Making Memories; *Ribbon:* C.M. Offray & Son; *Chipboard:* BasicGrey (chipboard letters) and Magistical Memories (stars); *Embroidery floss:* DMC; *Adhesive:* Scotch Tape, 3M; *Pen:* American Crafts.

**Photo sizes:** *4¼" x 2¾" (all photos)*

### DESIGN TIP

Use scraps of red, white and blue patterned papers to create a subtle flag look on your background. The flag design doesn't have to be a literal approach—here, Davinie Fiero shows how to don your inner Betsy Ross to create a flag with a shabby-chic approach.

### JOURNALING TIP

If parts of your tradition change each year, note it in your journaling. On this layout, Davinie shares how the tradition can vary. She says, "The Pet Parade is an annual tradition. Because of that, I'm going to have photos each year from this event, but things are always a bit different. Sometimes we bring our dog. Sometimes we use a stroller. Sometimes our kids are crying. On this layout, I wanted to document what the tradition was like on this particular year."

### DAVINIE'S STITCHED-ACCENT TIP

"Hand-stitching can change any layout. Use yellow embroidery floss to stitch a sun for backyard-swing photos or to create a flower for gardening photos. Use blue embroidery floss to stitch clouds on a rainy-day page or waves when you're scrapbooking a vacation at the beach. Hand-stitching adds texture and dimension to any layout, and it offers a fun opportunity when working on summer photos."

—DAVINIE FIERO

**4th of July** *by Brigid Gonzalez.* **Supplies** *Software:* Adobe Photoshop CS3; *Patterned paper:* Life and Liberty by Jesse Edwards; *Photo action:* Boutwell Magic Glasses by Doug Boutwell; *Fonts:* AL Charisma ("4"), Decker (journaling) and Jane Austen (title).

**Photo sizes:** 6¼" x 3¾", 3⅛" x 3¾" (six photos)

### JOURNALING TIP

Don't feel like you have to document every tradition on one page. If you have several traditions for a given event, document one aspect of it one year, another aspect the next year, and so on. It will help keep your journaling approach fresh from year to year. On this layout, Brigid Gonzalez shares her family's Fourth of July tradition of making T-shirts.

### BRIGID'S FAMILY-TRADITION ALBUM TIP

"I've wanted to create a 'Family Traditions' album for a long time, but it just keeps getting moved down to the bottom of my to-do list. My initial thoughts were to create a mini album using a coordinated kit, but then I realized it would be difficult to find a kit that would look good with the wide variety of family-tradition photos I have.

"I decided that instead of creating a matchy-matchy scrapbook, each tradition in my family-traditions album would have its own unique flavor, one that would highlight the specific tradition. Christmas layouts would have a Christmas theme. Summer vacations would have a beach theme.

"My advice is to scrapbook your traditions in the manner that best fits the theme. The pages don't all have to coordinate. The simple fact that the *subject matter* coordinates is enough to make a really great scrapbook."

—BRIGID GONZALEZ

# city
## *celebrations*

Every June, I kick back and clap my hands at the Strawberry Days rodeo in Pleasant Grove, Utah. Each July, I relax and enjoy the Pioneer Days parade and fireworks in Salt Lake City. And every September, I travel to Midway, Utah, to enjoy the music, dancing, food and fun at Swiss Days. These local celebrations are a part of my heritage, and attending them is a favorite tradition.

**What does *your town* celebrate each year?**

**The Fair** by C.D. Muckosky. **Supplies** *Ghost flower:* Heidi Swapp for Advantus; *Crystals:* Prima; *Label stickers:* 7gypsies; *Rub-ons:* Die Cuts With a View; *Corner rounder and foam squares:* Fiskars; *Watercolor paint:* Prang; *Font for arrow:* CK Good Point by C.D. Muckosky, www.scrapnfonts. com; *Pen:* Pigma Micron, Sakura; *Adhesive:* Aleene's Tacky Glue, Duncan Enterprises; EZ Runner, Scrapbook Adhesives by 3L; *Other:* Muslin, felt, graph paper, tickets, silk flower, bead, masking tape and embroidery floss.

My scrapbook wouldn't be complete without a page or two telling their stories. What local festivities belong in your scrapbook, and how can you create the perfect pages about them? You're on your own for the first question, but these six ideas are sure to help with the latter!

**SOFT & SWEET . . . & EASY**
C.D. softened the feel of a rigid grid photo arrangement with the following can-do techniques:

1. Round the corners of the photo mat.
2. Cut accents from felt or fabric.
3. Add cross-stitches to various accents with embroidery floss.
4. Paint freehand on the background, with no worry over creating straight lines.

**BY BRITTANY BEATTIE**

**Days of '47** *by Natalie Call.* **Supplies** *Patterned paper:* me & my BIG ideas; *Chipboard stars:* Fancy Pants Designs; *Chipboard numbers:* Chatterbox; *Die-cut journaling block and glitter frame:* Making Memories; *Paint:* Plaid Enterprises; *Fonts:* Fling, *www.linotype.com;* Digs My Hart, *www.abstractfonts.com.*

**The Fall Fair** *by Sheri Horton.* **Supplies** *Software:* Paint Shop Pro 9, Corel; *Cardstock: www.digitaldesignessentials.com; Patterned paper, right bracket and flower stamp:* Forever Grateful Kit Essentials; *Staple:* Modish Girl; *Fonts:* CK Maternal, *www.scrapnfonts.com;* Pea Stacy's Doodle Script, *www.kevinandamanda.com;* Trebuchet MS, Microsoft.

## NATALIE'S PERFECT MIX OF ELEMENTS

"I wanted to keep the layout simple so I could focus on the photos of my daughter (the pages are for her album)," says Natalie. "I used minimal accents that I felt enhanced the feeling of the celebration without taking away from the photos. The color scheme I used has everything to do with the colors of my photos and nothing to do with the actual celebration."

## SHERI'S PHOTO SELECTION TIPS

1. When scrapbooking a local celebration, try to capture the event in a way that when you look back on it you will remember what it was like to *experience that day.* For me, that meant lots of photos and journaling, but sometimes it can mean just one photo.

2. For this layout, I am most proud of the amount of pictures I fit on one page! I took *lots* of pictures that day, and I wanted to include so many of them to help tell the story of the day. I resized and arranged them to allow for lots of journaling.

3. When you have a lot of pictures, keep the rest of your layout simple . . . since it's the pictures that are the main focus.

**Time for Tulips** by *Jill Marie Paulson*. **Supplies** *Cardstock:* Bazzill Basics Paper; *Patterned paper:* American Crafts; *Rub-on numbers:* Making Memories; *Letter stickers:* Doodlebug Design; *Font:* Arial Narrow, Microsoft.

### EYE-CATCHING PHOTO ANGLES

Instead of taking photos from straight in front of your subject, take a couple steps to the side. It's a small adjustment, but it makes a big statement that will help take your scrapbook pages to a more sophisticated level.

### EMBELLISHED WITH COLOR

As Jill says, "Simple layouts do not need to be boring. This layout may not be highly embellished in product, but it is certainly high in colors, shapes and memories." Get more from your color by choosing bright hues for your summer pages. It's easy when you select complementary color combos like red and green, blue and orange or purple and yellow.

**Moose on the Loose** by *Sheila Doherty*. **Supplies** *Cardstock:* Prism Papers; *Brads, letters, tag and frame:* Making Memories; *Button:* Junkitz; *Fonts:* Century Gothic, Monotype Imaging; Times New Roman, Microsoft; *Software:* Adobe Illustrator 10, Adobe Systems; *Other:* Map and vellum.

### MEMORABILIA TRANSFORMATION

If you gathered some brochures or pamphlets at your festivities, turn them into a part of your scrapbook pages. Sheila incorporated a busy map (of the locations and artists for each moose in the city) on her layout without it overwhelming her photos by placing a layer of vellum on top. The combination is reminiscent of patterned paper.

# arts beats & eats

This year was the first time that we went to the Arts, Beats and Eats festival in Pontiac. We usually aren't in town over Labor Day weekend, but we were this year because we had traveled the two prior weekends and I can't handle being gone three weekends in a row.

It was a hot day, but we decided to go anyway. We hit the "eats" first, and pretty much struck out with icky food, except for the potatoes I got. They were a cross between a French fry and a potato chip and really, really good!

We checked out the art, but luckily we didn't find anything that we needed to spend oodles of money on. The carney rides and games were the big hit with the kids. I took both kids on the merry go round and Chris took Griffin on a spinning bear thing. I get sick easily, so there was no way I was going on that! Griffin played the dart game and won a stuffed penguin. He could have stayed in that area all day. He loved it! September 2007

**Arts, Beats & Eats** by Ashley Gailey. **Supplies** Cardstock: Bazzill Basics Paper; Patterned paper: Prima; Rub-ons: Making Memories; Letter stickers: Scenic Route; Chipboard circle: Li'l Davis Designs; Font: ER Kurier 1251, Internet; Other: Brads and thread.

## ASHLEY'S PHOTO SELECTION TIPS

❶ I decided to create a photo collage to cram as many photos on the layout as possible.

❷ Don't be afraid to crop your images. The photos on the merry-go-round were all taken horizontally, but I was able to crop them so that they fit with all of the other vertical photos.

❸ I love capturing all sorts of images to document a day. I took about 60–70 photos at this event. For the layout, I wanted an assortment that showed the fun we had. I just played with the photos until I created a collage that conveyed the right message and pleased the eye. I do tend to get most of my photos printed in 4" x 6" format and store the extras away.

## CARNIVAL-RIDE PHOTOS MADE EASY

Capturing family and friends on fast-moving rides can be difficult to get in clear focus, especially at night. An easy solution is to hop on the ride with your photo subjects. If you're both moving at the same speed, you'll capture the people in focus while the background will be blurred to reflect motion. Just be sure to place your camera strap around your wrist for security before the ride starts.

**Good Times** *by Jennifer Davis.* **Supplies** *Acrylic album:* Creative Imaginations; *Cardstock:* Bazzill Basics Paper; *Patterned paper:* Cosmo Cricket and Scrapworks (green and brown); *Ribbon:* Cosmo Cricket; *Rub-ons:* Scrapworks; *Font:* Century Schoolbook; *Adhesive:* Kokuyo and Ribbon Glue, Making Memories.

"In this busy *life*, we need to make time to enjoy family time spent at a lake or river. There is truly something to be said about spending time with *loved* ones in the great outdoors!"

**—JENNIFER DAVIS**

### RECORD MEMORIES THROUGH THE YEARS

If your visit to the lake or river is an annual vacation, make plans to create a mini album with photos taken throughout the years. After you've completed your layout for the trip this year, finding additional photos from the past to use in your mini album will be like a trip down memory lane. And if you recently vacationed, the details of favorite spots will be fresh in your mind to allow you to jot down all your favorite memories and traditions near the lake. What a mini album this will be!

### JENNIFER'S PHOTO ADVICE

"Anyone can get great photos in the outdoors. Getting great photos at a lake or river is really about taking a moment to look around you, to appreciate it and then to focus on what elements will best tell your story.

"I made sure I took photos of different scenes my family sees when visiting Lake George each year, such as the boats and a swing with the water in the distance. We visit this spot so many times and drag the boats down to the water and then back up again! It's an important photo. We spend time watching a sunrise or sunset from the swing, so I needed a photo of that as well. Great memories come from great and thoughtful photos!"

**—JENNIFER DAVIS**

**Seadoo** *by Lisa Swift.* **Supplies** *Cardstock:* Bazzill Basics Paper; *Patterned paper:* We R Memory Keepers (blue) and Scenic Route (all others); *Ribbon and pen:* American Crafts; *Letter stickers:* KI Memories (felt) and Making Memories (white); *Chipboard:* Scenic Route (circle and photo corner) and KI Memories (all others); *Buttons:* Jo-Ann Stores; *Tag and metal accent:* Making Memories; *Punch:* Fiskars Americas; *Embroidery floss:* DMC; *Font:* Decker; *Other:* Thread.

### MIMIC THE LOOK OF WATER

Blue patterned paper with a distressed design creates the perfect page element for lake and river layouts—it closely mimics the look of ripples and reflections on water.

### PHOTO TIP

While you're taking pictures of people, don't forget to photograph the canoe, boat or water craft your family enjoys spending time on throughout the day.

**Lake Michigan** by Kelly Purkey. **Supplies** *Cardstock:* American Crafts and Bazzill Basics Paper (kraft); *Patterned paper:* American Crafts; *Stamps:* Hero Arts; *Ink:* Stampin' Up!; *Letter stickers:* American Crafts (title) and Making Memories; *Circle cutter, adhesive, pen and circle, tag, border, corner-rounder, star and flower punches:* Fiskars Americas; *Buttons:* KI Memories; *Epoxy stickers:* Cloud 9 Design, Fiskars Americas.

### CAPTURE THE SUNSET

Sunrises and sunsets are made even more glorious with reflections on a lake, so be sure to capture them on camera. You can feature the sunrise and sunset photos together on a layout to show your relaxing time at the lake—from the beginning of the day to the end.

# Hip Color Palettes

Looking for the perfect color scheme for your lake and river pages? Try one of these creative combos.

**Pollen, Turquoise Mist, Curry Spice**
Bazzill Basics Paper
*BazzillBasics.com*

**Frosted Kiwi, Intense Kiwi, Baby Pink Dark**
Prism Papers
*PrismPapers.com*

**Boysenberry, Re-Entry Red, Orbit Orange**
Wausau Paper
*WausauPaper.com*

**The Lake** by April Massad. **Supplies** *Cardstock:* Bazzill Basics Paper; *Patterned paper, stickers and chipboard shapes:* BasicGrey; *Chipboard letters:* Colorbök; *Letter stamps:* Technique Tuesday; *Paint pen:* Elmer's; *Ink:* StazOn, Tsukineko (black) and Tim Holtz Distress Inks, Ranger Industries (red); *Tag:* The Paper Studio; *Font:* CK Journaling; *Adhesive:* E-Z Runner, Scrapbook Adhesives by 3L.

### CREATE AN EYE-CATCHING GRID

When we plan to create grid effects on layouts, it's often easy for us to worry about making sure photos of similar size are exactly the same size. But April Massad shows that they don't have to be—her layout showcases an eye-catching grid design with photos of slightly different sizes. Most of her photos align on the top and bottom, but not all of them. And it still looks stunning. On your layout about your water adventures, follow her lead and see what creativity arises when you're not focused on getting perfectly cut photo sizes.

# summer
## *wrap-up*

You have a lot of memories from this summer that you never want to forget. What's the best way to scrapbook them? You'll find everything you need right here: layout ideas, cool tips for embellishments, summer products, must-take photos (and tips!) and color schemes you'll love.

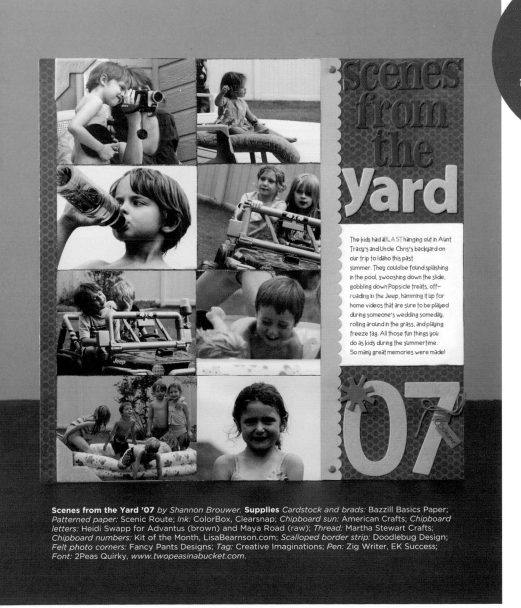

**Everything you need to *know* to scrapbook summer**

**Scenes from the Yard '07** *by Shannon Brouwer.* **Supplies** *Cardstock and brads:* Bazzill Basics Paper; *Patterned paper:* Scenic Route; *Ink:* ColorBox, Clearsnap; *Chipboard sun:* American Crafts; *Chipboard letters:* Heidi Swapp for Advantus (brown) and Maya Road (raw); *Thread:* Martha Stewart Crafts; *Chipboard numbers:* Kit of the Month, LisaBearnson.com; *Scalloped border strip:* Doodlebug Design; *Felt photo corners:* Fancy Pants Designs; *Tag:* Creative Imaginations; *Pen:* Zig Writer, EK Success; *Font:* 2Peas Quirky, www.twopeasinabucket.com.

**SAYS SHANNON:**

"When you have a collage of events to showcase but not really one main focal picture, a photo collage is a great way to go. When I looked at the pictures from a trip to my sister's house this past summer, many of them were of the kids just hanging out and having fun in the backyard. I wanted to capture the fun they had just being kids and doing the simple day-to-day stuff—my layout summarizes their activities."

**BY BRITTANY BEATTIE**

# summer embellishments tricks

**Limbo** by Cindy Tobey. **Supplies** *Cardstock:* Bazzill Basics Paper (green fringe and gold) and WorldWin (green); *Patterned paper:* Fancy Pants Designs; *Ink:* Clearsnap; *Brads:* Queen & Co.; *Paint:* Making Memories; *Buttons:* Autumn Leaves; *Chipboard, felt shapes and clear die cuts:* Fancy Pants Designs; *Journaling spot:* Heidi Swapp for Advantus; *Paper frill:* Doodlebug Design; *Pen:* Pigma Micron, Sakura; *Font:* Berlin Sans FB, Microsoft; *Other:* Thread and mesh.

> "I really love the felt tree branch and leaves made of various materials. I love the texture that it adds to the layout."
>
> **—CINDY TOBEY**

### SUMMER ACCENTS WITH FLAIR

- Use precut or hand-cut felt shapes to create a tree on your layout.

- Machine stitch with both straight and zigzag stitches to dress up felt (or other!) tree branches.

- Add texture to your accents with multiple materials. Cindy Tobey traced a felt leaf onto paper, then scanned it and enlarged it to different sizes to create templates for cutting additional leaves from patterned paper and cardstock.

- Create a grasslike border design by layering a cardstock strip with paper fringe and mesh. Secure them to the page with machine stitching for contrast if desired.

- Use diagonal patterned papers to add a sense of movement to a layout.

**Summer Feet** *by Gretchen McElveen.* **Supplies** *Patterned paper:* Love, Elsie for KI Memories (orange and yellow) and My Mind's Eye (blue and dot); *Ink:* StazOn, Tsukineko; *Brads and letter stickers:* Making Memories; *Chipboard letters and hearts:* Love, Elsie for KI Memories; *Circle die cuts:* QuicKutz; *Font:* My Type of Font, Internet.

### SUMMER ACCENTS WITH FLAIR

- Create a quick sun accent by die-cutting or hand-cutting circles in assorted sizes from patterned papers and layering them. Add scraps of paper for the sun rays.

- Use pinking shears to add dimension to paper borders—they're reminiscent of waves.

"I wanted this to be a fun, lighthearted summer layout about how flip-flops and painted toenails always remind me of summer."

**—GRETCHEN MCELVEEN**

# summer photos

Capture everything summer with these photo ideas and tips:

PHOTO BY EMILIE AHERN

### GORGEOUS GREENS

Green grass creates a bold background that captures the essence of summer in a photograph. Just remember that when taking pictures outdoors, be aware of the shadows created by the sun. Try taking pictures in the shade or using the fill flash on your camera to get the best photo. Emilie Ahern took this photo in the shade and used a Photoshop action to bump up the color at home.

FRESH FACE | PHOTO BY RACHAEL CHAMBERLAIN

**PHOTO MERGE**                                          PHOTO BY EMILIE AHERN

In Emilie Ahern's original snapshot of her daughter, you'll find a home and a van in the background. Emilie loved the pose of her daughter playing on the grass in the photo and wanted to use it to create an "essence of summer" photo.

The solution? Emilie used Photoshop to merge two photos, replacing the home and van in the background of the picture of her daughter with some clouds she'd captured in another photo. Emilie also used a cool Photoshop action available at *www.mindysphotoactions.blogspot.com* to enhance the colors.

**A NEW APPROACH**

Instead of taking photos from eye level, don't be afraid to kneel, sit or lie on the ground to change the height of your picture taking. Rachael Chamberlain obtained this shot because her camera was only inches from the ground. By using the Portrait mode on your camera, you can create a blurred background in shots of scenery.

# school *journaling* with a twist

If you're a mom, you likely have layout after layout about your children's first days of school over the years. But I imagine there's something in common with all those lay-outs besides the subject: they're journaled from your perspective, right? Switch up the memory-keeping this year and scrapbook back-to-school layouts that showcase your children's perspective about the first day of school. You'll all love it!

**memories from your *children's* perspective**

**Second First Day** *by Bethany Kartchner.* **Supplies** *Cardstock:* Bazzill Basics Paper; *Patterned paper:* Luxe Designs (aqua oval dot and pink grid) and My Little Shoebox, LLC (scallop circle, house elements, heart and "love"); *Rub-ons:* Prima; *Letter stickers:* Luxe Designs; *Pen and colored pencil:* Newell Rubbermaid; *Glitter glue:* Stickles, Ranger Industries; *Adhesive:* Scrapbook Adhesives by 3L; *Other:* Ribbon.

## 1 TELL A STORY

After your children return home, ask them to tell you about their first day in a story that begins, "Today was my first day of _____ grade" (or a similar statement). Take notes while they talk, and then transfer the sto-ries to your album.

BY BRITTANY BEATTIE

**While Waiting** *by Jacki Archibald.* **Supplies** *Software:* Adobe Photoshop Elements 6.0; *Patterned paper:* Monarch Mini Kit by Beth Long (yellow) and King Me Paper Pack by Katie Pertiet (stripe); *Ribbon:* Twilled Phrases by Jackie Eckles; *Scallop mask:* Serendipity Element Pack by Michelle Coleman; *Brushes:* Boho Flourish Brush Set by Michelle Coleman (brown), Delightful by Michelle Coleman (white swirl) and Grungy by in-vogue (grungy white); *Tag:* Apron Strings 2 by Leora Sanford; *Layout sketch:* Now We're Rockin' with Photoshop by Jessica Sprague; *Fonts:* Century Gothic (journaling) and unknown (title).

## 2 FOCUS ON ONE ASPECT

Ask your child about a specific aspect of the day. Consider one of these ideas:

- Waiting for the bus
- Meeting his or her new teacher
- Eating school lunch at the cafeteria
- Doing homework
- Learning a new concept like reading, writing, long division or history
- Playing at recess
- Using a locker
- Switching to a new school like junior high or high school

"I like to *include* my children's words on their layouts because they go to *school* without me and can share more about their *life* at school than I can."

**—JACKI ARCHIBALD**

# Back-to-School Photos

Use this handy checklist to make sure you don't forget any essential back-to-school photos this month:

- ☐ Pile of school supplies
- ☐ Backpacks in a row
- ☐ Height of each child (stand near the same location each year)
- ☐ School halls or classrooms

- ☐ Handwritten name or signature on homework
- ☐ Cubby or locker
- ☐ School desk
- ☐ Teacher
- ☐ Principal

- ☐ You with each child
- ☐ All of your children in one photo
- ☐ First week of homework or art projects (in a stack)
- ☐ School
- ☐ Cafeteria

**The Story** by Kim Watson. **Supplies** *Software:* Adobe Photoshop CS2; *Cardstock:* Prism Papers; *Patterned paper:* Chatterbox (floral), Crate Paper (pink dot and green), Heidi Swapp for Advantus (pink ledger) and Pink Paislee (pale yellow); *Rub-ons:* Kaisercraft (border strip) and Pink Paislee (sentiment); *Ribbon:* Cocoa Daisy; *Letter stickers:* American Crafts; *Transparency:* Pelikan; *Adhesive:* Scrapbook Adhesives by 3L and Mono Glue, Tombow; *Other:* Floral lace, paper clip and typewriter.

### JOT DOWN A CONVERSATION

Record a conversation between you and your child. Consider using names in front of the different snippets of conversation, or use a different color of pen, text or journaling strip for the words of each speaker.

# Hues to Use

Try one of these studious color palettes for your school-themed layouts:

**Red Devil, Kachina, Mocha Divine**
Bazzill Basics Paper
*BazzillBasics.com*

**Sunflowers Medium, Blush Red Medium, Razzleberry Dark**
Prism Papers
*PrismPapers.com*

**Kraft, Paprika, Olive (all from the Crinkles collection)**
Wausau Paper
*WausauPaper.com*

## TRY A Q&A APPROACH

Host a Q&A session with your child. For question ideas, check out the seven questions Pam Callaghan asked her son for her "First Day Q&A" layout at left. You can also try one of these ideas:

- Take various photos of your child during the day, like Pam did, and ask your child what he or she was thinking at each of these moments.
- Come up with questions on your child's level, such as "Why is first grade cool?"
- Use design elements on your page to focus on the questions and answers.

*First Day Q&A by Pam Callaghan.* **Supplies** *Cardstock:* Anna Griffin (green) and Bazzill Basics Paper (blue, kraft and white); *Patterned paper:* Anna Griffin (green and orange) and The Paper Company (stripe); *Letter stickers:* Bo-Bunny Press; *Chipboard:* Anna Griffin (letters) and Fancy Pants Designs (shapes); *Fonts:* Librarian and Times New Roman; *Adhesive:* Hermafix, Ek Success.

## CREATE A FILL-IN-THE-BLANK QUIZ

Create a quiz for your children to take. They'll appreciate how fun it is to fill out, and you'll get a record of their handwriting—it's a win-win situation!

**Product Tip:** To create white text on a colored background, use a white-opaque pen or apply white rub-ons. Or create a journaling block in a word-processing program, fill it with a colored background and select white for the text color.

*2nd Grade by Annette Pixley.* **Supplies** *Cardstock:* Bazzill Basics Paper; *Patterned paper:* Around The Block Products (purple), Luxe Designs (black and white) and Making Memories (green); *Mini rub-ons:* Doodlebug Design; *Chipboard number and butterfly rub-on:* American Crafts; *Letter stickers and brad:* Making Memories; *Pens:* American Crafts and Uni-ball Signo, Newell Rubbermaid.

**Starting 2nd Grade** *by Mou Saha.* **Supplies** *Cardstock:* Die Cuts With a View; *Patterned paper and letter stickers:* Piggy Tales; *Stamps:* Autumn Leaves; *Ink:* Tsukineko; *Colored pencil:* Newell Rubbermaid; *Embroidery floss:* DMC; *Pen:* American Crafts; *Adhesive:* Scotch, 3M.

## 6 COMPARE THOUGHTS

Recording your child's perspective on a layout doesn't mean you can't share your thoughts, too. Mou Saha shared her daughter's thoughts in journaling strips and added her own perspective in a journaling block on the right-hand page.

# { 6 back-to-school *jump-starts* }

The kids are going back to school today and are sure to come home with assignments tonight. Join them at the table (with scrapbook supplies in hand) and complete your own assignment this evening: a back-to-school layout. Try one of these six "assignments" to create your perfect layout this evening.

use this "homework" to *enliven* your pages

## english class

**YOUR HOMEWORK:**
Write down your feelings about watching your children leave for their first day of school.

**And He's Off** by Vivian Masket.
**Supplies** *Cardstock:* Prism Papers; *Patterned paper:* BasicGrey (stripe and test bubbles) and Scenic Route (lined); *Rub-ons:* Creative Imaginations (months); *Stamps:* 7gypsies (dotted circle) and Technique Tuesday ("and he's"); *Ink:* StazOn, Tsukineko; *Letter stickers:* American Crafts (apostrophe); *Sticker ("school today"):* Imagination Project; *Chipboard:* American Crafts (apple and leaf) and Scenic Route ("off" letters); *Font:* Times New Roman, Microsoft.

**BY BRITTANY BEATTIE**

**Officially Too Young** by Mou Saha. **Supplies** *Cardstock and patterned paper:* Frances Meyer; *Letter stickers:* American Crafts (title) and Making Memories (numbers); *Metal accents:* Making Memories; *Embroidery floss:* DMC; *Pens:* American Crafts (black) and Newell Rubbermaid (white); *Font:* Arial, www.dafont.com.

# home-ec class

**YOUR HOMEWORK:**

Use your sewing machine (or a needle and thread) to stitch a frame around your main photo. (This type of frame is especially helpful to let your main photo pop on the layout when all photos are the same size and right next to each other.)

**DESIGN TIP:**

If your layout feels unbalanced, try Mou's solution: "After adding all the elements toward the right side of the page, the left side looked a bit empty. I used a white pen to add the white page corners—they help balance the page elements better without competing with the page focus."

# time-management class

**YOUR HOMEWORK:**

Record the time schedule from a typical day at school. Heidi Sonboul used a mini-album format for a clever way to record the schedule, with each tab representing a different time of day (it's recorded on the back of each tab, and the month is recorded across the front).

**MINI-ALBUM IDEA:**

Heidi created this 4" x 6" album primarily from photos. Her cover and many interior pages are formed from printed photos serving as the background.

**Back-to-School Mini Album** *by Heidi Sonboul.* **Supplies** *Patterned paper and letter stickers:* Making Memories; *Stamps:* Purple Onion Designs; *Embossing powder:* Jo-Ann Stores; *Ribbon:* Ribbon Robbin; *Chipboard:* Scenic Route; *Other:* Pencil.

"For this theme, I wanted to *give* the breakdown for the day, from getting ready to walking in the door on the first day of *school*. Even brushing teeth was important to me."

**—HEIDI SONBOUL**

**Waiting for That Bus** *by Laina Lamb.* **Supplies** *Cardstock:* Archiver's; *Patterned paper:* Imaginisce; *Brads:* Stemma, Masterpiece Studios; *Chipboard letters:* American Crafts; *Font:* Century Gothic, Microsoft.

# design class

**YOUR HOMEWORK:**

Create a layout using accents, photos or embellishments in odd numbers—it's more aesthetically pleasing. Notice the use of odd numbers in this layout: three photos, three lines (see the title, the journaling and the paper strip) and three brads.

**COLOR TIP:**

Says Laina: "The focus of this layout was my son's nervous yet excited feelings about leaving home and going to school on a bus for the very first time. I chose simple and minimal primary colors to complement the photos and theme." Notice how the minimal use of color against the white background helps the photos and message stand out on Laina's layout.

**School Materials** *by Terri Davenport.* **Supplies** *Software:* Adobe Photoshop CS2; *Patterned paper:* Notebook No.2 Paper Pack by Katie Pertiet, *www.designer-digitals.com*; *Fonts:* TIA Miss Johnson, "15 Perfect for Journaling Fonts" CD, Autumn Leaves (journaling); Violation, *www.dafont.com* (title).

# accounting class

**YOUR HOMEWORK:**

Record the inventory of supplies purchased and gathered for the first day of school.

**PHOTO TIP:**

Terri placed her school supplies in front of a chalkboard when she photographed them to reinforce the school theme.

**Kindergarten** *by Natalie Call.* **Supplies** *Patterned paper:* BasicGrey (notebook and letter), Cosmo Cricket (red) and K&Company (ruler); *Rub-ons:* Autumn Leaves; *Ribbon:* Pebbles Inc.; *Paper clip:* Junkitz; *Chipboard:* Fancy Pants Designs; *Decorative scissors:* Fiskars; *Pen:* American Crafts.

"Find the *story* that made this year unique from the others and was most memorable, like the shoes your son had to have or the fact that your *daughter* asked you not to wait at the bus stop with her. For me, sharpening 91 pencils was a memorable part of the getting-ready-for-school process."

**—TERRI DAVENPORT**

# photography class

**YOUR HOMEWORK:**
Crop distracting backgrounds or elements from your photos, like your yard, students sitting at the table with your kids and cars parked in front of the bus.

**ACCENT IDEA:**
Check out Natalie's tips for using ruler-patterned paper on your layouts: "I wanted to make the 'ruler' (an old paper scrap) on this layout look dimensional, so I cut a piece of chipboard the same size and mounted the ruler paper on it. To make the ruler look like it was being held in place, like the loops in school binders that hold pencils, I looped ribbon around the background strip of patterned paper and secured it to the back with Glue Dots. I left it loose enough in the front so that the 'ruler' could slide through."

# *10 fun tricks* to treat you

Halloween is a holiday of creativity. You get to plan costumes, decorations, frightfully fabulous parties, spooktacular dishes and more. And when the holiday is over, you'll enjoy the creativity of scrapbooking all the monstrously fun photos. I've made it easy for you with these 10 tricks!

add a *new look* to your layouts

Include before and after photos of your jack-o'-lantern. It's a great way to showcase the transformation of your Halloween delights. You could also take before and after shots of your living room to show your Halloween decorations.

Add a circle accent behind one or more of your title letters. This technique adds a subtle look to reinforce the pumpkin theme. Don't you love how the "a" in Kelly Goree's "Jack" title looks like it's carved from the circle behind it?

**Jack** *by Kelly Goree.* **Supplies** *Cardstock:* Archiver's (black) and Bazzill Basics Paper (orange, yellow and white); *Patterned paper:* Heidi Grace Designs; *Ink:* ColorBox Fluid Chalk, Clearsnap; *Brads:* Queen & Co.; *Chipboard bookplate:* Heidi Swapp for Advantus; *Font:* Times New Roman.

**BY BRITTANY BEATTIE**

**Halloween Fair** *by Laina Lamb.* **Supplies** *Cardstock:* Archiver's (kraft) and Bazzill Basics Paper (black and orange); *Patterned paper:* KI Memories (stripe and circle) and Reminisce (graph); *Letter stickers:* American Crafts; *Stickers:* Pebbles Inc.; *Acetate house:* Making Memories; *Label:* Dymo; *Bat die cut:* AccuCut; *Software:* Adobe Illustrator; *Font:* News Gothic; *Adhesive:* Scotch ATG, 3M; All Night Media, Plaid Enterprises.

Add yellow cardstock behind a black haunted-house accent. The yellow backing will give the windows of the house an eerie evening glow.

Most trick-or-treating photos have dark backgrounds. To make sure they don't become lost against the background of your layout, mat them on a bright color—orange is a fabulous hue this month.

Set bold, black letters against orange papers for your title. It's an ideal way to showcase your Halloween photos.

**Halloween** *by Heidi Sonboul.* **Supplies** *Cardstock:* Bazzill Basics Paper; *Patterned paper:* cherryArte, GCD Studios and My Mind's Eye; *Ink:* Ranger Industries; *Letter stickers:* American Crafts; *Stickers:* Creative Café; *Chipboard:* Heidi Grace Designs; *Adhesive:* Scotch, 3M.

Glittered papers bring a festive feel to Halloween pages. Not only did Mou Saha punch squares from glittered paper to add to her photo-collage grid design, but she also cut a witch accent from the paper for the perfect accent above her title.

**Halloween '08** by Mou Saha. **Supplies** *Cardstock:* Die Cuts With a View; *Patterned paper:* Piggy Tales; *Ink:* Tsukineko; *Flower:* Prima; *Rhinestones:* Rusty Pickle; *Embroidery floss:* DMC; *Pinking shears:* Fiskars Americas; *Square punch:* Marvy Uchida; *Fonts:* American Typewriter (journaling) and Galleria (title); *Adhesive:* Scotch, 3M.

Don't forget to photograph the little details. This month, look for the following images through your viewfinder:

- Sprinkles on cupcakes
- Cups of cider on a table
- Glitter textures on Halloween decor
- Melting caramel dripping from an apple
- Sparkles and dye in costumed kids' hair
- Shiny, stitched or patterned pieces on costumes
- Halloween candy tucked carefully away until trick-or-treat night

## 10 Timeless Traditions

**Looking for something to do this month? Try one of these fun traditions from the designers whose work is published in "Seasonal Solutions" this month!**

1. Have a Halloween bonfire.
2. Find and carve a pumpkin.
3. Take a drive to watch a fall sunset.
4. Read Halloween books to your kids.
5. Take pictures of neighborhood decorations.
6. Attend a community Halloween fair or party.
7. Eat lots of candy corn throughout the month.
8. Answer the door to make the trick-or-treaters extremely happy.
9. Change your costume idea innumerable times before the big day.
10. Photograph your child on the doorstep to show his or her height.

If your layout has several photo blocks of the same size, fill a few of the spaces around your layout with a large image trimmed into smaller segments. Heidi Sonboul cut her colored tree accent into three adjacent squares placed in the center of her layout.

**Celebrate** by Heidi Sonboul. **Supplies** *Cardstock:* Bazzill Basics Paper; *Patterned paper and fabric letters:* Anna Griffin; *Rub-ons and brads:* Creative Café; *Stamps:* Purple Onion Designs; *Ink:* Stampin' Up!; *Ribbon:* American Crafts; *Flowers:* Prima; *Stickers:* Heidi Grace Designs; *Paint:* Crayola; *Adhesive:* Scotch, 3M.

## Striking Shades for the Season

If you can't decide what color palette to use for your layout, try one of these cool combos.

**Castle Copper (metallic), Midnight Blue, Umber**
Wausau Paper
*WausauPaper.com*

**Majestic Purple Dark, Intense Kiwi, Intense Teal**
Prism Papers
*PrismPapers.com*

**Butterfly/CC, Beetle Black, Pistachio**
Bazzill Basics Paper
*BazzillBasics.com*

**Trick or Treat** *by Sheri Horton.* **Supplies** *Software:* Corel Paint Shop Pro 9; *Template:* Yin Template 51 by Yin Designs; *Patterned paper and embellishments:* Boo to You by Digital Design Essentials; *Letters ("or"):* Cherishing Every Moment - Alpha by Weeds & Wildflowers Design; *Font:* Carter.

Felt accents and letters add a great feel to a fall page. Plus, they're inexpensive to create! Simply purchase sheets of craft felt from the store, photocopy or download a simple shape, trace the shape onto the felt and cut it out. Add googly eyes for the finishing touch on ghost or goblin accents.

Incorporating colors from costumes on your layouts doesn't have to be difficult. Simply add a patterned paper strip to one side, or ink or paint the edges of the layout in the color, just as Sheri Horton did.

# *seasonal solutions:*
# lifelong learning

BY LORI FAIRBANKS

**WHEN ALL THE KIDS** head back to school this month, you might feel a little nostalgic for freshly sharpened pencils and textbooks. But even without the school bell, September is a great time to recognize—and scrapbook—the skills, hobbies, and interests you're cultivating. Check out the following pages to see how six scrapbookers have documented their ventures in lifelong learning, then create a layout about your own endeavors.

**scrapbook your** *hobbies* **and interests**

I ran a marathon in

## these shoes

REMEMBER**THIS** *day*

This was such a great experience, from the beginning of training to the big day. It is true that you must walk before you can run, as I struggled to finish five miles during the first group run. But after four and a half months of training I ran 26.2 miles stopping only for water, a foot check and one bathroom break. Amazing! And the day was perfect. I was a little worried about San Francisco in October but we had a beautiful day! I will always remember how the Golden Gate Bridge looked as I ran by that morning - a blue sky, the brilliant red of the structure and puffy white clouds (or fog maybe) floating near the base of the bridge. A day to remember and a proud moment I will cherish forever. October 22, 2006

THE story

**These Shoes** by Julie DeGuia. **Digital Supplies:** *Software:* Adobe; *Cardstock, circle accent, and printed transparency:* Katie Pertiet; *Journaling spot:* Ali Edwards; *Fonts:* Bank Gothic, CK Ali's Hand, Times, and Skia.

**Scrapbook a layout about your accomplishments.** For your journaling, ask yourself

- What did I do to prepare for my achievement?

- What did I learn along the way?

### SCRAPBOOKING TIP FROM JULIE DEGUIA

"If you have something that you are proud of, don't be afraid to say so! Running a marathon is one of the most amazing things I think I have ever done (after giving birth and jumping out of airplanes!) and I am happy to share the experience. This is definitely something I had to 'learn' to do in small steps, gradually adding on the miles week after week."

**karate**

Japanese: kara (empty) + te (hand) A Japanese art of self-defense without the use of weapons by striking pressure-sensitive areas

**Karate** by Mou Saha.
**Supplies:** *Cardstock:* Die Cuts with a View; *Patterned paper, chipboard, and journaling spot:* Anna Griffin; *Stickers:* Chatterbox; *Stamp:* Recollections; *Ink:* Tsukineko; *Punch:* Martha Stewart Crafts and Marvy Uchida; *Pen:* American Crafts; *Adhesive:* 3M; *Other:* Karate school pass.

**Scrapbook things you're learning** in different areas of your life. Perhaps you've taken up a new sport like Mou Saha. Or maybe you learned a new scrapbooking technique, taught yourself three new recipes, or discovered a new passion for learning to speak another language.

### PHOTOGRAPHY TIP:

Ask a friend or family member to take pictures of you engaged in your favorite hobby or pastime. Although you may initially feel a little silly about having photos taken of you while you scrapbook, knit, play golf, or read, recognize that this is a part of your life that should be documented. Keep in mind that your friends and family want to see you represented in your scrapbooks too!

**Scrapbooking your activities, skills, and interests** is a good way to record another aspect of your life that your children and grandchildren will find fascinating.

### SCRAPBOOKING TIP FROM BARB WONG

"I think about the kind of details I will want to remember in years to come. I think about the kind of things I would like to know about my mom's younger days. I often try to make a connection between me right now and my boys in the future . . . what might they want to know about the person who nagged them about their homework every night, got on their case about dirty clothes on their bedroom floor, and asked them repeatedly if they washed their hands before dinner? I want them to know I was more than that."

**obsession**

I started taking lessons a few months ago so I'd be able to get on the outdoor courts with you and James this summer. We're still six weeks away from the official opening of those outdoor courts but that didn't stop me from dragging you out to the parking lot at a nearby school so we could hit balls against a windowless brick wall. I was in awe of the control you had over the ball, and I smiled when you gave me pointers to improve my shots. Thomas, you're pretty awesome. (March 17, 2010)

**Obsession** by Barb Wong. **Supplies:** *Brad, cardstock, and rub-ons:* American Crafts; *Patterned paper and sticker:* BasicGrey; *Embroidery floss:* DMC; *Ink:* Clearsnap; *Pen:* Newell Rubbermaid; *Adhesive:* Kokuyo.

# { *falling* for you }

Every year, fall comes faster than we expect it to. It reminds us how quickly time passes, and it nudges us to record the events of the year before the new year knocks on our door. Before this month slips away, schedule a day to scrapbook your photos from this fall. The layout ideas, techniques and journaling tips on the following pages will give you a great place to start.

**top** *tips* **for fall pages**

**LAYOUT IDEA:** Scrapbook outdoor play in the leaves. Bring your color scheme to life by punching leaf accents from multiple colors instead of just one.

**DESIGN TIP:** Finishing touches don't need to take much time. On this layout, Laurie Stenzel rounded two corners to set her photo and journaling mat apart from the brown background.

**Seasons of Change** by Laurie Stenzel. **Supplies** Cardstock: Bazzill Basics Paper; Brads: American Crafts; Leaf and corner-rounder punches: Creative Memories; Decorative paper strip: Doodlebug Design; Fonts: 1942 Report, Garamond and Stephanie Marie; Software: Adobe Photoshop CS3; Adhesive: 3M and Creative Memories.

**BY BRITTANY BEATTIE**

**JENN'S DESIGN TIP:** "If you're having a hard time combining patterns, cut your papers into small pieces or strips—it's less overwhelming."

**PAM'S PHOTO TIPS:** "Take your photos from different angles. Shoot some pictures on your knees and some standing up—that way you get both a blue sky and trees in the photos, along with the pumpkins on the ground."

*At the Patch* by Jenn Emch. **Supplies** *Patterned paper:* Collage Press and Maya Road; *Circle die cuts:* 7gypsies; *Punch:* Martha Stewart Crafts for EK Success; *Letter stickers and pen:* American Crafts; *Adhesive:* Tombow.

**LAYOUT IDEA:** Scrapbook a trip to the pumpkin patch.

**TECHNIQUE TIP:** To get a reverse rounded corner, like the one on the right-hand page of Pam Callaghan's layout, use a photo or paper block with a rounded corner as a template for tracing, and then hand cut the shape.

*Autumn Tradition* by Pam Callaghan. **Supplies** *Cardstock:* Bazzill Basics Paper; *Patterned paper:* Bo-Bunny Press (yellow) and Scenic Route (stripe); *Stickers and flower die cut:* Creative Café; *Corner-rounder punch:* Carl Mfg.; *Fonts:* Century Gothic and Partridge; *Adhesive:* Mono Adhesive, Tombow; *Other:* Embroidery floss.

**LAYOUT IDEA:** Scrapbook football activities at home or in a stadium.

**It's All about the Dance** by Cindy Tobey. **Supplies** Cardstock: Worldwin Papers; Patterned paper, felt and label stickers: Fancy Pants Designs; Ink: Clearsnap; Ribbon: Pebbles Inc.; Brads, epoxy buttons and paint: Making Memories (star) and Queen & Co.; Letter stickers: KI Memories; Chipboard: Heidi Swapp for Advantus; Photo corners: Canson; Border punch: Fiskars Americas; Pen: Sakura; Fonts: Allstar and Arial Narrow; Adhesive: Glue Dots, Glue Dots International; Scotch Mounting Tape, 3M; Tombow; Other: Embroidery floss and thread.

<< **TECHNIQUE TIP:** Trim a few notches into strips of patterned paper to re-create the feeling of yard lines painted on a football field.

>> **TECHNIQUE TIP:** Hand or machine stitch a motion path on your layout, like the one Cindy Tobey created, to add motion to a ball accent.

>> **PRODUCT TIP:** As you select the stickers or fonts for your title, look for something that supports the theme of your page. For a football layout, varsity-style letters are a perfect choice, and you don't need an entire collection of them. Add just a few varsity letters to change the feel of your layout.

BEFORE

AFTER

**LAYOUT IDEA:** Add personalized touches to tree designs on pages about fall leaves.

**New Discoveries from Shay** *by Julie Detlef.* **Supplies** *Cardstock:* Bazzill Basics Paper; *Patterned paper and buttons:* Harmonie; *Stamps:* 7gypsies; *Letter stickers:* Making Memories; *Pen:* Slick Writers, American Crafts; *Adhesive:* Adhesive Technologies, Inc.

**JOURNALING TIP:** Julie Detlef wrote the journaling on her layout from her daughter's perspective.

**FINISHING TOUCH:** Julie used a pen to draw a circle border inside the circles on her layout.

**Nature Walk** *by Julie DeGuia.* **Supplies** *Software:* Adobe Photoshop CS2; *Patterned paper:* Eco Paper Pack by Katie Pertiet (altered), Lucky Gardener by Katie Pertiet (journaling blocks) and The Shabby Princess (brown); *Frames:* Vintage Photo Frames by Katie Pertiet; *Stamps:* Fruehling ElementSet by Anna Aspnes (grass), Love Grows No. 1 Brushes and Stamps by Katie Pertiet (tree) and Katie Pertiet (grid); *Stitching holes, negative sleeves, flowers and rubber band:* Katie Pertiet; *Photo fasteners:* Fruehling ElementSet by Anna Aspnes; *Acrylic tab:* Absolutely Acrylic: Tabs and Tags by Pattie Knox; *Letters:* Chipboard Bytes Bare Tagboard Alphabet No. 04 by Pattie Knox; *Fonts:* American Typewriter, Angelina and Skia.

**DESIGN TIP:** Ground your hand-cut tree and leaf elements by adding a thin, green, decorative border strip at the base of the tree to resemble grass.

**JULIE'S PHOTO TIP:** "Remember to include yourself in a picture. This layout would not have been the same without a picture including me, because it was special that my son and I went for a walk by ourselves. I had to set my camera on my backpack (which was on the ground), set the timer and then run and lie down next to my son!"

**LAYOUT IDEA:** Scrapbook about finding leaves in your own backyard.

**Leaf Collector**
*by Rita Shimniok.*
**Supplies** *Cardstock:* Bazzill Basics Paper; *Patterned paper, die cuts and letter stickers:* SEI; *Brads:* Making Memories; *Stamps:* Autumn Leaves and Hero Arts; *Border punch:* Fiskars Americas; *Rickrack:* Wright's; *Thread:* Coats & Clark; *Ink:* ColorBox Fluid Chalk, Clearsnap; *Pens:* EK Success and Sakura; *Adhesive:* Fiskars Americas; Quick-Dry Tacky Adhesive, Scotch, 3M.

**TECHNIQUE TIP:** Stitch a branch design and then add epoxy leaves to the twigs. Rita Shimniok used a combination of straight and zigzag stitching for her branch design.

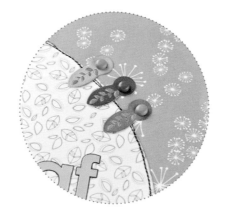

**PRODUCT TIP:** Give your photo turns a fall look by adding leaf rub-ons to the top.

**LAYOUT IDEA:** Showcase a walk through a forest.

**Fall** *by Marianne Hope.* **Supplies** *Patterned paper:* Cosmo Cricket; *Letter stickers:* American Crafts; *Paint:* FolkArt, Plaid Enterprises; *Software:* Adobe Photoshop CS4; *Adhesive:* Mono Adhesive, Tombow; *Other:* Opaque pen.

**TECHNIQUE TIP:** Paint a frame around a photo collage, and then use a white, opaque pen to journal over it. *Note:* Make your layer of paint very thin and flat; otherwise, it will be difficult to write on.

**DESIGN TIP:** Blue works well as an accent color on this layout because it's a complementary color to orange, which is showcased so beautifully in the photos.

**LAYOUT IDEA:** Scrapbook harvest time.

**Bára, Luky & Kaštany** *by Petra Alexova.* **Supplies** *Cardstock:* My Mind's Eye; *Patterned paper:* Efalin (brown) and My Mind's Eye (stripe); *Stamps:* Fancy Pants Designs; *Ink:* ColorBox, Clearsnap; *Brads:* American Crafts (brown), SEI (red) and unknown (white); *Chipboard:* BasicGrey; *Die-cutting machine:* Silhouette, QuickKutz; *Font:* Black Widow.

**CREATIVITY CHALLENGE:** For a fun creativity challenge, Petra Alexova of the Czech Republic trades photos with her friend Marketa, whose children are featured on this layout. This layout is one of the results.

# fall delights

If you can't decide which colors to use for your fall layouts, try one of these delicious combos:

**Desert Sun, Fern and Aspen**
Bazzill Basics Paper
*BazzillBasics.com*

**Sunflowers Dark, Desert Coral Medium and Suede Brown Dark**
Prism Papers
*PrismPapers.com*

**Wheat, Sparkling Merlot (metallic) and Burgundy**
Wausau Paper
*WausauPaper.com*

# *kid projects* for thanksgiving

While the grand Thanksgiving dinner is cooking, all will be quiet around the home, right? It won't be? You know there will be little ones running throughout the house? (What a blessing!) Well then, pull out your scrapbooking supplies on Thanksgiving Eve. You can use one of these fun-filled projects to keep the youngsters entertained on Thanksgiving Day while the cranberries are simmering and the turkey is roasting.

make these *cool projects* with your kids

**NOEL AND HER DAUGHTERS** make turkey hats each year on or around Thanksgiving. Says Noel, "Usually on Thanksgiving Day I'm very busy with meal prep and table setting, so it's great to have a simple craft that the kids can make all on their own. I'll precut the main strips for the headbands and legs, then trace the turkey heads. The kids can put together the rest!

"The kids love tracing their own hands for the turkey feathers. I have enough supplies out for each child that comes over, and the supplies are set out in piles with the names of the children on them (put the supplies in a Ziploc bag as a 'kit' if you prefer)." For step-by-step directions for this project, read on. **>>**

Turkey Hats *by Noel Culbertson.*
**Supplies** *Cardstock:* Wausau Paper; *Other:* Wiggly eyes, staples and glue.

**BY BRITTANY BEATTIE**

# turkey headband how-to

❶ Cut two 3" x 12" strips for the headband and four 1" x 12" strips for the legs.

❷ Sketch the turkey feet, the waddle and the turkey head, then trace your child's hands twice onto coordinating cardstock. Have the child cut out each piece.

❸ Fold a small square of orange cardstock in half and cut it into a triangle shape with the fold serving as the base; unfold slightly to resemble a beak.

❹ Accordion-fold the four leg strips. Staple two together to make long turkey legs; repeat with the remaining two strips.

❺ Glue the wiggly eyes, beak and waddle onto the turkey head. Glue the turkey head onto the center of one of the headband strips, then glue the hands onto the back of the headband strip behind the turkey head. Glue the turkey legs on either side of the turkey head on the bottom of the headband strip.

❻ Staple the two headband strips together to fit the child's head.

**Thanksgiving Busy Book** *by Heidi Sonboul.* **Supplies** *Cardstock:* Bazzill Basics Paper; *Patterned paper:* Anna Griffin; *Stamps:* Unity Stamps Company; *Ink:* ColorBox, Clearsnap; *Ribbon:* Bo-Bunny Press; *Other:* Thread.

# activity book

Create a Thanksgiving activity book that you can use year after year. Simply add handmade or downloaded-and-printed games, such as tic-tac-toe, word searches and Thanksgiving secret decoder messages, to several blocks of patterned paper. Then, laminate the pages and bind them together at home or at a copy center. Laminated pages will allow your children to use dry-erase markers that can be wiped clean so others can enjoy the activity book throughout the day.

**note:** Heidi secured several dry-erase markers onto a jump ring and a washcloth onto another jump ring. She then secured them onto the binding of her mini album so they couldn't become lost throughout the day.

**ACTIVITY-PAGE IDEAS**

Wondering what activities you can fill your activity book with? Here's what Heidi used:

- "Why do you love Thanksgiving?" (fill-in-the-blank boxes)

- "What did you eat for dinner?" (draw-in-the-circle dinner plates)

- Thanksgiving secret-decoder message (with key)

- "What are you grateful for?" (fill-in-the-blank boxes)

- "Draw a silly face" (draw-in-the-blank oval)

- Connect-the-dots turkey

- Word search

- Tic-tac-toe

# turkey handprint magnet

For a twist on the classic "handprint" turkeys, try Deena Wuest's design. She had each of her three children trace a hand onto patterned paper, then she layered the three pieces together to create one colorful turkey. She used clothespins (painted brown) for the legs and added magnets to the back of them. The magnets house children's art, except on Thanksgiving morning, when they hold a basket filled with goodies for the children to find and enjoy.

"This project was created with leftover *scraps* and things lying around the house. It took no money and such little effort to do this project with my kids, but they still *talk* about it."

**—DEENA WUEST**

**Turkey Handprint Magnet** *by Deena Wuest.* **Supplies** *Patterned paper:* Scenic Route; *Twill:* Rusty Pickle; *Ribbon:* C.M. Offray & Son; *Paint:* Plaid Enterprises; *Other:* Clothespins, antique buttons, raffia basket and adhesive magnets.

Mou created this mini album to teach her children the history of Thanksgiving Day in a fun and unique way. Her daughter suggested that they create "a little show" for the family to watch, and it ended up being the springboard for this project. Mou used the photos from the show as the pictures for her mini album, and she used the script from the play as her journaling.

## "THANKSGIVING STORY" HOW-TO

1. Write a brief children's story to summarize the history of Thanksgiving. (Stories are available online if you don't want to write one yourself.)

2. Sketch images (or download free coloring pages from the Internet) to support the story.

3. Let your children color in the images, then cut them out and glue them onto craft sticks.

4. Take pictures of your children holding the craft sticks as they tell the Thanksgiving story.

5. Use the pictures and your Thanksgiving story to create a mini book or mini album that you can continue to read in years to come.

**Learning about Thanksgiving** *by Mou Saha.* **Supplies** *Album:* Rusty Pickle; *Letter stickers:* American Crafts ("Thanksgiving") and Making Memories (mini); *Brad:* SEI; *Raffia:* Michaels; *Pen:* American Crafts; *Font:* American Typewriter, www.fonts.com; *Other:* Paper piercer and printer paper.

# great for the group

BY AMANDA PROBST

Thanksgiving may be all about food and gratitude, but what's a body to do while the food is cooking? My mom started a great tradition last year by "mandating" a coloring contest. She'd acquired an extra children's coloring page from a local store and made copies. As each person arrived to our Thanksgiving celebration, he or she was instructed to color. Amazingly, we all did as we were told and even had fun doing it. The crayons and coloring sheets remained out all day, and we taped our finished works of art to the bookcases anonymously. At the end of the day, a "judge" was brought in. Mom won. As it should be.

### COLORING CONTEST LAYOUT

I kept all the coloring contest pages, knowing I would use them to create a layout. I scanned them in (you could also photograph them), then reduced their size before printing to create this showcase of everyone's work.

**Turkey Gallery** by Amanda Probst. **Supplies** Cardstock: Prism Papers; Patterned paper, chipboard buttons and label: Chatterbox; Metal loops and brads: Creative Impressions; Circle sticker: Making Memories; Photo corners: Scrapbook Adhesives by 3L; Pens: Precision Pens, American Crafts; Mark-it, BIC; Fonts: CK Rough Housing, www.scrapnfonts.com; MC CEO, Internet; Rockwell, Microsoft.

### CHILDREN'S GRATITUDE BANNER

For a fun and easy way to keep little ones busy while you're finishing up Thanksgiving dinner, have them create their own banners to decorate the room. Print the design multiple times on solid cardstock or patterned paper, then let the children's imaginations lead. Hang the finished designs around the room to create a banner as they're completed. (I'm thinking I'll create a little album with them after the day is over.)

**note:** I simplified and just had the kids use pencil here, but one could easily set out a greater variety of supplies like markers, crayons, stamps and stickers.

**I Am Thankful for . . . Banner** by Amanda Probst. **Supplies** Cardstock: Prism Papers; Patterned paper: Chatterbox and Making Memories; Font: CK Taliatype, www.scrapnfonts.com; Other: Drawings by Noah (age 7) and Asher (age 5).

# a fun twist on place cards

This project combines "getting-to-know-you" bingo type games with creating your own place card. Here's how to create the project.

❶ Gather enough bingo cards so you have one for each table.

**Bingo Name Cards** *by Amanda Probst.* **Supplies** *Patterned paper:* Sassafras; *Bingo cards:* Jenni Bowlin Studio; *Pens:* Precision Pens, American Crafts; Mark-it, BIC; *Letter stickers:* Li'l Davis Designs; *Ribbon:* Creative Impressions; *Font:* Rockwell, Microsoft.

❷ Determine the number of guests at each table, then print that number of "getting to know you" questions on the back side of a double-sided patterned paper sized slightly larger than the bingo cards. Print enough copies to have one patterned paper for each table, and be sure to use a different patterned paper for each table.

❸ Adhere the bingo card to the back side of the paper with the "getting to know you" questions, then cut apart the "getting to know you" questions on the card.

❹ Flip the cutout cards over and use letter stickers to add the name of a guest to the bingo-card side. Punch holes in the top two corners of each question block and tie a 30" string through them to turn the card into a name tag for the guest to wear. Repeat for all guests.

When it's time to sit down to eat, guests must find the matching pieces to their card and can use the "getting to know you" questions as prompts for conversation starters. Name tags come off and become place cards.

If you're really adventurous, you can then play bingo by having all guests at the table put their name tags together to form one board, with the winning table getting to go through the food line first.

### ADDITIONAL GAME IDEAS

Still looking for more activities you can enjoy with the family? Try these ideas:

■ **Turkey scavenger hunts.** Hide turkey cards or turkey embellishments on the bottom of food trays and around the house. Give a prize to the first person to collect a certain number.

■ **Gratitude mini albums.** For a crafty crowd, why not make an annual gratitude album? Have each guest make a 6" x 6" (or some other size) page at his or her convenience during the day . . . just set out supplies.

■ **Gratitude guessing.** This one requires preparation in advance. Collect lists from each guest of the 10 things he or she is most thankful for. Have printouts of the lists at your gathering and let guests guess whose list is whose. The person with the most correct matches wins.

■ **Early ornaments.** Get a jump start on the holidays and set out supplies for guests to create their own Christmas ornaments. If you're feeling inspired, create kits for a number of different ornament projects and have several "stations" around the house.

# { 'twas the *month before* Christmas }

'Twas the month before Christmas and all through the house

You were searching for presents and treats and a blouse.

When what to your kids' "not again, Mom" eyes should appear

But the camera to capture more pictures this year?

As you gather the photos of comings and goings

You're not sure what to do with the picture pile that's growing.

You ask, "How can I make my holiday layouts look right?"

I answer, "Happy Christmas to all—use these 10 ideas tonight!"

**10 holiday *helps* for your pages**

**Christmas Bliss** *by Jill Marie Paulson.* **Supplies** *Cardstock:* Bazzill Basics Paper; *Patterned paper, stickers and die cuts:* October Afternoon; *Rub-ons:* K&Company ("Christmas") and Pink Paislee ("my holiday wish"); *Ink:* ColorBox, Clearsnap; *Chipboard:* American Crafts; *Journaling block:* Making Memories; *Punches:* Fiskars Americas (scallop) and Marvy Uchida (corner rounder); *Pen:* Sharpie, Newell Rubbermaid; *Adhesive:* Duck Products.

## PHOTO TIP

When piles of boxes and torn-apart wrapping paper clutter the background of your photos, crop them out. The result will provide a much cleaner look on your pages. Plus, with cropped photos you'll be able to fit more pictures on your layout.

**BY BRITTANY BEATTIE**

**Christmas Morning Surprises** by Julie DeGuia. **Supplies** Software: Adobe Photoshop CS2; Patterned paper: Hugs Paper Pack by Lynn Grieveson (tan) and Good Day Paper Pack (tan textured), Eco Paper Pack (cream) and King Me Paper Pack (green damask, recolored) by Katie Pertiet; Frames: Sketchy MultiFoto Frames No. 01 by Anna Aspnes; Vintage Frames No. 07 and Vintage Photo Frames Large Curled and Flat by Katie Pertiet; Stamps and letters: Messy Stamped Alphabet No. 02 Brushes and Stamps by Katie Pertiet; Ornaments: Mary Ann Wise; Yarn: Yarn Ties No. 01 by Katie Pertiet; Twill: Basic Twills: Holiday by Katie Pertiet; "Delight" circle: Simple Spots No. 04 by Katie Pertiet; Date tab: Tabbed Dates by Katie Pertiet; Embroidery stitch: Lil Bit Tags by Katie Pertiet; Scalloped journaling block and photo template: Christmas Memories Layered Template by Katie Pertiet; Staples: Absolutely Acrylic: Tabs and Tags and Fasten It! by Pattie Knox; Fonts: American Typewriter and Impact Label.

## DESIGN TIP

When you have a large area to fill on your layout, you don't need to include numerous accents. Simply place two or three ornament accents in the area and use string to connect the ornaments to the top of the layout.

**These Lights** by Stacy Cohen. **Supplies** Cardstock: Core'dinations (white) and unknown (green); Patterned paper and pearls: Melissa Frances; Ribbon: C.M. Offray & Son; Letter stickers: American Crafts (blue) and Making Memories (cream); Crystal flourish: Prima; Embroidery floss: DMC; Thread: Gutterman; Adhesive: Fabri-Tac, Beacon Adhesives; Tombow; Other: Eyelets.

## EMBELLISHMENT TIP

This holiday season, look through your supply stash for embellishments that will resemble twinkling lights or a candle glow. Stacy Cohen used crystal flourishes, glitter letter stickers and star eyelets to create the motif on her page.

## BORDER TECHNIQUE

Cut horizontal slits in a vertical paper strip, and then weave ribbon between the slits. Add stars or gems in the open spaces between the ribbon for a beautiful border design.

PJs *by April Massad.* **Supplies** *Cardstock, patterned paper, stickers and brads:* BasicGrey; *Chipboard:* BasicGrey (shapes) and Colorbök (letters); *Ink:* ColorBox, Clearsnap (red) and StazOn, Tsukineko (black); *Fonts:* CK Cheer Squad (dates) and CK Chemistry (journaling); *Software:* Adobe Photoshop Elements 5.0; *Adhesive:* E-Z Runner, Scrapbook Adhesives by 3L; The Paper Studio; *Other:* Thread and gems.

### APRIL'S JOURNALING TIPS

- "Before I print my photographs, I add the date and name of the photo subject(s) to each photo in Photoshop. I think of who will look at my pages years from now, and I want them to know whom my pages are about!"

- "I try to journal as if I'm telling a story. I assume the reader doesn't know anything about the photos. That way, years from now my descendants will get a glimpse into our lives and know us a little better!"

### EMBELLISHMENT TECHNIQUE

To create incredibly cute circle accents like April Massad did, simply follow these steps:

❶ Punch a small circle from four scraps of patterned paper.

❷ Cut each of the four small circles into four quarters.

❸ Mix and match the quartered sections to create a quilted circle, and then stitch or adhere the pieces together.

❹ Punch a medium circle from patterned paper, and adhere the quilted circle to the top.

# holiday hues

If you're wondering which colors to use on your next layout, try one of these sensational schemes.

**Slipper, Pirouette, Deep Blue**
Bazzill Basics Paper
*BazzillBasics.com*

**Spring Willow Dark, Rose Medium, Iced Yellow**
Prism Papers
*PrismPapers.com*

**Chalice Silver, Old Towne Red, Cotton**
Wausau Paper
*WausauPaper.com*

**BUDGET TIP**

Die-cut papers can be included on your layout in more than just block sections. Kim Watson cut five snowflakes apart from a sheet of snowflake die-cut paper and used them as individual accents on her layout.

**Reluctant Reindeer** by Kim Watson. **Supplies** *Cardstock:* American Crafts and Bazzill Basics Paper; *Patterned paper:* K&Company, KI Memories (snowflake), October Afternoon and Pink Paislee; *Die-cutting machine:* Slice, Making Memories; *Punches:* EK Success (corner rounder), Fiskars Americas (border) and Marvy Uchida (corner rounder); *Ribbon, letter stickers and pen:* American Crafts; *Adhesive:* Mono Adhesive, Tombow; *Other:* Thread.

**DESIGN TIP**

Cutting your journaling into strips and grouping them vertically on your page creates a fantastic look. But the straight edges can sometimes feel too abrupt when used on a lay-out with circles, flowers or rounded corners. Soften your grouping of journaling strips by placing a circle outline around the set—this tech-nique adds more consistency to the soft feel of the layout.

**Kisses for My Santa Girl** by Sheri Horton. **Supplies** *Software:* Corel Paint Shop Pro; *Template:* Sketch Collection #18 by Jen Caputo; *Kit:* Jubilant by Gina Cabrera and Twas the Night by Shabby Princess; *Letters:* Corduroy Alpha Essentials ("Santa") by Gina Cabrera; *Numbers:* Cozy Comfy Fall by Gina Cabrera; *Font:* 2Peas Old Type.

**Sweet Holiday Tradition** *by Mou Saha.* **Supplies** *Patterned paper:* Anna Griffin (white), BasicGrey (white with green) and Die Cuts With a View (green); *Stamps:* Autumn Leaves; *Ink:* Ranger Industries; *Letter stickers:* Piggy Tales; *Punch:* EK Success; *Embroidery floss:* DMC; *Gingerbread man accent:* Colorbök; *Pen:* American Crafts; *Adhesive:* Scotch, 3M.

## TITLE TIP

When your title deserves extra attention to communicate a main point of your story, don't just confine it to a corner of your layout. Use this layout design from Mou Saha to place your photos around the outside of your pages and give your title prominence in the center.

## FUN FACT

Mou Saha originally had 10 photos on this layout, but it left her with no room for journaling. Her solution was to remove one "nonessential" photo and use its space for a journaling block.

## PHOTO PLACEMENT TIP

Outdoor winter shots may lead to less-than-magical objects in your pictures, such as electrical wires or telephone poles. Rather than cropping out entire edges of your photos to remove them from the background of the picture, try a little creative placement with the photos on your layout.

You can position a corner of another photo to cover the distracting elements without covering the entire edge of a photo. Or, layer a decorative border strip or circle embellishment over part of the photo. Both solutions look natural in your design and will allow you to keep the rest of the photo in view.

**Santa's Visit** *by Lynn Ghahary.* **Supplies** *Cardstock:* Core'dinations; *Patterned paper:* Black River Designs; *Letter stickers and buttons:* American Crafts; *Snowflake stickers:* Heidi Swapp for Advantus; *Die-cutting machine:* Cricut Expression, Provo Craft; *Die cartridge:* Opposites Attract, Provo Craft; *Punches:* Fiskars Americas (border and circle) and Stampin' Up! (file tab); *Font:* Rough Typewriter; *Adhesive:* Herma Dotto, EK Success; Pop Dots, All Night Media, Plaid Enterprises.

# *holiday*
# { journaling ideas }

The holiday season always helps us reflect on what's truly important—things like faith, family, friends and the memories we share. Although it's a busy time, the pleasure of reflecting on these blessings brings joy and meaning to each day. That's what I love about scrapbooking—it's a chance to record the memories most dear to us—that way we can actually reflect on them all year round. So even while the hustle and bustle is going on around you, take time to record those precious moments of this year's holiday season.

Happy holidays . . . and happy journaling!

**Favorite Christmas Memory** *by Lisa Swift.* **Supplies** *Cardstock:* Bazzill Basics Paper; *Patterned paper:* KI Memories; *Rub-ons:* Autumn Leaves ("Christmas Day"), Doodlebug Design (green swirl) and Hambly Studios (frame above title); *Brads:* Autumn Leaves and Doodlebug Design (white, green and red); *Letter stickers:* Doodlebug Design ("favorite" and "memory") and Making Memories ("Christmas"); *Stickers:* Imagination Project ("December"); *Epoxy sticker:* KI Memories; *Pens:* Uni-ball Signo, Newell Rubbermaid (white) and Zig Millennium, EK Success (black); *Journaling card:* Dude Designs; *Photo corners:* Jo-Ann Stores; *Buttons:* Autumn Leaves; *Font:* Decker, Internet; *Other:* Thread.

**seven journaling *ideas* for your pages this month**

## JOURNAL YOUR FAVORITE HOLIDAY MEMORY FROM CHILDHOOD

When I asked Lisa Swift why she created this page, she answered: "So much of what I scrapbook is centered around my daughter, so I wanted to take a different approach here to capture my husband's childhood holiday memories. I could not believe how vividly my husband remembered things!"

You are bound to remember holiday traditions from your childhood as well. Have you written them down yet? Today is the perfect day to do it!

**BY BRITTANY BEATTIE**

### JOURNAL ABOUT THE HOLIDAY DECOR IN YOUR HOME

Home-decorating traditions change from generation to generation. Capture your home decor on a layout today so that it's documented for years to come!

"I think having most of the photos the same size helped *unify* the pages and add order to my layout."

**—ELISABETH CASS**

**Joy** *by Elisabeth Cass.* **Supplies** *Cardstock:* Bazzill Basics Paper; *Patterned paper:* Making Memories; *Stickers:* 7gypsies; *Pen:* Zig Millennium, EK Success.

**Favourite** *by Barb Wong.* **Supplies** *Cardstock:* Bazzill Basics Paper; *Patterned paper:* BasicGrey (green and dark-pink dot), Chatterbox, K&Company, Karen Foster Design, KI Memories (brown), Luxe Designs, My Mind's Eye and Scenic Route (blue snow); *Ink:* VersaColor, Tsukineko; *Brads:* Making Memories; *Ribbon:* May Arts; *Glitter glue:* Stickles, Ranger Industries; *Foam letter stickers:* American Crafts; *Glaze:* Crystal Effects, Stampin' Up!; *Corner-rounder punch:* EK Success; *Chipboard star:* BasicGrey; *Pen:* Pigma Micron, Sakura.

### JOURNAL ABOUT THE "FAVORITE"
### GIFTS GIVEN OR RECEIVED

There's usually at least one gift given or received each year that draws a lot of excitement. Be sure to share the story around it to complete the journaling on your layout. Try one of the journaling prompts above to help you get started.

### JOURNALING PROMPTS FOR GIFT-THEMED LAYOUTS

■ How long did you search for the perfect gift?

■ Who was most excited: the gift giver or the recipient?

■ How long was the "perfect gift" on the wish list?

■ What memorable stories occurred when *finding* the gift?

■ Did a gift receive an unanticipated response?

## paper-scrap trees

To create a tree like Barb's, follow these steps:

**1** Draw a tree outline onto a large scrap of cardstock.

**2** Turn the cardstock over and cover it with small blocks of green patterned paper.

**3** Return the paper to the side with the tree sketch, and cut it out.

**4** Ink the edges of the tree. Complete it with a chipboard star and a paper pot and trunk.

### JOURNAL ABOUT THE HOLIDAY'S DIFFERENT COMPONENTS

Pick a specific theme to showcase the different components of your holiday, then make a list for your journaling. For a fun challenge, find a monogram accent and list all the holiday items beginning with the letter. Or, showcase:

- People you give gifts to
- People who give gifts to you
- Favorite holiday movies you watch
- The foods you eat at specific parties
- People you visit during the holiday season
- The decorations in each room of your home

**Hanukkah Is Special** *by Lisa Swift.* **Supplies** *Cardstock:* Bazzill Basics Paper (black) and SEI (blue); *Patterned paper and tags:* SEI; *Rub-ons:* Autumn Leaves ("December"), K&Company (stitches) and Scenic Route ("miracle"); *Ink:* Tsukineko; *Brads:* Doodlebug Design; *Flowers:* Making Memories (blue) and Prima (pink); *Letter stickers:* Mustard Moon; *Die-cuts:* Dude Designs ("eight"), Luxe Designs (oval) and My Mind's Eye (monogram); *Sequins:* Queen & Co.; *Buttons:* Making Memories; *Pen:* Uni-ball Signo, Newell Rubbermaid; *Font:* Decker, Internet; *Other:* Thread.

### JOURNAL ABOUT THE ACTIVITIES OF THE HOLIDAY

Write down a list of the activities you participated in (including their order and location). Yes, journaling can be *that easy*!

## get more from paper scraps

Dawn Hagewood used a scrap of tree-patterned paper to cut out individual trees. She then added them to her layout directly above the title using Pop Dots. The finished result looks like die-cut accents, but she made them all with a scrap of paper—what a great way to use your supplies!

PAPER BY SCENIC ROUTE

**Christmas Morning** *by Dawn Hagewood.* **Supplies** *Cardstock:* Bazzill Basics Paper; *Patterned paper:* Scenic Route; *Brads:* Making Memories; *Letter stickers:* American Crafts (black) and Scenic Route ("Christmas"); *Chipboard:* Queen & Co.; *Photo turn:* 7gypsies.

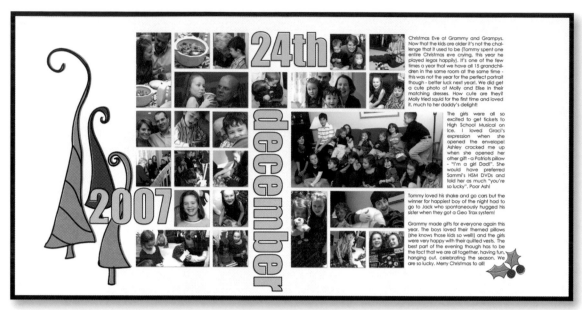

**December 24, 2007** *by Paula Gilarde.* **Supplies** *Template:* Tortuga Template No. 62 by Kellie Mize; *Patterned paper:* Daylily Paper Pack (white) and Rejoice Paper Pack (green and red) by Katie Pertiet; *Brushes:* Festive Song BrushSet by Anna Aspnes; *Font:* Century Gothic (journaling) and Impact (title), Microsoft. *Note:* All digital elements were downloaded from *www.designerdigitals.com.*

## JOURNAL ABOUT THE EXCITEMENT OF OPENING GIFTS

The opening of presents is sure to bring lots of emotional reactions—joyful smiles, fun-filled laughter and perhaps even a few pouts. Sadly, these memories often fade if we don't record them right away. Don't let that happen this year—just jot down what happened within a few days of the event. Don't worry about recording your memories in complete sentences or with perfect grammar. Simply write them down so the memories will never fade.

## JOURNAL ABOUT THE SOUNDS YOU HEAR DURING THE HOLIDAYS

Kim Watson incorporated the sounds she hears during the holidays as a portion of her journaling, and it brings the events that fill her holiday season to life on the page. This journaling approach makes it easy for viewers to imagine themselves surrounded in the same scene.

**Season for Giving** *by Kim Watson.* **Supplies** *Patterned paper:* Autumn Leaves, Craftstock, KI Memories and Luxe Designs; *Tag and epoxy brad:* Autumn Leaves; *Rub-ons:* SEI; *Felt snowflake:* Michaels; *Letters stickers:* American Crafts, Doodlebug Design and Making Memories; *Other:* Typewriter, silver trim from gift wrap, silver jewel star, thread and paper napkin.

THIS LITTLE PIGGY BY ELIZABETH KARTCHNER. AS SEEN IN OUR SEPTEMBER 2008 ISSUE.

## CK & Me: A Reader's Take on a Published Layout

**Elizabeth Kartchner** has inspired me in so many ways. When I saw her "This Little Piggy" layout in the September 2008 issue, I fell in love with the geometric elements and the idea of featuring a child's book. My "Guess How Much I Love You" resulted from the inspiration.

—Angela Lenssen, Pullman, WA

**Guess How Much I Love You**
*by Angela Lenssen.* **Supplies**
*Software:* MemoryMixer V2;
*Cardstock and brads:* Bazzill
Basics Paper; *Patterned paper:*
BasicGrey and MemoryMixer
V2; *Ink:* Ranger Industries,
*Fonts:* Arial, Complete in
Him and TXT Delicate Script;
*Adhesive:* Duck Products and
EK Success; *Other:* Page from
*Guess How Much I Love You?*
by Sam McBratney.

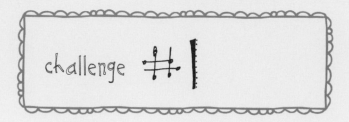

challenge #1

## Scraplift a Color Combination

I loved the blues, browns and oranges on Mellette's layout, so I decided to scraplift her color combination for my pages at right. For this challenge, you can scraplift me— or Mellette—or open up this book to any page and challenge yourself to scraplift the color scheme!

You are **pure potential**, son. In your eyes I see so much love, kindness, and the ability to do remarkable things.

PURE POTENTIAL (on opposite page) by Mellette Berezoski

**SUPPLIES** *Patterned papers: Wild Asparagus, My Mind's Eye; Déjà Views, The C-Thru Ruler Co.; Scenic Route Paper Co.; BasicGrey; Making Memories; Coin mounts: Whitman; Metal frame, metal word charm, screw-top eyelets, circle cutter and floss: Making Memories; Ribbon: Making Memories and May Arts; Photo corner: Heidi Swapp for Advantus; Computer font: AL Songwriter, downloaded from www.twopeasinabucket. com; Times New Roman, Microsoft Word.*

**10 THINGS I LOVE** by Elsie Flannigan

**SUPPLIES** *Textured cardstock: Bazzill Basics Paper; Patterned papers, stickers, tags and acrylic accents: KI Memories; Photo corners: Canson and Heidi Swapp for Advantus; Letter sticker: American Crafts; Other: Buttons and thread.*

**SOULMATES** by Elsie Flannigan

**SUPPLIES** *Embroidery Floss: DMC; Circle Punch: EK Success.*

## Scraplift a Technique

Vicki's layout inspired me to take out my sewing machine and sew a simple stitched frame around the focal point of my layout. Even though our layouts are actually quite different, they show how one technique can be adapted to any design.

PRE-TEEN (on opposite page) by Vicki Harvey

**SUPPLIES** Patterned papers: Chatterbox; Red chipboard letters, flower and index tabs: Heidi Swapp for Advantus; Pink chipboard letter squares and button: Making Memories; Ribbon: C.M. Offray & Son; Lace: Europa Imports; Embroidery floss: DMC; Computer font: Avant Garde, Microsoft Word.

POSH PUPPY by Elsie Flannigan

**SUPPLIES** Patterned papers, ribbon, transparency and stickers: KI Memories; Large letter stickers: Gin-X, Imagination Project.

MOMENTS LIKE THESE by Elsie Flannigan

**SUPPLIES** Patterned paper: Chloe's Closet, Imagination Project; Ribbon: American Crafts and Doodlebug Design; Pen: Sakura; Acrylic paint: Making Memories; Computer font: 2Peas Flower Garden, downloaded from www.twopeasinabucket.com; Other: Staples, buttons, thread and chalk.

## Scraplift a Topic

Rachel's layout about how her camera is her baby inspired me to scrapbook about my camera, too. I really love the shot of Rachel holding her camera and the way she layered those open letters right over her photograph.

NAME                                          71
                                        FOLIO

MY CAMERA

baby

*i adore MY CAMERA! ever since i got it, LAST APRIL, i HAVE HAd So Much fun documenting OUR Life iN PHotos. it is So fun ANd there is ALWAYS MoRe to LEARN! ♡♡♡ —elsie'05

A B C D E F G H I J K L M M⁵ N O P

A photograph | can be as | striking and | as haunting | as a great painting | or a | fine poem. | —Unknown

MY CAMERA IS BABY NO. TWO (on opposite page)  by Rachel Ludwig
**SUPPLIES** Textured cardstock: Bazzill Basics Paper, Letter stickers: Marcella by Kay; Fabric letters: Scrapworks; Rub-ons: Scrapworks and Fontwerks; Letter stamps: Fontwerks, Stamping ink: Nick Bantock, Ranger Industries.

MY CAMERA BABY  by Elsie Flannigan
**SUPPLIES** Textured cardstock: Die Cuts With a View; Patterned paper: Making Memories; Acetate letters and shapes, photo tape, flower jewels, photo corners and acrylic paint: Heidi Swapp for Advantus; Tabs: Autumn Leaves; Quote sticker: KI Memories.

As a scrapbooker, you may want to create a page about how you love your camera— or maybe you just want to flip through the pages of Creating Keepsakes and find a topic that inspires you! What layout topics reach out and grab your attention?

## Scraplift a Journaling Style

I loved how Joy started the journaling on her page with the word "free." When I look at her page, I see the word free! I decided to use a similar idea on my page, using the word "fresh." Here's your challenge: Choose one word that summarizes your layout and repeat it several times in your journaling. You'll see that it can make a powerful impact!

Free to wander
Free to jump
Free to run
Free to learn
Free to skip
Free to laugh
Free to cry
Free to be
Just the way it
should be for
a six year old girl.
No obstacle seems
too big
No trial without end.
You have big
dreams, you know
you will live them.
So good for me to
see you being free.
This day you
did cartwheel after
cartwheel on the
front lawn as I
watched you smiling
Be free.
Free to wander
Free to jump
Free to learn
Free to skip
Free to laugh
Be free.

free

There are tons of different ways to add journaling to a page. One of my favorite ideas is to journal around the edge of a cluster of photographs. It's a fast and simple way to add both journaling and a border at the same time!

Fresh Air.
Fresh Flowers.
Fresh Art.
Fresh Water.
Fresh Fruit.
Fresh Ideas.
Fresh Color.
Fresh Music.
Fresh Fashion.
Fresh Perspective.
Fresh Life.

love

FREE (on opposite page) by Joy Bohon
**SUPPLIES** Patterned paper: Karen Foster Design; Chipboard letters, stars and acrylic paint: Heidi Swapp for Advantus; Other: Chipboard.

FRESH  by Elsie Flannigan
**SUPPLIES** Textured cardstock: Bazzill Basics Paper; Patterned papers: KI Memories, Sassafras Lass, Scenic Route Paper Co. and American Crafts; Ribbon: C.M. Offray & Son and Doodlebug Design; Photo corners: Heidi Swapp for Advantus; Stickers: Making Memories; Other: Staples, button and thread.

"RING OF FUN" BY CINDY TOBEY, AS SEEN IN THE *JULY/AUGUST 2010* ISSUE, P. 27.

## CK & ME: A READER'S TAKE ON A PUBLISHED LAYOUT

The minute I opened the page and saw this layout I knew I had to use it for inspiration on a page. I loved the scalloped mats Cindy Tobey created; they made me think of waves, [inspiring me] to create a pirate page featuring my son.

**–BECKY CUTSHAW
PENSACOLA, FL**

### We love how Becky

- Used the sails of the boat for journaling.

- Adapted a two-page layout for a one-page layout.

*A Pirate's Life for Me* by *Becky Cutshaw.* **Digital Supplies:** *Software:* Adobe; *Patterned paper, coins, and die cuts:* Faith True; *Font:* Pea Doodle Deb.

# let's make it happen

USE YOUR SUPPLIES TO ACHIEVE YOUR GOALS THIS YEAR!

BY BRITTANY BEATTIE

A couple years ago, I accepted a friend's challenge to run a half marathon in the summer. I could barely run for a minute when I started, but by setting daily goals and creating a visual reminder—I posted a daily check-off calendar on my fridge (and the perfectionist in me couldn't bear to have a day left unchecked)—I was able to reach my goal.

Something about having that visual reminder of my small goals was just what I needed to actually follow through and meet my larger goal. So I'm doing the same thing this year with my four top goals for 2009. Try it with me—let's meet our goals together! I'll share six great ideas of how you can display those goals in your home as daily motivation. Notice that each shows small goals to help achieve the larger end goal. Together, we can do this!

*Create* a "vision board" that showcases your goals as the vision of what you want to accomplish by the end of the year.

**My Vision Board** *by Elizabeth Kartchner.* **Supplies** *Patterned paper:* American Crafts and October Afternoon (blue grid); *Letter stickers:* American Crafts and Making Memories (small); *Felt flowers, buttons and pen:* American Crafts; *Stamp:* Bam Pop; *Ink:* StazOn, Tsukineko; *Font:* Another Typewriter; *Other:* Magnet board, magnet, paint, clip and fabric.

**KEY TO SUCCESS:** Create a weekly to-do list specific to your goals.

Although she's already created sub-goals for herself, Elizabeth wanted to make it even easier to apply them to her daily life. She created a space on her vision board to post a list of specific things she wants to do each week. At the end of the week, she has specific tasks completed and can write a new list for the next week. (What a great record of her year those lists will be when they're kept together!)

*Use* pages from an acrylic album to create a vertical hanging for your bathroom mirror.

"By placing my album on the bathroom *mirror*, I see my *goals* each night before I go to bed and first thing in the morning. My goals *focus* on 'getting it together' in the morning, so I used *bright* colors that would spark my senses. Using a large font for the key *words* helps keep them the center of attention on a *project* with no pictures."
—*Noel Culbertson*

**KEY TO SUCCESS:** Hang it where you'll see it.

Location, location, location. Put your daily reminder where you'll see it . . . daily! I love how Noel created this project for the bathroom mirror (she used a suction cup to hang it). She'll still be able to see through the album while she gets ready for the day, but she'll also be reminded of her goals each morning—because, really, who doesn't spend at least a little time in front of the mirror each day!

**Every Morning** *by Noel Culbertson.* **Supplies** *Acrylic album:* Rusty Pickle; *Cardstock:* Bazzill Basics Paper; *Patterned paper:* American Crafts (yellow) and Making Memories (green); *Rub-ons, translucent cards, beaded chains and chipboard:* Maya Road; *Brads and punch:* Stampin' Up!; *Flowers:* Prima (red paper) and Stampin' Up! (red felt); *Letter stickers:* Adornit - Carolee's Creations (small red), American Crafts (green), Jenni Bowlin Studio (large red) and Making Memories (black); *Journaling cards:* Making Memories (green edge) and My Mind's Eye ("what to wear").

*Turn* your goal into a
word-only decor project
for your wall.

**KEY TO SUCCESS:** Communicate
the message.

Deena Wuest wanted to keep her project "simple
yet bold, so every single time I glance at it, the
message is communicated." She matted the main
part of her goal behind the frame, then added
the "think" letters with chipboard in front of the
glass for extra impact.

**Think about Such Things** *by Deena Wuest.* **Supplies** *Patterned
paper:* Esme Paperie by Anna Aspnes; *Chipboard letters:*
Rusty Pickle; *Spray paint:* Krylon; *Font:* Avant Garde; *Software:*
Adobe Photoshop Elements 4.0; *Other:* Frame.

*Create* a multicolor
display for your walls.

**KEY TO SUCCESS:** Use colors that will catch your eye.

Suzy Plantamura chose a bright color
scheme with several colors—it will
stand out against the wall and remind
her of her goals. Your project doesn't
have to include bright colors—just
choose a color scheme that draws your
eye and suits your pleasure so you'll
look at it regularly and stick to your
everyday goals.

**Get Fit in 2009** *by Suzy Plantamura.* **Supplies**
*Patterned paper:* Autumn Leaves, Chatterbox,
Déjà Views by The C-Thru Ruler Co., KI Mem-
ories, Paper-fever, The Paper Loft and SEI;
*Chipboard accordion album:* Maya Road; *Rib-
bon:* Love, Elsie for KI Memories; *Embroidery
floss:* DMC; *Sticker strips, rubber charms and
chipboard:* KI Memories; *Letter stickers:* Adornit
- Carolee's Creations (white), Doodlebug Design
(large black) and Making Memories (small black);
*Markers:* Sakura and Sharpie, Newell Rubbermaid;
*Other:* Images cut from magazines.

*Create* a mini album you can refer to frequently and add "progress report" pages to.

**KEY TO SUCCESS:** Keep the mini book short.

Why keep it short? As Shelley Aldrich says, "I can flip through my album in only a minute—and just like that I am reminded of my main goal and the basic steps to get there. It's a great reminder that goals don't have to be overwhelming—they can be as easy as five simple steps."

Shelley designed the book so she could add more pages later. "At the end of the album," says Shelley, "I plan to add monthly 'progress pages' that list what I did to achieve my goal each month. Not only does this plan motivate me to fill up the pages, but it's inspiring to look back and see what I've accomplished so far."

**Express Your Creative Side** by Shelley Aldrich. **Supplies** *Black album:* Cosmo Cricket; *Patterned paper:* 7gypsies (black buttons), BasicGrey (test bubbles) and Scenic Route (red, checkbox and numbers); *Rub-ons:* 7gypsies (numbers), BasicGrey (birds and butterflies), Creative Imaginations (borders) and Making Memories (repeating numbers); *Stamps:* Impress Rubber Stamps (dot) and Tim Holtz (numbers); *Ink:* VersaMagic (edges) and StazOn (numbers), Tsukineko; *Paint:* Liquitex and Distress Crackle Paint, Tim Holtz, Ranger Industries; *Numbers, quotes and date:* Tim Holtz; *Chipboard:* Heidi Swapp for Advantus, Making Memories and Sizzix (flower die); *Transparencies:* 3M; *Colored pencils:* Prismacolor, Newell Rubbermaid; *Pen:* Zig Writer, EK Success; *Fonts:* CanCan de Bois, Reservoir Grunge and Mom's Typewriter; *Other:* Playing cards.

**KEY TO SUCCESS:** Leave the album open to the page that shows your most challenging goal.

Says Cindy Tobey, "If I am struggling with one goal in particular, I can leave the album open to the page that tells that step." And sometimes the page with the "needed reminder" may be one that gives you words of encouragement. Again, Cindy comments, "I added a photo of myself and a word of encouragement to myself at the end of the album. Since I have to make these choices for myself every day, having a photo of me—telling myself that I can do it—just seems like the perfect way to end the album." I also love that, on her album's opening page, Cindy reminded herself why she set these goals.

**Healthy Choices Every Day** by Cindy Tobey. **Supplies** *Album, patterned paper, chipboard, mini file folders, clip and rub-ons:* Fancy Pants Designs; *Ink:* Clearsnap; *Ribbon:* May Arts; *Flowers and decorative borders:* Doodlebug Design; *Letter stickers:* EK Success; *Fonts:* Calibri and Impact.

# Finding Your
# Creative Muse

### Let home, outdoors and the media inspire your next page!

**by Maurianne Dunn**

WHAT INSPIRES YOU? What makes you want to run home and create the perfect project? For quite a few years, I've been inspired by all things vintage—letters, cards, books and clothing. Each item feels like a newly discovered treasure.

I recently rediscovered some old aprons my grandmother made long before I was born. These aprons have inspired me in many ways—from the vintage patterns and fabric to the shapes and careful stitching. Inspiration can come from anywhere, and if you keep your eyes open, you're bound to find the perfect muse for your next layout. I'll share a few places you can look to find inspiration.

# At Home

We love surrounding ourselves with beautiful things in our homes because that's where we *live*. Sometimes a look at the ordinary is all we need to get a creative jump-start. Try looking at your clothes, the labels on products in your house or decor on your walls.

Kelly Purkey found inspiration in a Starbucks mug. She took the outlined letters from the mug and used them in her journaling for a unique and fun look.

**Now Hear This** *by Kelly Purkey.*
**Supplies** *Cardstock:* Bazzill Basics Paper (white) and Heidi Grace Designs (blue); *Patterned paper:* Love, Elsie for KI Memories (brown and blue) and Scenic Route (red); *Brads, stickers and pen:* American Crafts; *Chipboard and rub-ons:* Heidi Grace Designs.

Result

**font inspiration**

Inspiration

Result

**shape & color inspiration**

C.D. Muckosky was inspired by a chandelier that hangs in her mother-in-law's home. Notice how she replicated the chandelier's colors and shapes in the background to represent her daughter's tears.

Inspiration

**Tough Days** *by C.D. Muckosky.* **Supplies** *Software:* Adobe Photoshop CS3, Adobe Systems; *Cardboard:* Designs by Lili, www.scrapartist.com; *Patterned paper, blue ribbons, foil hearts, frame and wings:* Gina Cabrera, www.digitaldesignessentials.com; *Staples:* JennPatrick.com; *Watercolor paints:* Prang; *Watercolor paper:* Canson; *Painted letters:* Michelle Coleman, www.littledreamerdesigns.com; *Font:* CK Chocolate Sundae by CD Muckosky, www.scrapnfonts.com; *Other:* Embroidery floss, jump rings and masking tape.

# Out and About

Look for inspiration in unfamiliar surroundings. Discovering the quaint decor of an unfamiliar café or the color combinations in a newly planted flower bed is so much fun. Observe carefully in the stores you visit (even the online ones), in parks you frequent or on signs you pass. You'll be surprised how many items jump out at you that can translate into a page design, color scheme or theme.

Result

Inspiration

**project/ theme inspiration**

Celeste Mores, a Fresh Face, was inspired by something she saw on eBay. While looking in the Turner's Collectibles store (http://stores.ebay.com/Turners-Collectibles), she fell in love with this old set of letterpress type and created her own version using chipboard.

**Chipboard Letterpress** by Celeste Mores. **Supplies** Cork paper: Creative Impressions; Ink: ColorBox, Clearsnap; Chipboard: BasicGrey, EK Success, Fancy Pants Designs, Heidi Swapp for Advantus, Jo-Ann Scrap Essentials, Making Memories, Rusty Pickle and We R Memory Keepers; Paint: Making Memories; Other: Kraft paper.

Result

Inspiration

**color & texture inspiration**

Emily Falconbridge saw this card in IKEA and had to buy it for its delicious colors! In this layout, she replicated the textured wall for her background (by spreading gesso on cardstock with a blunt knife and painting over it) and used a color scheme similar to the one in the card.

**Can I Hold Yindi?** by Emily Falconbridge. **Supplies** Cardstock: Bazzill Basics Paper; Patterned paper and acrylic stamps: Autumn Leaves; Rub-ons: BasicGrey and Creative Imaginations; Gesso and cobalt turquoise paint: Matisse Derivan; Other: Flowers, hemp and Indian mirror.

# In the Media

We are surrounded by media full of ideas. I love seeking out inspiration in books, catalogs and magazines. In addition, I'm inspired by so much online media. Try flipping through a store's catalog or visit your favorite blog. A duvet cover's pattern from a catalog might lead to the perfect layout!

Inspiration

Result

**Boston Children's Museum** *by Paula Gilarde.* **Supplies** *Software:* Adobe Photoshop CS2, Adobe Systems; *Kraft paper:* Doodled Daydreams by Katie Pertiet; *Alphabet:* Paper Bag Alphabet by Lynn Grieveson; *Paint brushes:* Touch Up Paint Brushes-n-Stamps by Katie Pertiet; *Frames:* Dirty Photo Frames Curled-n-Flat (No. 1 and No. 2) by Katie Pertiet; *Embellishments:* Between the Lines by Katie Pertiet. All digital elements downloaded from *www.designerdigitals.com.*

Paula Gilarde saw an advertisement in a magazine with a lot of framed pictures in a unique shape. She sketched this general layout of the pictures and used her photos in a similar layout on her page.

Result

**A Time for Growth** *by Karen Wilson-Bonnar.* **Supplies** *Software:* Adobe Illustrator and Adobe Photoshop, Adobe Systems; *Digital elements:* Botanist Notebook No. 09 and Ledger Journalers Brushes-n-Stamps by Katie Pertiet, *www.designerdigitals.com*; *Digital brushes:* Cabaret by Rhonna Farrer, "Designing with Digital" CD, Autumn Leaves; Good Times by Jesse Edwards, *www.designerdigitals.com*; *Fonts:* Caecilia and Zapfino, Internet.

Inspiration

Karen Wilson-Bonnar used an advertisement from Anthropologie's website for inspiration. Notice how she put similar flourishes around the photo just like in the advertisement.

# GET INSPIRED BY LIBRARY BOOKS

"CHECK OUT" INSPIRATION
FOR YOUR NEXT LAYOUT.

I'VE ALWAYS LOVED GOING TO THE LIBRARY.
Each and every aisle is full of new delights and
tons of inspiration. I'm not talking about actually *reading* the books for inspiration—my inspiration comes from the beautiful cover designs,
the typography treatments and the little details
and images inside the books that catch the eye.
Schedule a visit to your local library or bookstore
and examine the books in a completely new way.
The images, colors and even the fonts can inspire
your next scrapbook page!

BY LORI ANDERSON

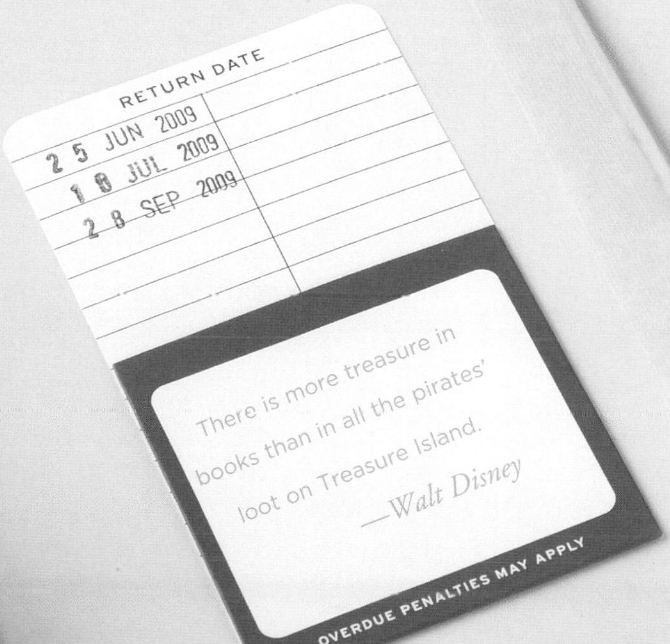

RETURN DATE

2 5 JUN 2009
1 0 JUL 2009
2 8 SEP 2009

There is more treasure in
books than in all the pirates'
loot on Treasure Island.
—*Walt Disney*

OVERDUE PENALTIES MAY APPLY

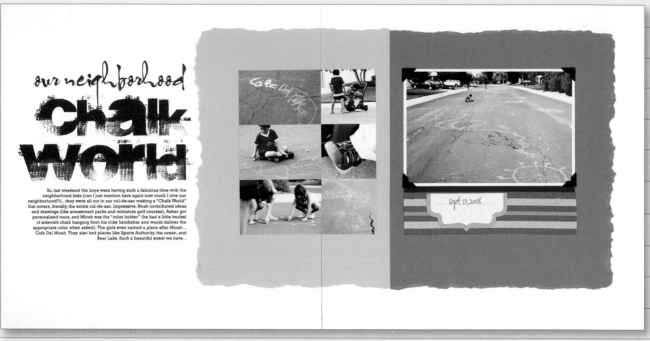

**Chalk World** *by Amanda Probst.* **Supplies** *Cardstock:* Prism Papers; *Pastel pencils:* Koh-I-Noor; *Ribbon:* May Arts; *Journaling paper:* Making Memories; *Pen:* American Crafts; *Fonts:* Rockwell, Sidewalk and VNI-HL Thuphap; *Adhesive:* E-Z Runner, Scrapbook Adhesives by 3L; *Other:* Photo corners.

## GET INSPIRED BY A TECHNIQUE

Inspired by the rough edges around the color blocks on this *Harry the Dirty Dog* book cover, Amanda Probst applied the same technique to her layout about her neighborhood's attempt at making their very own "chalk world" in their cul-de-sac. After a first effort of painting acrylic blocks on her layout (which she wasn't happy with), Amanda decided to instead tear the edges of colored card-stock to achieve the same effect. After adding her photos, journaling and title, the layout was complete.

Technique tip: Just a touch of pastel pencil on the title supports the chalk theme of the layout while also imitating the title on the book cover.

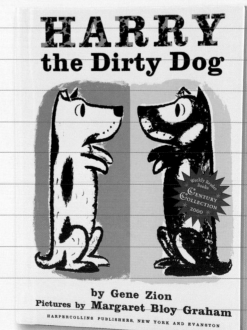

**39 Things I Can Do Without** *by Kim Watson.* **Supplies** *Patterned paper:* Jenni Bowlin Studio (red damask), Kaisercraft (red dot, teal stripe and green damask), Luxe Designs (green grid) and Piggy Tales (red floral); *Chipboard tag:* Autumn Leaves; *Letter stickers:* Karen Foster Design (black) and Pink Paislee (blue); *Ribbon:* Making Memories; *Transparency:* Pelikan; *Corner-rounder punch:* EK Success; *Pen:* Zig Photo Signature, EK Success; *Fonts:* Mom's Typewriter, Rough Typewriter, Teletype 1945–1985 and Traveling Typewriter; *Adhesive:* E-Z Runner, Scrapbook Adhesives by 3L; Mono Adhesive, Tombow; *Other:* Buttons, embroidery floss and thread.

## GET INSPIRED BY A SUBJECT

When Kim Watson saw the book *Throw Out Fifty Things* by Gail Blanke, it immediately caught her eye. With her fortieth birthday only weeks away, Kim thought, "It's about time I get my life in order." The idea of throwing out clutter inspired her to make a list of 39 things she can do without as she approaches this milestone. She chose fun and serious items to document in a list, printed the list onto a transparency and attached it to her layout. This list serves as her journaling and as a reminder of where she is as a person at this point in time.

Color tip: Check out the bits of color inspiration Kim took from the book and applied to her layout—red and black with extra colors thrown in.

*THROW OUT FIFTY THINGS BY GAIL BLANKE*

# favorites

by Zach (age 3)

**things to do:**
help Dad, build cars, watch tv,
help clean the house, help Sissy

**things to play:**
animal train, blocks

**foods:**
baked potatoes, rice, eggs

**drinks:**
water, milk

**friend:**
Seth

**color:**
green

**treat:**
popsicles

january 2009

**Favorites by Zach** *by Wendy Sue Anderson.* **Supplies** *Heavy photo paper:* Ilford; *Chipboard frame, circle accent and letter stickers:* American Crafts; *Software:* Adobe Photoshop; *Font:* Delicious; *Adhesive:* Glue Runner, Adhesive Technologies, Inc.

## GET INSPIRED BY A DESIGN STYLE

The clean, graphic and playful style of the book *Dinosaur Soup* is inspiring and easy to duplicate. To create her layout, Wendy Sue Anderson created an 8½" x 11" canvas in Photoshop and colored the right side of the layout to match her son's shirt using the Eyedropper Tool. After adding white text, she printed the layout and added dimension with letter stickers, a chipboard frame and an adorable circle accent. She kept the design clean and simple, just like the book design, yet she still made the look her own.

Inspiration tip: Finding inspiration from a design style doesn't mean you can't make your project your own. Adding pieces of "you" will make your project personal.

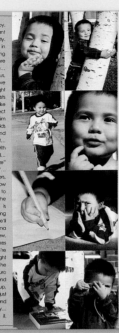

Feb/March 2008. This boy. He's been our constant entertainment recently. And he thinks he's in charge. He's talking more and doing more and expecting more... amazing & humoring us, often simultaneously. I love everything about him right now. I love how he insists his name is "Little Mike Brother" and will correct anyone who dares call him otherwise...how he holds a pencil "correctly" and has right from the start... how he loves to draw with pencil or doodle board... how he says "sorry-gize" instead of "I apologize"... how he tells his brothers, "you in trouble!"...how he has the patience to sit with puzzles...how he asks what everything is called by demanding "this name?!"...how he'll tell you, with all the drama that goes with it, "whew, close one"...how he likes to tell us all that we're crazy (he does this right before bed)...how he loves to have his picture taken and to take pretend pictures himself. Yup, pretty much this boy just has us all wrapped around his little finger lately... and he totally knows it.

# Don't Let the Boy Run the Show!

**Don't Let the Boy Run the Show!** *by Amanda Probst.* **Supplies** *Cardstock:* Prism Papers; *Pen:* Precision Pens, American Crafts; *Fonts:* Century Gothic and Typist; *Adhesive:* E-Z Runner, Scrapbook Adhesives by 3L; Foam Squares, Therm O Web.

## GET INSPIRED BY A VISUAL ELEMENT

Sometimes a visual element immediately grabs your attention, calling, "Look at me!" Use that element to your advantage and create a layout with the same element. The talk bubble on the cover of this book by Mo Willems inspired Amanda Probst's layout about her adorable son and the persuasive personality he's developing. To include multiple photos in her design, Amanda blocked the photos and added them next to the journaling. All the important pieces are included but don't interfere with the overall feel of the layout.

Color tip: Your photos don't always have to match the colors on your layout. The subtle tones on the book's cover are perfect for use on Amanda's layout—they keep the focus on the words and photos.

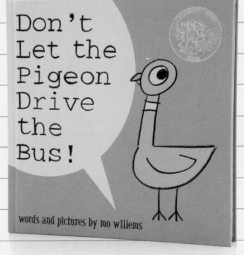

DON'T LET THE PIGEON DRIVE THE BUS BY MO WILLEMS

**Be Amazing** by Maggie Holmes. **Supplies** *Patterned paper:* Sassafras and Studio Calico; *Flowers:* American Crafts and Prima; *Stamp:* Crate Paper; *Ink:* ColorBox, Clearsnap; *Decorative tape:* TapeSwell; *Glass pebbles:* Prima; *Brads:* Heidi Swapp for Advantus and Making Memories; *Self-adhesive fabric:* Studio Calico; *Rhinestones:* me & my BIG ideas; *Pins:* Jenni Bowlin Studio; *Letter stickers:* American Crafts and Making Memories; *Metal letters:* Making Memories; *Punch:* EK Success; *Decorative-edge scissors:* Provo Craft; *Pen:* Zig Writer, EK Success; *Other:* Pom-pom trim.

## GET INSPIRED BY TYPOGRAPHY

Quote books can be so inspirational. Each page you turn reveals a new message, and sometimes a new journey begins for the reader. Maggie Holmes loves the typography in this book compiled by Kobi Yamada just as much as she loves the quotes. (By the way, she'd love to make a layout for each quote in the book!) Notice how she mimicked the way the words are laid out, the colors of the letters and even the different word sizes on her layout.

Inspiration tip: You don't need a quote book to create a layout inspired by typography. Check out ads in magazines or on TV, and transfer the type treatments to your page. **ck**

# FROM BLAH to *Ahh*

## 25 simple strategies to make ordinary layouts dazzle • BY BETH OPEL

Each January, I get a little melancholy when the Christmas decorations come down. Yes, it's nice to get back to normal, but it's always a little sad to say farewell to all the pretty adornments for another year. It doesn't help that sunshine is scarce and temperatures are frigid. Those winter blahs can settle in with a vengeance, and I just want to hibernate. If you're like me, your creativity may be at a low, too, and you may be struggling to bring your layouts out of the doldrums.

Help is on the horizon! You're about to discover how easy it can be to take a ho-hum page and elevate it to excellent with some minor adjustments. Just a few small design fixes can lift your layouts above January's clouds.

# Consider the balance.

In Kelly Purkey's original layout, the red on the right-hand side was hogging the spotlight and making her spread feel unbalanced. To remedy the situation, she rearranged the small circle photos and added lots of embellishments on the red cardstock circles to temper the boldness of the color and give the layout a more festive vibe. In addition, she enlarged her title to give comparable weight to the left-hand side.

**BEFORE**

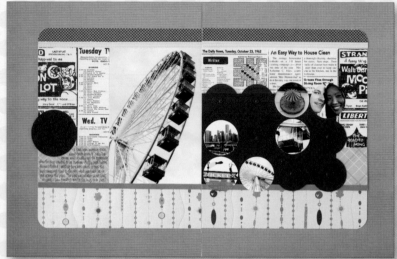

### DID YOU NOTICE?

Kelly elevated her second layout's title and photo circles with foam dots to vary the dimension on her pages. She also added stitching to give her layout a nice, finished look and carried out her rounded motif with a scalloped border at the top.

*Original layout* by Kelly Purkey. **Supplies** *Cardstock:* Bazzill Basics Paper; *Patterned paper:* Heidi Grace Designs (green, orange, tinsel and yellow), Li'l Davis Designs (blue) and October Afternoon (newsprint); *Corner-rounder and circle punches:* Fiskars; *Brads, pen and stickers:* American Crafts.

**AFTER**

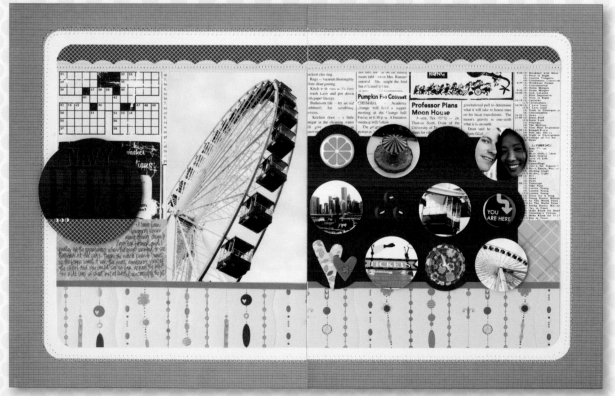

**Navy Pier** *by Kelly Purkey.* **Supplies** *Cardstock:* Bazzill Basics Paper; *Patterned paper:* Heidi Grace Designs (green, orange, tinsel and yellow), Li'l Davis Designs (blue) and October Afternoon (newsprint); *Jewels and stamps:* Hero Arts; *Ink:* StazOn, Tsukineko; *Buttons:* 7gypsies and Li'l Davis Designs; *Chipboard:* Heidi Grace Designs; *Corner-rounder and circle punches:* Fiskars; *Pen, pins, rub-ons and stickers:* American Crafts; *Other:* Thread.

**Original layout**
*by Emily Merritt.*
**Supplies** *Software:*
Adobe Photoshop
CS3; *Digital card-
stock:* Catrine
(brown, green and
tan) and Creashens
(white square);
*Digital kit:* {Fall}
ing for Retro kit
by Paislee Press
and Leora Sanford;
*Alphabets:* Amber
Clegg; *Paper block
templates:* Emily
Merritt Designs;
*Fonts:* CK Double
Mou and CK Erin.

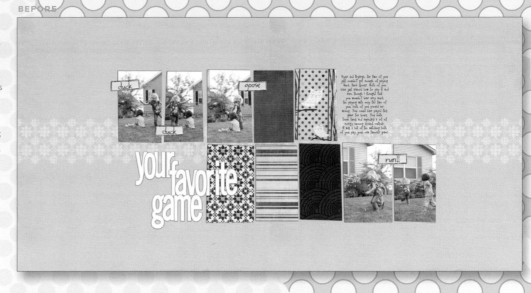

AFTER

**Your Favorite Game** by Emily Merritt. **Supplies** *Software:* Adobe Photoshop CS3; *Digital cardstock:* Catrine (brown, green and tan) and Creashens (white square); *Digital kit:* {Fall}ing for Retro kit by Paislee Press and Leora Sanford; *Brackets and alphabets:* Amber Clegg; *Tree template:* Amy Wolff Designs; *Border:* Jenna Desai; *Paper block templates and wire clouds:* Emily Merritt Designs; *Background word art:* Press Lines by Paislee Press; *Fonts:* CK Double Mou and CK Erin.

## Claim the sweet spot.

Emily Merritt's original version is nice, but it doesn't have a strong focal point. Utilize the design-based "rule of thirds" to locate your layout's "sweet spots." Divide each page into thirds both vertically and horizontally and place your most important elements at the intersections of those lines. By inserting the charming tree near one of these intersections, Emily created a strong focal point for her spread.

### DID YOU NOTICE?

Emily inserted a subtle line behind her photographs and added a whimsical border on her second design. She also clustered some clouds in another of the layout's sweet spots and included numbers to show the progression of her photos.

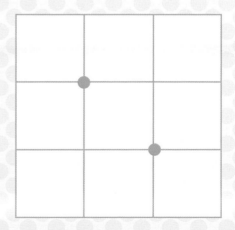

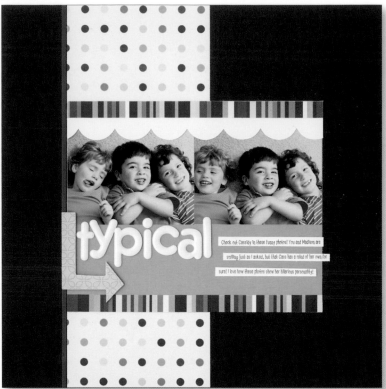

## Coordinate the theme.

Think of the elements on your layout as a whole, not just as separate components. The difference between Kelly Noel's layouts seems subtle visually, but thematically her second version is much more cohesive. By simply changing the placement of the arrow treatment, Kelly directs the eye to the subject of her journaling and title—little goofball Cassidy.

**Original layout** *by Kelly Noel.* **Supplies** *Cardstock:* American Crafts (orange and pink) and Bazzill Basics Paper (brown and white); *Patterned paper:* KI Memories (green and stripe) and Making Memories (dot); *Letter stickers:* American Crafts; *Chipboard arrow shape:* Scenic Route; *Font:* Glass Gauge.

AFTER

**DID YOU NOTICE?**
Kelly also improved her second layout in small but effective ways by bulking up the vertical line to the left of her photo and adding dashes to the scalloped edging.

**Typical** *by Kelly Noel.* **Supplies** *Cardstock:* American Crafts (orange and pink) and Bazzill Basics Paper (brown and white); *Patterned paper:* KI Memories (green, floral and stripe) and Making Memories (dot); *Letter stickers and brads:* American Crafts; *Border sticker and chipboard arrow shape:* Scenic Route; *Pen:* Zig Writer, EK Success; *Font:* Glass Gauge.

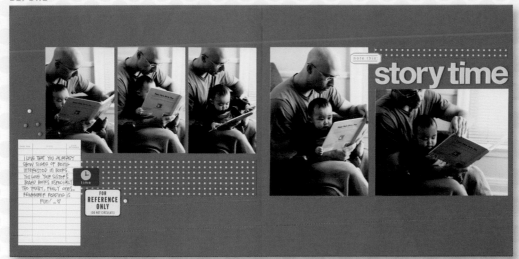

**Original layout** by Angela Urbano. **Supplies** Cardstock: Prism Papers; Patterned paper, letter stickers, metal plate and pen: American Crafts; Word stickers: FontWerks ("note this") and Knock Knock ("for reference only"); Library card: Knock Knock; Brads: Bazzill Basics Paper.

**Mister Ryan's Pick** by Angela Urbano. **Supplies** Cardstock: Bazzill Basics Paper; Patterned paper: American Crafts and KI Memories; Letter stickers: Autumn Leaves ("Pick") and Doodlebug Design ("Ryan's"); Tab: Autumn Leaves; "Mister" embellishment: KI Memories; Felt trim: Fancy Pants Designs; Library card, sleeve and sticker: Knock Knock; Brads: Making Memories; Chipboard, foam stickers, metal plate, photo turns and pen: American Crafts; Other: Staples.

# Correct the color.

Your first instinct might be to match your cardstock color to the clothing of your photo subjects. However, when you choose a contrasting background, your pictures can really take on greater vibrancy. Before she adhered her elements, Angela Urbano changed out the background to a darker blue, making her photos stand out against the cardstock.

## DID YOU NOTICE?

In her updated version, Angela also adjusted the gutters (the margins around her photographs) to make them consistent, included two detail shots for variety, and used patterned paper to emulate book spines. In addition, her new embellishment choices better fit the subject of her layout.

Original layout *by Cindy Tobey.* **Supplies** *Cardstock:* Bazzill Basics Paper; *Patterned paper:* Cosmo Cricket (white) and Luxe Designs (blue); *Stamping ink:* Clearsnap; *Letter stickers:* Doodlebug Design ("sled") and EK Success ("fun"); *Chipboard:* BasicGrey (letters) and Scenic Route (circle); *Ribbon:* Li'l Davis Designs; *Journaling spots:* Jenni Bowlin Studio; *Paint:* Pebbles Inc.; *Pen:* Pigma Micron, Sakura; *Font:* Courier New; *Other:* Scrap chipboard for stars.

**A Boy and His Sled** *by Cindy Tobey.* **Supplies** *Cardstock:* Bazzill Basics Paper; *Patterned paper:* Bo-Bunny Press (red), Cosmo Cricket (white) and Luxe Designs (blue); *Stamping ink:* Clearsnap; *Letter stickers:* American Crafts ("a boy and his") and EK Success ("fun"); *Chipboard:* Melissa Frances (stars) and Scenic Route (circle); *Felt:* Fancy Pants Designs; *Embroidery floss:* DMC; *Ribbon:* Li'l Davis Designs; *Journaling spots:* Jenni Bowlin Studio; *Pen:* Pigma Micron, Sakura; *Font:* Courier New; *Other:* Thread.

# Change the proportion.

Cindy Tobey's first design is fine, but definitely not as fabulous as her second version. The reason? Proportion. Her first title was too puny and didn't add much energy to her pages. In her final layout, she focused even more on the word "Sled" in the title. The large curve of the "S" adds a sense of movement and suggests the curve of a hill. Plus, it makes a more interesting division between her two patterned papers.

## DID YOU NOTICE?

Cindy knotted the ribbon in the top-left corner of her second layout and brought in some wintry touches with felt and glitter to really amp up her design from its original look.

# Title How-To

Want to replicate Cindy's big title treatment on your own layout? Here's how:

**1.** In a word-processing or drawing program, type each letter in its own text box and enlarge each one, making the first letter much larger than the rest. Rotate and arrange the letters until you achieve the effect you want. Print.

**2.** Trace the largest letter onto tracing paper. Place it over your layout and make adjustments if necessary. (Cindy slimmed down the "S" so it wouldn't obstruct what she wanted to show in her photos.) Trace the remainder of the word.

**3.** Flip the tracing paper over so the title reads in reverse and use repositionable adhesive to secure it to the back side of your paper. Use a craft knife to cut out the word. Remove the tracing paper and attach the word to your layout.

# 5 Products You'll Love

Whether you add them on, change them up or move them around, you, too, can use products like these to create "ahh"-worthy layouts:

**The Daily Grind Collection, Fancy Pants Designs**
*FancyPantsDesigns.com*
These ready-made embellishments could be just the finishing touch your design needs.

**Mini Charms, Karen Foster Design**
*KarenFosterDesign.com*
Get your page cooking with adorable add-ons in several themes, like this "Baking" selection.

**Flair Adhesive Badges, American Crafts**
*AmericanCrafts.com*
Funky and fun, you'll want to snap up these badges for all your projects. (Check out how Kelly Purkey used them on her "Navy Pier" layout on page 104.)

**Frames and Hardware, Close To My Heart**
*www.closetomyheart.com*
Check out the Foundry metal frames and Spring Blossom hardware in luscious sherbet colors.

**Sparkle Fibers, Clearsnap**
*Clearsnap.com*
Simultaneously soft and bold, these fibers can upgrade your layout from coach to first-class.

# TOTALLY WICKED TEEN LAYOUTS!

ILLUSTRATION BY NICOLE LARUE

DUDE, YOU GOTTA SEE THESE COOL PAGES & ACCENTS—THEY'RE SICK!

Let's face it: teens have a style that's all their own—and chances are what was "in" last month is probably on its way out this month. One thing's for sure, when it comes to teens you can always count on changes in fashion, music, and lingo. Unless you're in the know, you might miss the 411 on what's totally sick! IDK about you, but in addition to deciphering my daughters' unique language, creating layouts about them can also be very overwhelming. But it doesn't have to be. We have 16 awesome ideas, including accents, for creating layouts about the teens in your life—with tips and techniques that will have you straight up feeling non-parental. True that!

BY JOANNIE McBRIDE

**Got Friends** by Jamie Harper. **Supplies:** *Cardstock:* Bazzill Basics Paper; *Patterned paper:* Teresa Collins; *Letters:* American Crafts; *Flowers:* Me and My Big Ideas; *Adhesive:* Tombow.

# PHOTO TIP

Show your teens' personalities by taking action group shots and printing them out in color to highlight fashion and charisma.

**Life** by Leslie Ash. **Supplies:** *Patterned paper, stickers, and pearls:* Glitz Design; *Chipboard:* Magistical Memories; *Letters:* Jenni Bowlin Studio; *Decorative tape:* 7gypsies; *Spray ink:* Shimmerz; *Paint and staples:* Ranger Industries; *Pen:* Newell Rubbermaid; *Adhesive:* Glue Arts.

# BUDGET TIP

Patterned paper scraps are not only great for decorating the tops of chipboard shapes and letters, they also allow you to create personal touches on your teen layout.

**Fabulous Fashion Finds** *by Brigid Gonzalez.* **Digital Supplies:** *Software:* Adobe; *Patterned paper:* Vector Jungle; *Grunge frames:* Anna Aspnes; *Fonts:* Bleeding Cowboys and Chalkduster.

## BUDGET TIP

A great budget-friendly solution is to use free downloadable backgrounds, the perfect solution to getting just the right page accent to fit the teen in your life.

## GR8 ACCENTS

These sa-weet accents will help transform your pages from cute to cool! You'll find even more accents like these throughout.

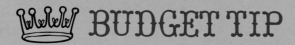

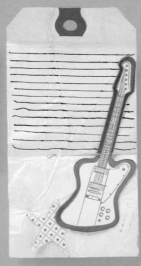

### DESIGN TIP
Punch a hole in the guitar pick and add a brad to create a swivel closure. Super cute!

### DESIGN TIP
Layer bits of patterned paper in varying sizes to create a bright and colorful page accent.

# DESIGN TIP

To create a funky background that creates a hip and edgy feel, use an empty chipboard letter sheet as a mask, and spray ink over it.

**Edvin @ 13** *by Gudrun Loennecken.* **Supplies:** *Cardstock:* Bazzill Basics Paper; *Letters:* American Crafts; *Chipboard:* Cosmo Cricket; *Stamps:* My Stamp Box; *Ink and color wash:* Ranger Industries; *Spray ink:* Tattered Angels; *Tags:* Panduro Hobby; *Pen:* Marvy Uchida; *Adhesive:* Scrapbook Adhesives by 3L; *Other:* Chipboard letter sheet.

# TECHNIQUE TIP

Create a "favorites" or "about me" layout that includes photos of everything your teen loves right now.

**Me** *by Becky Pogatchnik.* **Digital Supplies:** *Software:* Adobe; *Patterned paper and overlay:* Katie Pertiet; *Brushes:* Anna Aspnes, Susan Bohannon, Emily Merritt, and Katie Pertiet; *Logos:* Abercrombie & Fitch, Facebook, Hollister, and YouTube; *New Moon book cover image:* Little, Brown, and Company; *New Moon poster image:* Filmofilia.com; *Gossip Girl DVD cover image:* The CW Television Channel; *Justin Bieber CD cover image:* The Island of Def Jam Music Group; *Band Hero box cover image:* Activision; *Seventeen magazine cover image:* Hearst Corporation; *Fonts:* Angelic War, Display, and Impact.

**Let's Get This Party Started** by Becky Olsen. **Supplies:** *Cardstock:* Prism Papers; *Patterned paper:* Cosmo Cricket; *Paint:* I Love to Create and Ranger Industries; *Templates:* I Love to Create; *Letters:* American Crafts; *Pen:* Sakura.

 **TECHNIQUE TIP**

Use craft templates and paint to create your own backgrounds that are fresh and that highlight the personality of your teen.

# EVEN MORE AWESOME ACCENTS

**TIP**
Rather than thread the ribbon through the tins, sandwich it behind your photos, and close the tins. This will hold everything in place.

**TECHNIQUE TIP**
Dress up a sticker with some decorative trim.

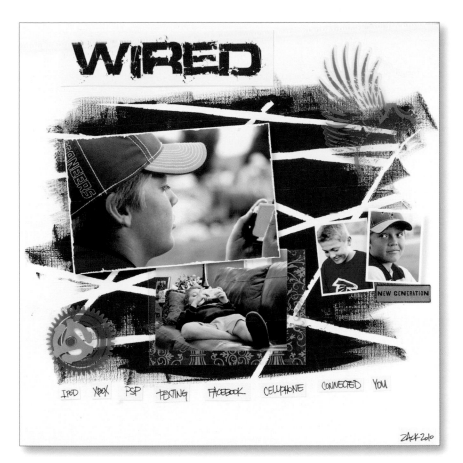

# TECHNIQUE TIP

To create a grunge feel like Lori Anderson did, mask the background with blue painter's tape, cut in different size strips, and then paint over it.

*Wired* by Lori Anderson. **Supplies:** *Cardstock:* Bazzill Basics Paper; *Transparencies and sticker:* Little Yellow Bicycle; *Paint:* Delta Creative; *Pen:* American Crafts; *Font:* Defused.

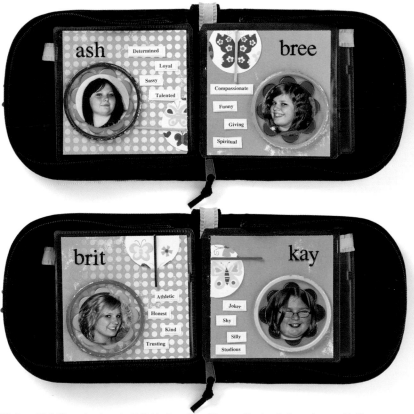

# DESIGN TIP

Use thin plastic bracelets as frames. They highlight cropped photos perfectly!

# BUDGET TIP

Use old CD cases to create mini albums. It's a great way to use wallet size school photos that your teens can add inside along with fun descriptions of their friends.

**CD Case Mini Album** *by Joannie McBride.* **Supplies:** *CD case:* Staples; *Patterned paper:* Making Memories; *Letters:* Karen Foster Design; *Butterflies:* Hallmark; *Flowers:* Bazzill Basics Paper and Prima; *Bobby pins:* Forever 21; *Bracelets:* No Boundaries; *Rhinestones:* KaiserCraft; *Brads and ribbon:* American Crafts; *Font:* Times New Roman; *Adhesive:* Therm O Web.

# DESIGN TIP

For a fun way to include teen jewelry on your layout, consider outlining a journaling spot with a friendship bracelet or beads.

**When You're the Best of Friends** by Brittany Laakkonen. Photography by Breanna and Brittany Laakkonen. **Supplies:** *Tags and letters:* BasicGrey; *Leaves and flowers:* Prima; *Adhesive:* Beacon Adhesives; *Other:* Bracelet, cardstock, fishing line, and wire. **Digital Supplies:** *Software:* Adobe; *Journaling block:* Two Peas in a Bucket; *Swirl brush and frame:* Prima.

# COOL ACCENTS

## TECHNIQUE TIP

Punch shapes out of patterned paper from different sheets within the same collection. Everything matches—but now it's a one-of-a-kind accent.

## DESIGN TIP

Scraps of paper can create journaling spots to fit any layout. Decorate with flowers, bling, or letters to customize it.

Only if you have been in the deepest valley, can you know how magnificent it is to be on the highest mountain. —R.M.Nixon

glimpses

You are such a strong girl with a beautiful smile & heart
Babes I know your life is complicated I wish it was different, easier & a little more carefree.
....all I wanted to say was that I see babes, I see the glimpses of your hurt & I am here for you.

love Mama xx

**Glimpses** *by Kim Watson.* **Supplies:** *Patterned paper:* BasicGrey, Lily Bee Design, Pink Paislee, Prima, and Sassafras; *Flowers:* Prima; *Letters and pen:* American Crafts; *Journaling spot:* Cocoa Daisy; *Rhinestones:* BasicGrey; *Stamp:* Croxley Stationary; *Ink:* Close to My Heart; *Corner-rounder punch:* EK Success; *Border punch:* Fiskars Americas; *Die-cutting machine:* Making Memories; *Software:* Adobe; *Photo paper:* Canon; *Adhesive:* Elmer's; *Other:* Thread.

# DESIGN TIP

Create whimsical stitching to house part or all of your journaling.

# { *letter to a new* scrapbooker }

I started scrapbooking in 2002. I can vividly remember the *intense* excitement I felt as I quickly found myself deeply engaged—in the stories, the photos, the supplies and the message boards. I remember the creative rush I got from linking my memories and photos together. My heart actually beats a bit faster thinking back to the very beginning.

**10 lessons every scrapbooker should know**

**Practice Your Letters** by Ali Edwards. **Supplies** *Cardstock:* Bazzill Basics Paper; *Patterned paper:* BasicGrey; *Stamp:* Hero Arts; *Word stickers:* 7gypsies and Love, Elsie for KI Memories; *Letter sticker:* American Crafts; *Strip sticker:* Creative Café, Creative Imaginations; *Circle punch:* Fiskars; *Pens:* American Crafts and Newell Rubbermaid; *Ink:* StazOn, Tsukineko.

Over time, that super-intense passion has both ebbed and flowed. Many of you reading this may be lifelong scrapbookers and know just what I mean. Some of you are learning about scrapbooking for the very first time as you read the pages of this magazine. If this is you, *welcome*. This month I want to talk to **you**, the new person who is just getting started.

Here are some things to look out for, to plan, to not miss and to think about. Some of these things are really simple and others will take more thought.  **>>**

**BY ALI EDWARDS**

**Check You Out** by Ali Edwards. **Supplies** *Cardstock:* Bazzill Basics Paper; *Patterned transparency:* Hambly Studios; *Stitched ribbon:* K&Company; *Circle tags:* Staples; *Brads:* Making Memories; *Pen:* American Crafts; *Other:* Stamps.

## Here's *looking back* with a bit of perspective:

**1 THERE'S NO "RIGHT WAY" TO SCRAPBOOK.** Regardless of anything else, there's no right or wrong way to approach scrapbooking. It's the creative expression of your memories—the personal documentation of you and your family's life experience.

If you feel like scrapbooking only one photo, go for it. If you want to include 12 photos on a page, go for it. If you want to make an entire book with no photos, go for it. Don't get caught up in comparisons with friends and their pages. These are *your* memories and *you* get to choose how to create with them.

**2 PRINT YOUR PHOTOS.** Digital photography has changed scrapbooking—*and the way we take photos*—forever. Rather than having rolls of film lying around, we have files on our computers just waiting to be printed.

Figure out a system that works with your photos. Make sure you back them up (an external hard drive and burning to DVD works well) and print them just in case your computer crashes.

**3 DON'T BUY EVERYTHING IN SIGHT.** You don't need to have all the latest and greatest products to record your memories. As you get going, take a bit of time to assess what you really need to make pages you'll love. Look around on your desk—what elements have you already purchased that you could use right now on a layout? As you scrapbook each page, use your supplies to emphasize the two most important aspects: **words + photos.**

**4 SCHEDULE TIME TO CREATE.** Go to a crop at a local store, gather up a group of friends and literally make time to scrapbook. Get up a bit earlier or stay up a bit later if it's tough to find time during the day.

**5 DON'T THINK YOU HAVE TO SCRAPBOOK IN CHRONOLOGICAL ORDER.** Record the stories that inspire you most—this could be a story from yesterday or from 10 years ago. It could be in the order events occurred, or it could be random everyday moments. I hear people talk about being "years behind." Remember that there will always be another story to tell,

**The Story of Us** by Ali Edwards. **Supplies** Cardstock: Bazzill Basics Paper; Patterned paper: Iron Orchid Designs, A Cherry on Top; Stamps: Catslife Press, CK Media and Paperbag Studios; Ink: Close To My Heart and StazOn, Tsukineko; Stickers: 7gypsies; Other: Playing cards.

**6 USE YOUR HANDWRITING.** It's a part of you. Regardless of what you think of your handwriting, your family will LOVE that they have this little piece of you when you're gone. If you absolutely hate it, don't feel like you have to use it on everything you create, but make sure it's there somewhere. Your family will thank you.

**7 DON'T FORGET THE DATE.** In looking back on my work, I've noticed pages where the date is missing. *What?* This totally defeats one of my main purposes in creative documentation: identifying when an event occurred. Now I often use a simple office-supply date stamp to make sure I can quickly add the date to projects I create.

**8 BECOME A TRANSLATOR.** I love looking at scrapbooking magazines and idea books for design ideas. A *translator* is someone who can look beyond the page theme and see the cool design or a cool accent and be able to adopt that for his or her own layouts.

Can you look at a baby page and see elements you could adopt for a sports page? Don't just look at a great layout—rather, take a look and then take a closer look. What pieces and ideas can you pull out and use in your scrapbooks?

**9 LEARN BY DOING.** This magazine is here to inspire you, educate you and empower you to tell the stories of your family. Take our ideas and run with them! Translate them (see step 8 above) and make them your own.

**10 GET YOURSELF ON YOUR PAGES.** Hand your camera over to your spouse, partner, friend or kids and make sure that you are present and represented in the story of your family.

## CK & ME: A READER'S TAKE ON A PUBLISHED LAYOUT

I haven't been motivated to work on any scrap-booking project lately, but all of that changed when I got the February 2010 issue of *Creating Keepsakes*! I particularly liked "All We Need is Love" by Stephanie Howell. I loved the white space, the collage, and the theme. So I got to scrapping and created this version. On a whim I wrote to thank Stephanie on her blog for the inspi-ration, and she suggested I submit this layout.

—Aubree Greenspun, Cherry Hill, NJ

"ALL WE NEED IS LOVE" BY STEPHANIE HOWELL, AS SEEN IN THE FEBRUARY 2010 ISSUE, P. 43.

**We sure are glad Aubree followed Stephanie's suggestion.**

We love how Aubree

1 Converted a two-page layout to a one-page layout by condensing the large white borders.

2 Changed the orientation of the title and added extra embellishments to maintain the balance of the design.

3 Used the photo template from the original left-hand page, switching up the photo coloring to emphasize the black-and-white photo against the deeper red background.

It's All About Love *by Aubree Greenspun.* **Supplies:** *Cardstock and ink:* Close to My Heart; *Patterned paper:* BasicGrey and Colorbök; *Chipboard:* BasicGrey; *Flowers and sequins:* Prima; *Paint:* Making Memories; *Rub-ons:* BasicGrey and Daisy D's Paper Co.; *Journaling tab:* Heidi Swapp; *Stamp:* Technique Tuesday; Punch; Fiskars Americas; *Adhesive:* 3M.

# hot spot

BY LORI FAIRBANKS

Adorn your scrapbook layout with a fancy fair ribbon.

**VINTAGE FRILLS ARE SUPER-POPULAR ACCESSORIES,** and one in particular that we're excited to show you is the fancy fair ribbon. You'll see this fresh alternative to flower accents in advertising, stationery, clothing, and even home décor. A fair ribbon accent can lend a fun, celebratory feel to your scrapbook layout, making it a great choice for pages about birthdays, successes, and other cheery events and happenings—just like Kim Watson's layout. And you'll love how easy these are to make try one out on your next scrapbook page.

**Champ** by Kim Watson. **Supplies:** *Cardstock:* American Crafts and Bazzill Basics Paper; *Patterned papers:* American Crafts and October Afternoon; *Ribbon:* American Crafts; *Die cuts:* Bazzill Basic Paper and Collage Press; *Stickers:* AdornIt-Carolee's Creations, American Crafts, and Collage Press; *Dimensional glaze:* Ranger Industries; *Software:* Adobe; *Font:* Another Typewriter; *Adhesives:* American Crafts, Scrapbook Adhesives by 3L, and Tombow; *Other:* Ribbon and thread.

*Blouse: Panoplusfriend Garden; Card and coasters: Rock Scissor Paper.*